English Unlimited

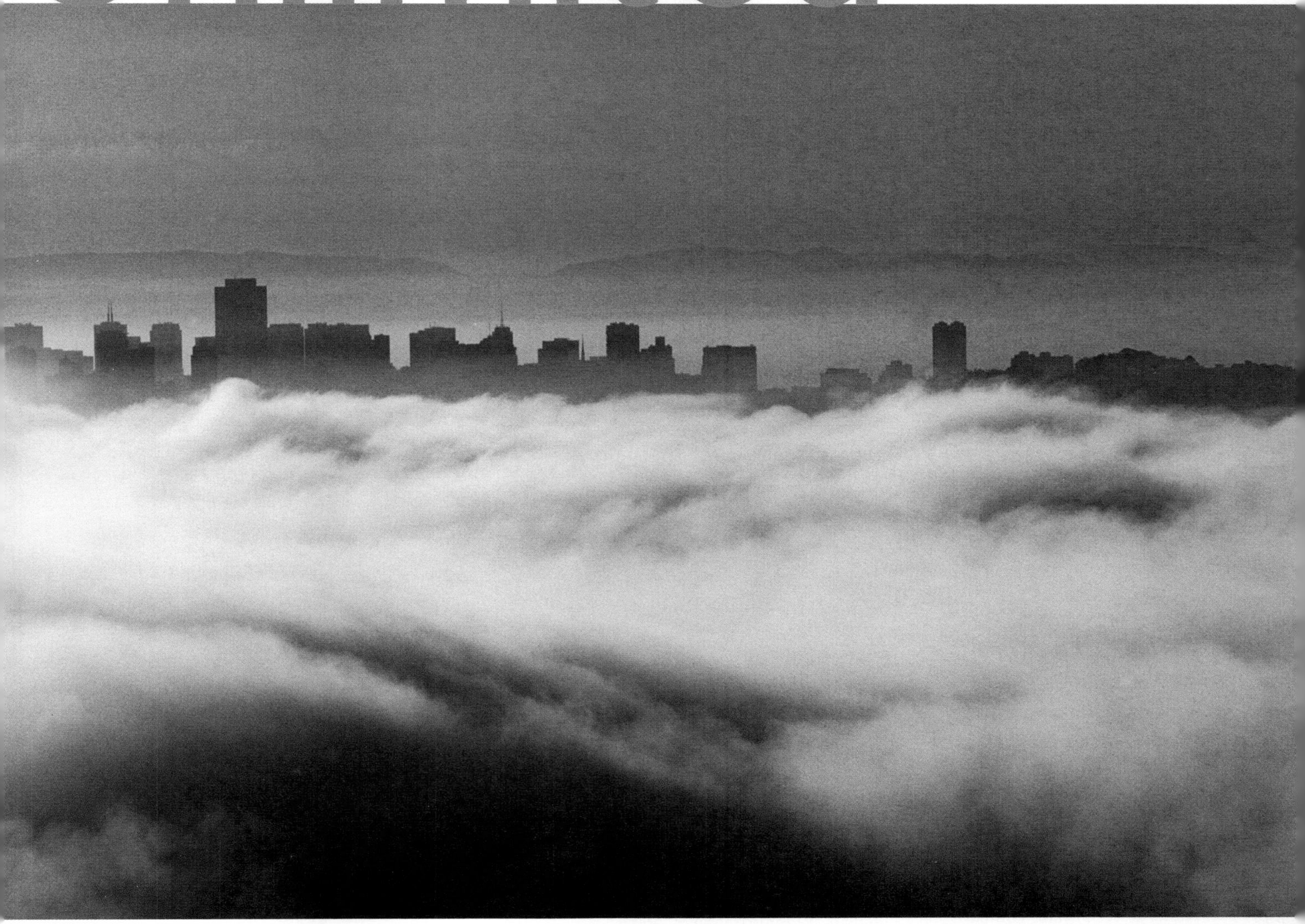

C1 Advanced
Coursebook with e-Portfolio

Adrian Doff & Ben Goldstein

Contents

Contents

Contents

How to use this coursebook

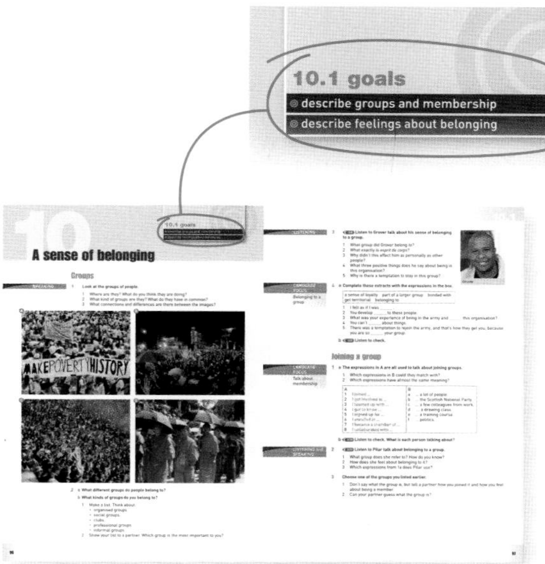

Every unit of this book is divided into sections, with clear, practical **goals** for learning.

The first four pages of the unit help you build your language skills and knowledge. These pages include speaking, listening, reading, writing, grammar and vocabulary activities. They are followed by a **Target activity** which will help you put together what you have learned.

The **Explore** section of the unit includes an **Across cultures** page, a **Keywords** page, which looks at useful and commonly confused words, and an **Explore speaking** or **Explore writing** page. The Explore section gives you extra language and skills work, all aiming to help you become a better and more culturally aware communicator in English.

The **Look again** section includes detailed work on the advanced-level grammar and vocabulary you have met in the unit, helping you review and extend your learning. Sometimes you will also find this recycling symbol with the goals, to show when a particular goal is not new but is recycling language that you have met before.

The **e-Portfolio** DVD-ROM contains useful reference material for all the units, as well as self-assessment to help you test your own learning, and **Word cards** to help you test your vocabulary learning.

You can do more practice by yourself using the **Self-study Pack**, which includes a workbook and interactive DVD-ROM. Work you do on this DVD-ROM can be saved to the e-portfilio.

The DVD-ROM contains authentic video clips and over 280 interactive activities.

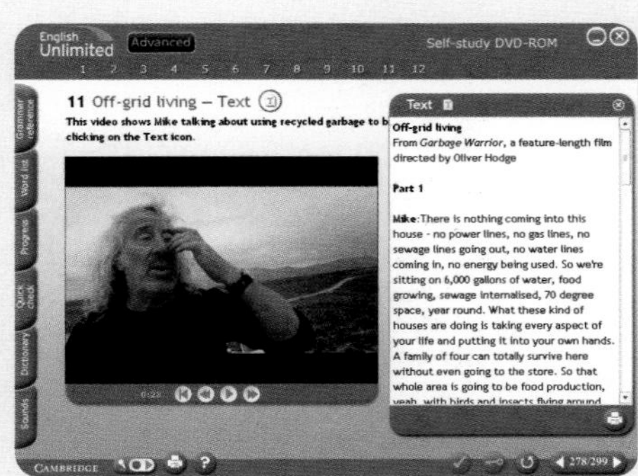

1.1 goals

◎ talk about adapting to different cultures

1 Childhood

Born everywhere, raised in Britain

READING

1 a Look at the photos of the children. Where do you think they are from? What do they have in common?

b Read what the children said. Try to guess who is who in the photos.

"Mauricio, aged 11 (Brazil)

My dad, he decided he just want to stay here one year, because the problem is we don't have a nanny here. In Brazil we had a lot of them. On the weekend in Cambridge, I usually tidy up the house with my mum and brothers and dad, and then go to read or play video games. In Brazil we didn't do anything at the house. People did. Nannies."

"Amna, aged 15 (Bahrain)

My school's really friendly. It's easy to find somebody in common because of the diversity of the people and the nationalities. People are accepting within this whole city. I guess because everyone moves in and out of here, and it's filled with people from all sorts of places. ... I even hear Arabic a lot around this area and it makes me feel that I'm still connected with my culture, and at the same time I'm learning about other cultures."

"Inza, aged 16 (Ivory Coast)

In Africa, if you see anyone walking around, you just say hello. But in England if you see anyone and say hello, they will not say hello back. They have to get to know you properly. When I arrived here I was saying hello to everybody but they wasn't answering me back so I stopped. I tell myself there's no big deal me saying it again."

"Indi, aged 15 (St Lucia)

There are a lot of differences. In St Lucia people pray when they wake up, before they go to sleep, before they eat. Religion is a big thing. If a person's older than you, you call them madam or auntie, even if you don't know them. It's just respect. And in St Lucia people take education seriously. If you don't go to college, you can't get a job. Here, if you fail, you can probably work in KFC."

"Luis, aged 15 (Peru)

Even though racial discrimination is a crime, I still feel it's there. Here, people take the mick out of accents, they act differently towards immigrant people. Sometimes they're just nasty. Most people don't know I'm Peruvian because I've worked very hard at my accent."

"Sara, aged 12 (Macedonia)

I just wonder if English children need to learn to be more free, to go out, to be more kid-like. Because sometimes I get kind of tired of shopping because it's a bit grown up. I still want to live the life of a little child, play hide and seek and stuff like that."

"Collins, aged 10 (Uganda)

In Uganda, I spent my days playing with the dogs, chasing the chickens, watching my uncle cut a goat – which is quite gruesome, but it looks good. In London, I'll just stay home and watch TV."

2 a Who comments on:

1 nostalgia for their home country and culture?
2 their identity as children?
3 personal relationships?
4 differences in behaviour and attitude?
5 domestic life?

b Are the children negative, positive or ambivalent about the changes they have to make? What specific expressions indicate the children's attitudes?

c What examples of non-standard and colloquial English can you find in the quotes?

LANGUAGE FOCUS
Adapting to another culture

3 a 1.1 Listen to Daniel and Sarah talk about adapting to life in Germany. Who finds it most difficult? Why?

b 1.1 Listen again. Tick the expressions they use. Who says them and what do they say?

1 fit in
2 welcoming
3 feel at home
4 make friends
5 be / feel accepted
6 adapt to
7 an outsider
8 expats
9 make an effort
10 integrate
11 get used to
12 miss

SPEAKING

4 a Talk together.

1 Have you, or has anyone you know, lived in a foreign country? What were the first impressions of that country?
2 Do you know anyone who has come to live in your country from abroad? Was it easy or difficult to integrate? Why / Why not?

b Talk about a country you could imagine living in, or have lived in. From what you know of the country and its culture, what things in the box would / did you find:

1 easy to adapt to?
2 interesting or exciting?
3 difficult to adapt to?

values and beliefs	food and eating habits	making friends
leisure time and going out	the way society is organised	climate
language and culture	family life and relationships	safety

1.2 goals

◎ talk about memory

A

Athabasca University 2012/13

Student Identification & Library Card

Julia Gates

1563237

Stephen White, Registrar

Canada's Open University

B

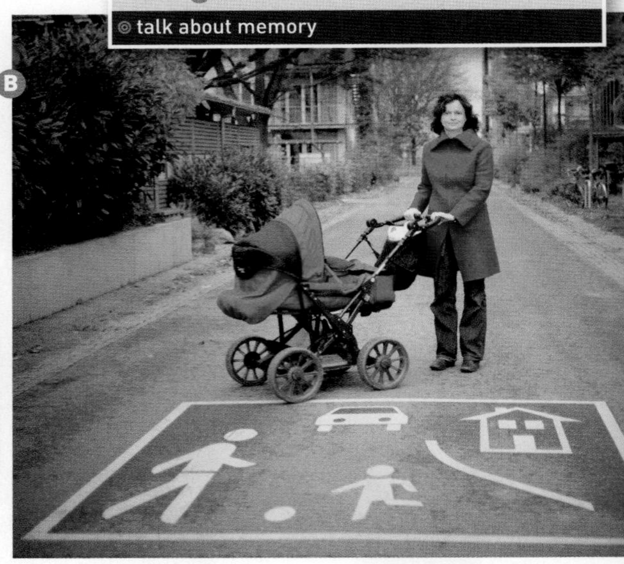

Memory

SPEAKING

1 a How well do you remember things? Look at these photos for one minute, then look on p126.

b Talk together. Who seems to have a better:

- short-term memory?
- memory for names and numbers?
- long-term memory?
- visual memory?

LISTENING

2 a How do you think these photos are connected with memory?

A

B

C

D

E

b 1.2 Listen to five people talking about different aspects of memory.

1 Match each person with one of the images in 2a.
2 Does each person have a good or a bad memory?

c 1.2 Listen again and correct these statements about each speaker.

1 Liam recalls where he is immediately and always has a good visual memory.
2 Jane doesn't check her pockets before leaving the house because she doesn't have time.
3 Olga keeps the passwords in her head but forgets them easily.
4 Uri's memory is very good for his age, especially when it comes to numbers.
5 Tina can't remember names of anything or anyone.

d Which of the five people do you most identify with? Why?

READING

3 a Look at the title of the article. What do you think the author will say about memory?

b Read the article quickly. What is the writer's main point about childhood memory? How do we know this?

c How does the writer grab our attention in the first few sentences?

Childhood memories are *fairytales*

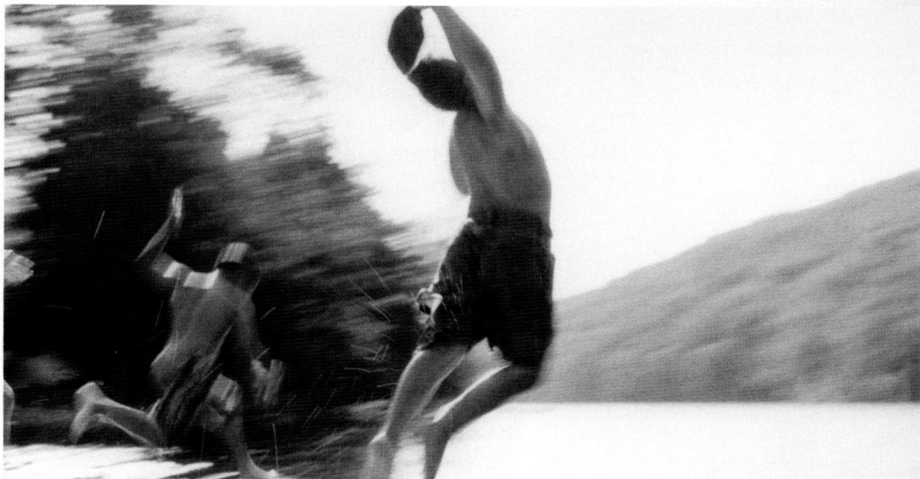

Most of us have treasured memories of the events that shaped our lives as a child. Or do we? Controversial new research claims that those recollections may be as real as fairytales. Leading psychologist Elizabeth Loftus, of the University of California, believes your memories are more likely to be dream-like reconstructions of stories told by your parents. When we think we are reminiscing, we are simply 'rewriting' our memory to suit ourselves. She adds: "Our biases, expectations and past knowledge are all used in the filling-in process, leading to distortions of what we remember." She maintains there is no evidence that perfect memories are stored by individuals.

In one study, volunteers were asked to read about events that happened to them as children. One of these was made up – a shopping trip when they were five, in which they got lost and were rescued by an elderly person. Later, some participants recalled the event in detail, with self-assurance and emotion. You could argue that these people might have genuinely lost their mum in a shop at some point during childhood. But Loftus later carried out similar studies where the fake event was an attack by a vicious animal, or being responsible for knocking over a punch bowl at a family wedding and spilling it all over the bride. The results were the same.

Dr Jaime Quintanilla, professor of psychiatry at the Texas School of Medicine, agrees that our earliest recollections are far from accurate and often complete distortions or figments of our imagination. He says: "It's a proven fact that young children take fragments of experience and build them into distorted memories. For example, one 40-year-old man distinctly remembers his parents once punished him by refusing to buy him shoes. In fact, when he was three, he cut his foot on a piece of glass and developed a nasty infection. For two weeks, he was confined to the house in his socks so his wound would heal. When he wanted to go out, he was told he couldn't, because he had no shoes." These false suggestions about childhood events can profoundly change people's attitudes and behaviour in adulthood.

d **Read the article again.**

1 Why do we choose to 'rewrite our memories'?
2 What would you say is the 'filling-in process'?
3 What do the anecdotes about the shopping trip and wedding reveal?
4 How are these findings shown to be important in later life?

LANGUAGE FOCUS
Remembering

4 **a** **Look at the article.**

1 What synonyms can you find for remember and memory? How are they different in meaning?
2 'One 40-year-old man distinctly remembers ...'. What other adverbs could collocate with remember?

b **Look at the script for 1.2 on p146. Explain the expressions in bold using remember.**

'Jog my memory' means something makes or helps me to remember.

SPEAKING

5 **Discuss these questions.**

1 Do you have a clear idea of your earliest memory? What do you think it might be?
2 Do you think this memory is your own, or was it told to you by family or friends?
3 Why do you think this memory stayed? How did you feel about what happened?
4 Do you agree that we tend to distort our earliest memories?

Target activity

Describe a childhood memory

1.3 goals
- talk about a personal memory
- evoke the feelings and moods of a past event

TASK LISTENING

1 a What images of childhood does the photo bring to mind?

b Which moments can you most easily recall from your childhood?

holidays / journeys
moving house
your grandparents
a new school
your best friend
a particular day / place

c What helps trigger that memory: an image? a feeling? a smell?

2 a 1.3 Listen to Andrew, Julia and Ben describing their memories. Which topics in 1b do they talk about?

b 1.3 Listen again. Try to 'picture' the scenes the speakers describe.

1. What images stand out? Make notes.
2. What feelings or moods are associated with each description? Note adjectives and nouns.
3. Why is the memory still significant for each speaker?

TASK LANGUAGE
Talking about a personal memory

3 a Look at the script on p146. Divide each memory into four different sections:

- focusing on time and place.
- describing background / participants.
- relating a sequence of events.
- giving an evaluation.

b You can use different expressions to structure your memory. Complete the gaps.

Focusing on time and place	Describing background / participants
• I remember [1]________ I was little ... • I remember [2]________ to the beach ... • The thing I [3]________ remember is ... • One of my [4]________ memories is ...	• I [8]________ just started primary school. • I must [9]________ about four years old. • We [10]________ in a kind of forested area. • She [11]________ getting married. • We [12]________ stay in a cottage ...
Relating a sequence of events	**Giving an evaluation**
• [5]________ we got towards the coast ... • We're [6]________ really close friends ... • [7]________ the time we arrived ...	• [13]________ back now on this occasion ... • That's a [14]________ of meeting someone. • ... has just [15]________ with me forever.

c Why is *would* used so frequently in Andrew's story?

TASK

4 Talk about a childhood memory.

1. Think of a significant childhood event from which you learned something. Decide how you want to tell it.
2. Divide the memory into four clear sections. Choose expressions from 3b to help you.
3. Tell your story. Listen to each other's memories and talk about what personal significance they still have.
4. Talk about the differences and similarities between your stories.

Across cultures Attitudes to children

1 These photos accompany a feature about Norway called *Babyland*.

1 What do you think the photos show?
2 What do you think the feature will say about Norwegian society?

A
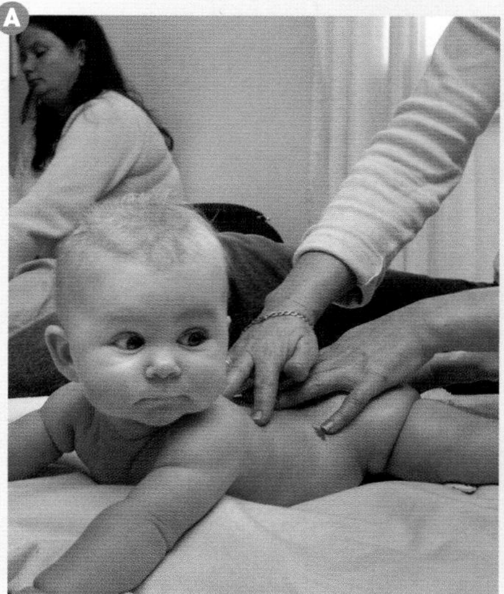

B
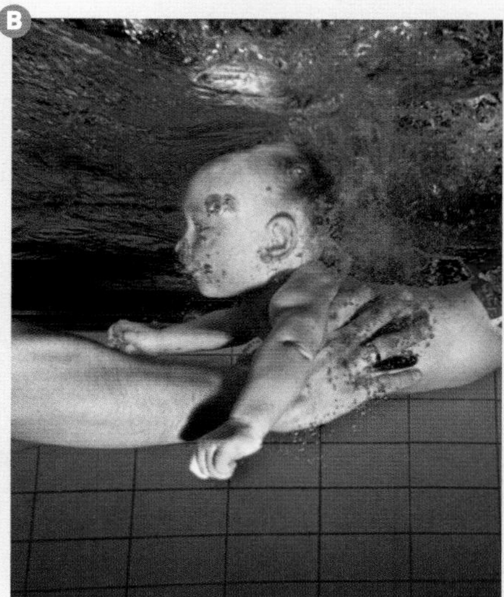

C
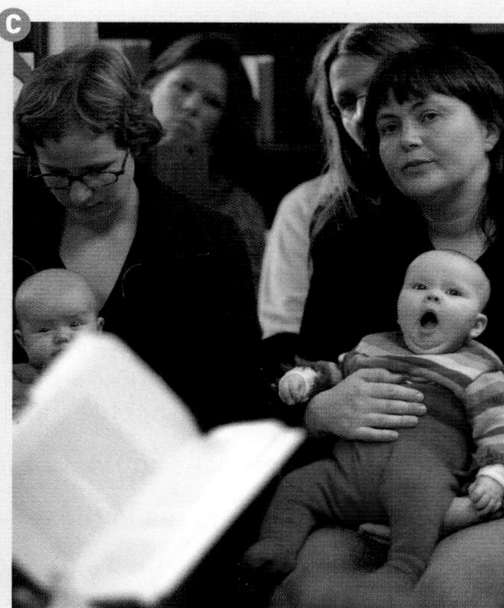

2 Read the introduction to the feature.

1 What, if anything, surprised you?
2 Could this article be a description of your country? What would be different?

Babyland

According to the UN's Human Development Index, Norway is the best place to live on the planet. It certainly seems to be one of the best places to be a baby. In contrast to most European countries, the Norwegian birth rate is a healthy 1.9. Norway's reputation as a child-friendly society is partially founded on a succession of government initiatives to improve parents' rights and economic circumstances. Maternity leave is 42 weeks with full pay, and paternity leave is four weeks. There is financial support for those who choose to look after their children rather than return to the workplace. And the baby industry is booming, giving birth to a plethora of new activities: baby-massage, baby-cinema, baby 'n' book days at the library, even *baby-au-lait* (a term for breastfeeding-friendly cafés).

3 Talk about whether your country is 'child-friendly'.

1 How much support is there for mothers or fathers and babies?
2 What facilities are there for small children?
3 How safe is it for children?
4 What are people's attitudes towards children?
Do they tend to:
- ignore them?
- make a fuss?
- expect them to behave well?
- disapprove?

5 Is it considered important to have children?
Do most people want to have them?
Has this changed in recent years?

Keywords describing habits and tendencies

1 a Look at these examples from the unit. What meaning do will and would have? Could you express the same meaning in another way?

```
1  If you see anyone and say hello, they will not say hello back.
2  In London, I'll just stay home and watch TV.
3  As we got towards the coast, the trees would start to thin out.
4  … and we'd pack all our things up and set off for the beach …
```

b In these sentences, people are talking about childhood. Add will or would and a verb.

1. When he was little, he *would sleep* when you didn't want him to!
2. If you're not careful, they ______ on their video games all afternoon.
3. She ______ with her twin sister but not with the oldest one, not any more.
4. Babies ______. That's how they start talking, by mimicking us adults.
5. As a kid, I ______ hours on my own, I was a real loner.
6. He was a very impolite kid. He ______ 'please' or 'thank you'.

c In which sentences could we also use used to? Would this change the meaning?

d Correct the mistakes in these sentences.

1. I use to ride my bike with my friends.
2. I would have lots of friends when I was little.
3. I'm still remembering my fifth birthday.

2 a These sentences show other ways to talk about habits, or things that often happen. Underline the expressions that convey this idea.

1. Young children *have a tendency* to take fragments of experience and build them into distorted memories.
2. In Western societies, we tend to share precious memories of childhood and relate these openly in public.
3. I'm afraid I'm always forgetting people's names and faces.
4. As I get older, my memory starts to fade a bit, and I'm liable to forget things I've done.
5. People like me, who are prone to put on weight, can't eat like that. You're OK – you're really skinny.

b Which expressions often have a negative connotation? Which means 'it's annoying' in this case?

3 a What tendencies might you associate with these photos? Use expressions from 2a to talk about them.

A

B

C

D

b 1.4 Listen to the conversations. Match them with the photos.

1. Where are the two people?
2. What is each speaker warning the listener about? Why?

4 Think of someone with an irritating or attractive habit. Describe it using will / would or expressions from 2a.

EXPLORESpeaking

Goals

- tell an anecdote effectively
- keep people interested in a story

1 Talk together.

1 What are the children doing in the photo?
2 What is their attitude?
3 What makes a story captivating?

2 a 1.5 **Cover the script on this page and listen.**

1 Why was the story not very effective?
2 What could the speaker have done to make it more effective? Think about:
- tone of voice.
- attitude.
- pace.
- use of language.

b 1.6 **Listen to a second version of the same story.**

1 What is the difference between the ways they are told?
2 How is the second speaker's story-telling more effective?

3 1.6 **Listen again and look at the script on this page. The speaker uses various strategies to keep the listeners interested. Find examples of:**

1 rhetorical questions.
They say the youngest are the spoilt ones, don't they?
2 visual details.
3 direct speech.
4 addressing the audience directly.
5 comments which are not part of the story.
6 repetition.

4 Find more colourful synonyms in the story for these expressions.

1 visible *in full view*
2 smiling a lot
3 disappeared
4 shocked
5 found it amusing
6 allowed me to do what I wanted
7 behaving badly

5 a Work in groups. How could you make the story below more interesting?

I was 10. We were on holiday in Italy. We were walking down a street and stopped to watch some street performers. I went to the front of the crowd to get a better view. I was watching the performers and forgot everything else. When the performance finished, I looked round and couldn't see my parents. I was scared and started running down the street. Then I realised I should stay in one place, so I went back to the street performers. After a few minutes I saw my parents. They bought me an ice cream.

b Practise telling the story.

I'm the youngest of three. So, as I'm sure you can imagine, when I was little I was always up to no good. They say the youngest are the spoilt ones, don't they? I suppose my parents just let me get away with it, because I was the youngest. I'd spend half the time showing off, breaking my brothers' toys, ruining their games, attracting attention to myself. You know, the usual, just terrible … Anyway, I'd better get back to the anecdote!

Well, my dad did a lot of public speaking for his work, and sometimes all of us – the whole family – would go and see him. I remember being told how important it was to be on our best behaviour then. So, if I started messing about, my brothers would just pretend that they didn't know me. It was like a very formal setting with cameras and everything. At first, they would try to keep me quiet, or stop me fidgeting or whatever, but then they used to just ignore me, 'cos it was too embarrassing otherwise.

Anyway, my brother Gary tells me that one day, I was sitting there with all of them and I just disappeared. So my mother asked, "Where's he gone now? Where's that troublemaker?" One minute I was there it seems, the next minute I'd vanished into thin air. So, anyway, everyone got a bit panicky because no one knew where I'd got to. Then, suddenly … you should have seen everybody's faces … suddenly, there I was in full view. I'd only got up on the stage with my dad, hadn't I? Waving to everybody and beaming like mad in front of the cameras. Can you believe how cheeky you have to be to do that, can you?

Apparently, what I'd done is edge out of the seat without anyone seeing and then crawl down to where my father was speaking. At first, my dad was horrified … but then he saw the funny side, and the audience did too. I mean, I simply couldn't bear anyone else to get the attention! I wanted to be the star! Nothing's changed really. Unbelievable!

Grammar

would

1 a Match groups A–F with these uses of would.

1 past habits *B*
2 polite requests and offers
3 the past of 'will' in reported speech
4 the 'future-in-the-past'
5 hypothetical situations
6 giving advice (softening)

A They said that there would be hundreds out of work.
He said he would be back in time for the film.
B In those days, we would walk home late at night with no problem.
Sometimes we'd go to work, just for fun.
C After that goal, it was clear they wouldn't win the match.
She decided that she'd spend the rest of her life there.
D Without the land, we would have gone bankrupt a long time ago.
Would you ever leave this country?
E Would you mind having a look at this with me?
Which hotel would you prefer to stay in?
F I wouldn't worry about it, if I were you.
You'd be a complete fool not to take that job, you really would.

b In which cases can would have a similar meaning to 'was going to' and 'used to'?

2 a Change these sentences to include would.

1 Open the door.
2 I asked him, but he didn't say a word.
3 Do you prefer to go by bus?
4 She never forgot that favour.
5 I went there every year in August.
6 He said he might leave early today.
7 That's so typical of her to say that.

b What effect, however subtle, do these changes have on each sentence?

c 1.7 Listen to check. Is would stressed in any of the sentences?

3 a Complete these sentences so they are true for you.

1 I wouldn't be surprised if ...
2 I would always recommend ...
3 When I was younger, I thought I would ...
4 I can't imagine what I'd do if ...
5 I wish people wouldn't ...
6 I'd rather ... than ...

b Listen to each other's sentences. Ask questions to find out more.

Grammar reference, p140

using the *-ing* form

4 Look at these examples. In which is the -ing form:

a the subject of the sentence?
b after a preposition?
c after a verb?

1 Looking back now on this occasion reminds me of how beautiful the village childhood was.
2 Sometimes all of us – the whole family – went to see him. I remember being told how important it was to be on our best behaviour then.
3 Apparently, what I'd done is edge out of the seat without anyone seeing and …

5 Look at these verbs.

1 Which of these verbs can be followed by -ing forms?
2 Which can be followed by to + infinitive?
3 Which can be followed by both?

remember finish manage offer regret decide mind suggest imagine agree enjoy postpone prepare give up risk avoid

6 a Add prepositions to these sentences from the unit.

1 I get kind of tired shopping.
2 I've no problem remembering pin numbers.
3 That's a happy memory meeting someone.
4 That's how they start talking, mimicking us adults.

b Which sentences are also possible without the preposition? Would they mean the same?

7 a Complete these sentences using an -ing form.

1 I wouldn't mind ...
2 I get really fed up with ...
3 You can't always avoid ...
4 I vaguely remember ...
5 I'm quite used to ...

I get really fed up with receiving junk mail.

b Listen to each other's sentences. Ask questions to find out more.

Vocabulary

Memory

8 a How many collocations with memory can you remember?

Short-term memory.

Jog someone's memory.

b In what context do you think you would hear these expressions? Which is the odd one out?

1 They're the worst in living memory.
2 He's suffering from short-term memory loss, but there's nothing to worry about.
3 You've got a memory like a sieve.
4 This model has plenty of memory.
5 I think I can do it from memory.
6 Sorry, memory's playing tricks again.

c 1.8 Listen to check.

just

9 Look at these sentences from the unit. What does just mean? More than one answer may be possible.

only really simply

1 My dad, he decided he just want to stay here one year. *only*
2 In Africa, if you see anyone walking around, you just say hello.
3 I'll just stay at home and watch TV.
4 If a person's older than you, you call them madam or auntie, even if you don't know them. It's just respect.
5 They act differently towards immigrant people. Sometimes they're just nasty.

10 a Look at these examples with the expression it's just too much. What situations might they be used in and what would they mean?

1 I can't do it, working full-time, it's just too much.
2 It's just too much pressure right now.
3 I'm not sure, it's just too much of a risk.
4 Living like this – it's just too much to handle.
5 It's just too much for her, she's had enough.

b Look again at the expressions in 10a. Decide which words or syllables you would stress.

c 1.9 Listen to check.

d Imagine you are in one of these situations. Talk to another student about it using expressions from 10a. Then ask for advice.

- You're working very hard.
- You want to invest some money.
- You're moving to a new home.
- You're looking after someone's children.

11 a What do you think the people are saying in the cartoons? Use It's just so / That's just too ... .

b 1.10 Listen to check.

c 1.10 Listen again to how the speakers stress the key words. Which is the most important information in each case?

1

2

3

4

Self-assessment

Can you do these things in English? Circle a number on each line. 1 = I can't do this, 5 = I can do this well.

talk about adapting to different cultures	1	2	3	4	5
talk about memory	1	2	3	4	5
talk about a personal memory	1	2	3	4	5
evoke the feelings and mood of a past event	1	2	3	4	5
tell an anecdote effectively	1	2	3	4	5
keep people interested in a story	1	2	3	4	5

- For Wordcards, reference and saving your work → e-Portfolio
- For more practice → Self-study Pack, Unit 1

2 Self

2.1 goals

- talk about personality traits
- talk about identity

Your online self

SPEAKING

1 Look at this profile image used on a social networking site. Discuss these questions.

1. What aspect of his personality do you think he wants to show?
2. Have you ever uploaded an image to represent yourself? What was it for and how did you choose it?
3. Do you have an online page? Do you regularly update it or comment on other people's?
4. Do you think these pages generally portray an accurate impression of people's character?

READING

2 Read the article. Does it have similar views to yours?

Social networking sites such as Facebook, MySpace and Orkut are now estimated to have more than 700 million users worldwide. As users can create any profile of themselves they choose, you might expect them to portray themselves in the best possible light. When putting up a profile, it would be reasonable for them to present flattering images, choose sophisticated and discerning interests, and carefully express their thoughts so as to appear more intelligent than in real life. But according to recent research, this is not the case. Far from presenting themselves in a flattering way, most users' profiles reflect their true personalities, and reveal both psychological weaknesses and natural physical flaws.

Research was carried out on 250 Facebook users who filled in a personality questionnaire. Results were compared with the same people's Facebook profiles. The survey set out to assess not only the participants' actual personality, but their 'ideal' personality – in other words, what kind of person they would be if they actually possessed all their ideal characteristics. These results were then compared with the participants' Facebook profiles. What emerged was astonishing: far from being idealised versions of themselves, people's online profiles conformed closely to what they were really like. Their profiles accurately reflected how agreeable, extroverted, conscientious, neurotic and sociable they were in real life.

It's not entirely clear why online profiles depict users' personalities so accurately. It could be that users want to portray themselves as they really are, or it could be that people attempt to present an ideal image of themselves but in fact fail to do so. One thing seems clear: social networking sites can in no way be considered a false online world that is idealised and removed from reality; rather, they are simply another way in which people choose to interact with each other.

3 a Read the article again. Identify the parts which make these points.

1. We are not calculating in the way that we present ourselves to others.
2. We don't attempt to hide our eccentricities or our appearance.
3. Online profiles are not fantasy representations, but match reality.
4. People want to present – or are unable to hide – their true selves.
5. In spite of what many people think, networking sites encourage us to be who we are.

b Look at the opening paragraph. How does the writer arouse the reader's curiosity about the differing viewpoints?

LANGUAGE FOCUS
Presenting a self-image

4 a Find eight adjectives in the article which refer to different personality traits.

b Cover the article. Can you remember what nouns collocated with these verbs?

create	portray	put up	present	choose	reflect	express	reveal

5 **Discuss these questions.**

1 In what other ways can people present themselves online (e.g. role-playing games or professional websites)?
2 Look at these online profile images. Why do you think each person chose them?
3 Can you think of other types of profile photo? What would you typically see in them?

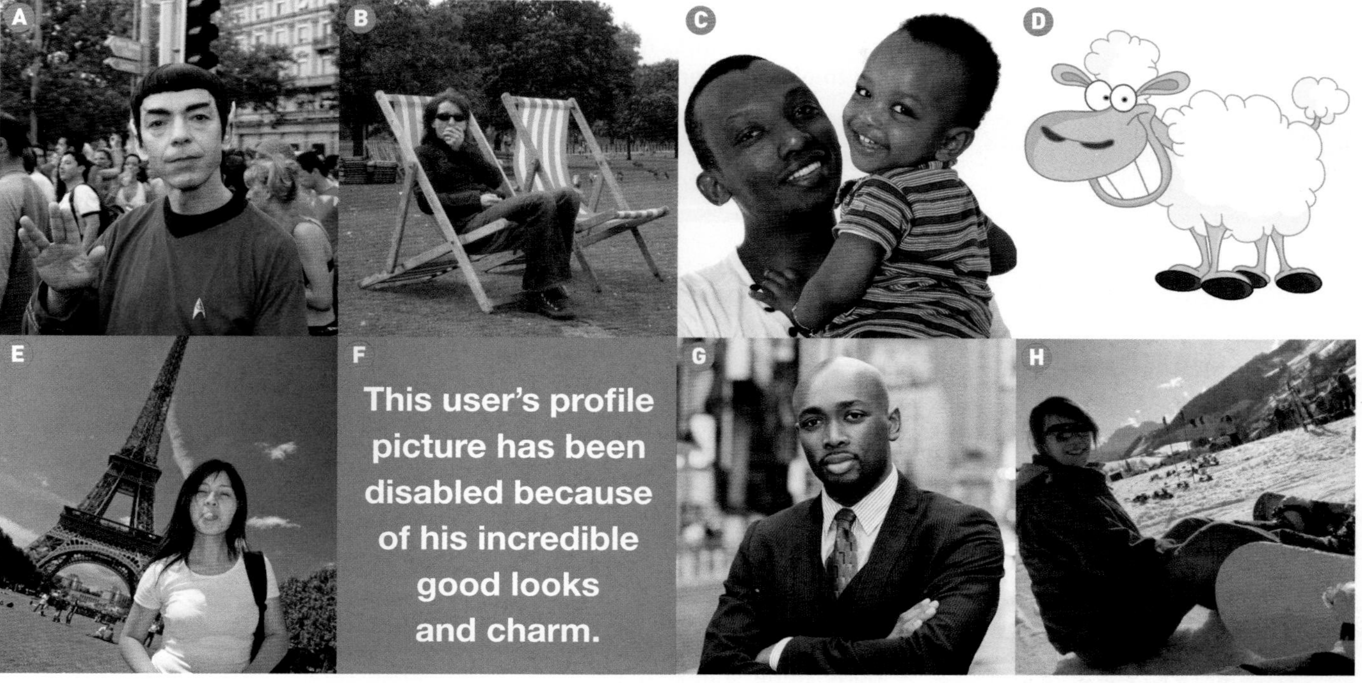

What defines you?

LISTENING

1 **a** 1.11 **Listen to Norman, Olga, Liam and Jane answering the question 'What defines you?' What is the defining factor in each case?**

b 1.11 **Listen again and make notes on these questions.**

1 Which two people mention other countries or cultures? How were they influenced by them?
2 Which two people talk about when they were younger? How was their sense of self different then?
3 What people do they all mention as being important in defining who they are?

LANGUAGE FOCUS
Talking about identity

2 **a Match expressions 1–8 from the recording with sentence endings a–h.**

1 I think of my identity partly in terms of
2 I need to feel part of
3 My life is centred a lot on
4 What defines me most is
5 I'm a product of
6 I see myself as
7 I like to think that I'm reflected in
8 What has also had a great influence on me was

a my friends.
b my background.
c a happy person.
d my stay in other countries.
e the people I like.
f my children rather than on myself.
g where I come from.
h a close circuit of friends.

b Check the script on p147.

SPEAKING

3 **What defines you as a person?**

1 Work alone. Think about these categories:
- nationality.
- religion.
- clothes and appearance.
- language.
- your family.
- where you grew up.
- your work or job.
- belonging to a group.
- personality traits.

2 Think about expressions in 2a you could use to talk about your identity.
3 Compare with other students. Did you define yourselves in similar ways?
4 Which categories do you think are the most and least important?

Dating agencies

2.2 goals

- understand promotional language
- say how you met someone

READING

1 **Talk together.**

1. Why do you think online dating agencies are gaining popularity?
2. Do you know anyone who met their partner in this way?

2 **Look at the three websites. What different ways of meeting people do they provide? How do you think each service works?**

A

➡ ClubM8 is a brand-new community that gives you the chance to chat, exchange text messages and interact with other cell-phone users, anytime, anywhere. It's 100% fun and 100% safe! How does it work, you ask? It's simple. You tell ClubM8 what your desires and criteria are. You'll receive the profiles of members that match yours, while your profile is sent out to members you match with. You'll immediately be able to exchange text messages with him or her however, whenever, wherever you want! No boring forms to fill in, or expensive subscriptions to pay. Send a text message now and enter the fun! You may find your perfect ... cell mate!

B

Solo's

Nobody understands the needs of the single traveller more than we do, which is why you have made us the UK's number 1. Established in 1969, ours is a name our customers trust, that's why they come back to us, time after time. Solo's isn't just another holiday company. Solo's is a travel community, and we fondly welcome new 'members' to enjoy the experiences of solo travel. We know that our success is completely down to our customers, and that's the ethos upon which our business has grown over the last quarter of a century. The service we offer is personal, yet unobtrusive – group sizes do vary, but you will doubtless be holidaying with other single travellers who share a passion for life and discovering new, exciting destinations in the UK, Europe and around the world. Love is nearer than you think.

C

Make it happen!

Stop waiting around for Mr or Ms Right, and simply log on to the dating agency for professionals. It's OK to look, and with a million members online, you're sure to love what you see. Start a subscription, create your profile and start enjoying all we have to offer. If you don't find that someone special in three months, we'll give you the next three months absolutely free! Not convinced by online love? Then our Singles' Events may be your thing. Aimed at professionals, these are a great way to find like-minded people in a relaxed party atmosphere. For the not-so-confident, we even have our staff on hand to help you mingle and make you feel at ease. You'd be a fool not to give it a try ...

3 **Which website does each sentence describe?**

1 Other people are available to help you meet the right person.
2 The company has existed for a long time.
3 It compares its services to others.
4 It targets a specific type of customer.
5 It stresses the number of people available in the service.
6 The service emphasises the ease with which you contact someone.
7 It compliments its customers.
8 It makes an offer if the customer is unlucky in love.

LANGUAGE FOCUS
Promotional language

4 a **What devices do the adverts use to sell their product? Find examples of:**

1 a promise or prediction.
2 a boast.
3 a slogan.
4 an exclamation.
5 a joke or pun.

b **What kind of language do they use? Find examples of these forms in the adverts.**

imperatives · rhetorical questions · conditional sentences · positive adjectives · inversion · modal verbs

c **What other techniques are used?**

How we met

LANGUAGE FOCUS
Say how you met someone

1 a **Read this testimonial about dating agency C. Fill in the gaps with the most appropriate form of the verbs in brackets.**

"We met at the London Singles' Events in July. He [1]______ (say) he [2]______ (see) my photo on the wall and just [3]______ (know)! I [4]______ (be) there with friends – we [5]______ (see) the advert in the paper and we [6]______ (decide) to give it a try, just for a laugh. I [7]______ (sit) in a corner having a drink and he [8]______ (come) to find me. We [9]______ (chat) for the rest of the evening and then he [10]______ (call) the next day and we [11]______ (be) together ever since. We [12]______ (have) tons in common. We both [13]______ (work) in the media and [14]______ (have) an amazing time. So thank you! It does work and I'm so glad I [15]______ (come), or I never [16]______ (meet) the love of my life!"

b 1.12 **Listen to check. What different verb forms are there? Make a list. Are these the only forms that could be used in each gap, or would others be possible? Why / Why not?**

WRITING and SPEAKING

2 a **Writing game. Invent a story about meeting someone for the first time.**

1 Write a few sentences starting with 'We met …'. Pass it to another student.
2 Add a few more sentences starting with 'I was …'. Pass it to another student.
3 Continue, starting with the expressions in the box. Pass each new section to another student.

- He / She was …
- We … and then …
- And since then …
- We have tons in common. We both …

b **Read out your story.**

3 **Work with a partner. Describe how you met someone important to you. Talk about:**

- when and where you met.
- how it happened.
- what you first talked about.
- what you had (or have) in common.

Promote yourself

2.3 goals
- use effective introduction strategies
- promote yourself

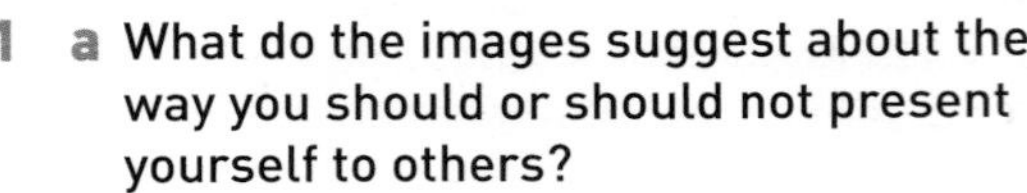

TASK LISTENING

1 a What do the images suggest about the way you should or should not present yourself to others?

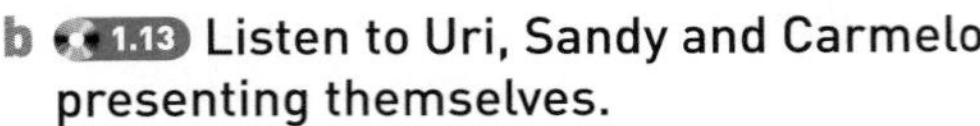

b 1.13 Listen to Uri, Sandy and Carmelo presenting themselves.

1 What do you think are the situations? What words helped you decide?
2 What is wrong in each case with the way the candidates present themselves?
3 What advice would you give the people?

c 1.14 Listen to new versions. What has improved?

TASK LANGUAGE
Introduction strategies

2 a Match these strategies to the highlighted examples in the scripts.

1 backtracking and reformulating *b*
2 choosing an equivalent term for a word you can't remember
3 selecting an expression in order to gain time and keep the floor
4 expanding and developing the point
5 handling interjections well
6 considering the effect on the listener

A

AMANDA So, Uri, would you like to say a little bit about yourself first, just to get the ball rolling, you know?
URI Of course, well, my name is Uri Salemi. [a]I have worked in the marketing ... area for many years, as you might have seen from my CV and I studied economics, so that's why working with Deutsche Bank really was appealing ... [b]why it really appealed to me, I should say. I believe I have a number of characteristics that would be suitable for the job.
A Such as?
U [c]My experience of working in a team, the need to plan strategically, and decisiveness when having to take difficult, tough decisions. I think these facets are crucial.

B

MICHAEL So, Ms Faber, it's nice to meet you at last!
SANDY [d]Hi, Sandy Faber. Likewise, Michael! It's always nice to meet somebody face to face after emailing such a long time. It's wonderful to be here!
M Yes, that's right, it's always good to put a face to a name.
S [e]Absolutely, the thing is ... sometimes you never get to meet that person and that can be even more frustrating, can't it?
M Well, I'm glad that's not the case this time. Well, it's time for you to meet the others now... come this way, please. The seminar begins in a few minutes.

C

AMANDA Mrs Santos, it's really nice to have you back here with us.
CARMELO Thanks a lot. Pleased to meet you, [f]I don't think we've been introduced. Carmelo Santos.
A Amanda Woods.
C It's a pleasure, Amanda. And, well, it's great to be back. So, I suppose the other candidates are here? Should I go through?
A Oh yes, we're keen to get started, as you can imagine. Is there anything else you need?
C I was wondering if I could borrow a pen, I seem to have left mine behind for some reason.
A Of course, no problem. Follow me.

b How do the people introduce themselves? Who is more formal / informal?

c How do the interviewers attempt to put the candidate at ease?

TASK

3 Conduct a job interview. Together, look at this job. Then, Student A, look on p126. Student B, look on p134.

Public relations manager

We need a high-energy, motivated professional to take responsibility for external communication and growing our company's reputation.

Responsibilities. You will be the main point of contact for the media, writing press releases, presentations, customer success stories and case studies. You will be building the company's presence online (Facebook, Twitter, etc.) and driving programmes for winning awards, gaining positive product reviews in the media, and so on.

Required experience. You should have 3–5 years of public relations and marketing experience, as well as a university / college degree, preferably in business or marketing.

Required skills. Superior written and oral communications skills are a must. You are a creative thinker who can develop unique ideas and marketing programmes, someone who is passionate about growing our company every day.

Across cultures Your cards

1 a Look at these business cards. What do you think the cards say about the people who own them or the company they work for?

b In your country, do people use business cards as a way of expressing themselves?

c What do individuals or companies need to bear in mind when designing a business card for themselves?

2 a Read the article and check your answers. Where do you think this article originally appeared?

Business cards are something that we take for granted when we shouldn't. The look, feel, and message on a card help people determine how they view you, and more importantly, if they will even remember you. When you leave a conversation and the other party has your business card, your identity is that piece of paper. Because of this representation, your business card should not only state who you work for, your contact information, and what you do, but it should also state something about you – not in a written sense, but more of an impression of your overall image. For example, if I were to hand you my business card, you would probably get the feeling that I am a warm and caring person (the card is thick, yet feels soft; the corners of the card and the typography are rounded; it's green), because that's just the message I wanted to communicate.

b Look at the business cards again. Do you notice any features mentioned in the article?

3 a Think about the people below. What image of themselves or their company might they want to convey through their card? How might this be reflected in the card itself?

1. the sales manager of an international company
2. a singer
3. an architect
4. a yoga teacher
5. a website designer
6. the owner of a furniture shop

b Work in pairs. Choose one of the people and design a card for them. Think about:

- information.
- images.
- colours.
- texture.
- uniqueness.
- font.

c Find other students who chose the same person. Compare your ideas.

4 **Discuss these questions.**

1. Do people in your country present cards to each other? In what situations?
2. Do you know any other societies where cards are: more important? less important? Why is this?
3. Do you think the society in which you live encourages people to stand out or fit in?
4. What other cards in your possession communicate things about you to others? (Consider different cards: membership cards, loyalty cards, identity cards, etc.)

Keywords describing skill and ability

1 a Look at these examples.

1. Do you think they are written or spoken?
2. Where would you read or hear them? What are they about?

a Natasha is settling in very well at Lancaster and doing lots of sport, apparently. She seems to have a real talent _______ _______ new sports - she took up volleyball this term ...

b We are based in Glasgow and still small, but set to expand rapidly. We need someone who has acquired skills _______ _______ a business and who would be committed to hard but rewarding work.

c So United still three down, and nowhere near their usual form. But as they proved last season against Bolton they do have this ability _______ _______ the match in the last minute ...

b Add a preposition and a verb to each sentence. What do you notice about the verb forms?

in	to	for	win	learn	run

c How could you express each sentence using these words?

a talented
b skilled
c capable

2 a Which of these words frequently occur before talent? Which frequently occur before skills?

leadership real natural academic
basic computer considerable
technical intellectual

b Which of these words can also come before the word ability?

c Talent can refer to people or the ability itself. Which do you think these expressions refer to?

1 new talent *people*
2 creative talent
3 young talent
4 home-grown talent
5 athletic talent
6 artistic talent

3 a What type of talent or skill do you think is being illustrated in the photos opposite?

b 1.15 Listen to check.

1. Which expressions do you hear?
2. What are the people talking about?
3. Which of the skills can you easily learn?

4 Think of someone who has a particular talent for something. What would you say are his / her skills? Talk about this person's achievements.

2 EXPLOREWriting

Goals
- write a cover letter
- describe experience and ability

1 a You are going to read a letter applying for an MBA grant. How do you think the words in the box will be used?

skills familiar relevant future aptitude challenges hesitate specialty application accustomed

b Add words to the gaps.

Dear Sir/Madam,

I am writing to provide you with some background information so you can better judge my scholarship [1]______ for the MA in Business Administration (see attached form and résumé).

Regarding my academic experience, I am currently completing my degree in Economics at the University of Stony Brook, New York, where my current [2]______ is in Marketing. So far, I have received excellent grades in all subjects, and I am on course to graduate with distinction at the end of the semester. Enclosed you will find photocopies of all [3]______ certificates.

As you will see from my attached résumé, I am [4]______ to working in the financial sector. I've worked for the last three summers for Citibank in the customer service department here in New York State, where I honed my personal [5]______ and became [6]______ with the banking world at first hand.

I believe my greatest strengths lie in my ability to work well in a team and an [7]______ for taking on whatever [8]______ that come my way. For these reasons, at this stage in my life, I strongly believe I am able to take on the demands of a full-time Masters degree. My [9]______ career in banking would be greatly enhanced by earning an MBA at your university.

Should my application be successful, I am available for interview whenever it is convenient. If you require any further details or references, please don't [10]______ to contact me.

I look forward to hearing from you.

With best wishes,

Sharon Partridge

Sharon Partridge

2 a Does the writer use US or British English? How can you tell? Do you think it is important to adopt one variety or the other?

b How does the writer present herself in a positive light? Find expressions in the letter which show optimism and self-confidence.

c Cover the letter. How do (or could) these sentences continue?

1 My greatest strength is an aptitude …
2 I am accustomed …
3 I became familiar …
4 I believe my greatest strengths lie …
5 I am available …

d Look at the letter and check.

e How is the letter structured?

1 Describe the function of each paragraph.
2 What kind of language is required for each?

3 Write a cover letter. Choose one of these options.

- Apply for a further education grant in an academic field of your choice.
- Respond to a job advert in the professional field of your choice.

Grammar

Verb tenses in narration

1 **Can you remember the story in *How we met* on p19? Which different tenses did you use?**

2 **Which tenses can be used to:**

1. set the scene of the story?
2. describe actions in progress up to a point in the past?
3. describe the story's main events?
4. clarify that one event happened before another?

3 **Put these pictures in order to make a story.**

A

B

C

D

E

F

4 **Read the story and fill in the gaps with the most appropriate form of the verbs in brackets.**

"I [1] *had spent* (spend) a year off in France and [2] ______ (look for) a partner there for months but I [3] ______ (not find) anybody I could relate to, or who also liked me. Anyway, that all [4] ______ (change) the day I [5] ______ (leave) France. I [6] ______ (wake up) early and [7] ______ (take) the six-hour train journey to the airport. So far, so good. I got to the airport fine, no problem. But then chaos [8] ______ (strike). When checking in at the airport I found that my flight was full and I was on standby. They told me that I [9] ______ (do) the online check-in wrong or something. I [10] ______ (travel) a long time already, was really tired and this was the last thing that I needed. Anyway, I [11] ______ (wait) patiently at the gate, hoping to get my place, when the pilot of the plane [12] ______ (arrive), looked at me and asked the stewards what [13] ______ (happen). Can you believe he intervened and got a seat for me in the cockpit? Well, that's how we met. Incredible isn't it? Funny thing is, he's not French, and I [14] ______ (not go back) to France since."

5 **Work in A/B pairs.**

1. Prepare to tell your partner something that happened to you. Use one of these ideas or your own:
   - an important event in your life.
   - an interesting travel experience.
2. Think of the background to your story and any effects it still has for you now.
3. Tell your story.

Grammar reference, p140

Phrasal verbs; verbs + prepositions

6 a **Look at these examples from the unit. Which of the highlighted expressions are:**

- verbs + prepositions?
- phrasal verbs?

What is the difference between them?

1. 250 Facebook users who filled in a personality questionnaire.
2. When putting up a profile, it would be reasonable for them to present flattering images.
3. It gives you the chance to interact with other cell-phone users.
4. Aimed at professionals, these are a great way to find like-minded people …
5. I have worked in the marketing area for many years.
6. I am able to take on the demands of a full-time Masters degree.

b **Add prepositions or particles to these verbs. Underline the phrasal verbs.**

1. I didn't succeed ______ passing the test.
2. I'm lacking ______ practical experience.
3. I decided to look ______ 'avatar' on wikipedia.
4. I would benefit ______ living abroad for a year.
5. I relied ______ bluffing to get through the interview.
6. What really appealed ______ me was working in a new field.
7. I can't quite make ______ what he's saying.
8. Given the choice, I'd opt ______ both work and study at the same time.
9. You need to immerse yourself ______ the culture in order to learn a new language.

c **Try expressing the sentences in 6b using a different part of speech. Is it always possible?**

I wasn't successful in passing the test.

d **Test each other.**

1. Student A, choose a sentence and read it as far as the verb.
2. Student B, cover the page and continue the sentence so it is true for you.

I would benefit …

I would benefit from exercising more often.

Vocabulary

self-

7 Look at these examples of self used as a prefix. Can you think of other examples of each structure?

- self-doubt (self + noun)
- self-aware (self + adjective)
- sense of self (self is a noun in its own right)

8 a Add self- to these words to make adjectives.

evident	contained	centred
made	sustaining	fulfilling

Which could be used to talk about:

1 a system?
2 an idea?
3 a prophecy?
4 a flat?
5 a person?

a self-made person

b What would the adjective mean in each case?

c Add expressions from 8a to the gaps. In what context would you find them?

1 This motel offers 12 fully ______ units in a well-kept modern building.
2 She was a ______ millionaire, and now she's left with nothing.
3 Soon after independence, the country became a ______ economy.
4 The details of the case are ______. The suspect is clearly guilty.
5 His paranoia became a ______ prophecy. He behaved so strangely, people really did start talking about him.
6 He plays a ______, corrupt individual in the film of the same name.

9 a Add these words to make nouns with self-.

interest	discipline	esteem
confidence	pity	defence

1 Anorexia can be related to low self-______.
2 The police claimed they acted in self-______.
3 You need self-______ to work from home.
4 Speaking in public is to do with having plenty of self-______.
5 His decisions were motivated by self-______.
6 He's not really depressed, he just wants our sympathy. It's a question of self-______.

b Which of the nouns have a negative connotation? How many can become adjectives?

self-pity → self-pitying

10 a Think of someone (a fictitious person or a celebrity) who you consider to be:

- self-satisfied.
- self-taught.
- self-conscious.
- self-disciplined.
- self-critical.
- self-sufficient.

b Talk about the person and explain your opinions.

Reformulating what you say

11 a Look at this example from the unit. Can you think of other expressions Uri could have used to reformulate what he was saying?

> I studied economics, so that's why working with Deutsche Bank really was appealing ... why it really appealed to me, I should say.

b 1.16 Listen to the conversation. How many of the details in the image turn out to be incorrect?

c What different ways of reformulating did you notice? Check the script on p148.

12 a Work in A/B pairs. Have conversations, continuing for as long as you can.

1 Student A, say something (not necessarily true) about someone in your family, a friend or neighbour, or your own past life. Whenever B responds, reformulate what you say. Use the expressions from 11c.
2 Student B, respond to what A says, showing interest or surprise.
3 Now change roles.

b Think about your conversation.

1 Which expressions did you use?
2 Which were easiest to use?

Self-assessment

Can you do these things in English? Circle a number on each line. 1 = I can't do this, 5 = I can do this well.

talk about personality traits	1	2	3	4	5
talk about identity	1	2	3	4	5
describe how I met someone	1	2	3	4	5
understand promotional language	1	2	3	4	5
promote myself	1	2	3	4	5
use effective introduction strategies	1	2	3	4	5
write a cover letter	1	2	3	4	5
describe my experiences and abilities	1	2	3	4	5

- For Wordcards, reference and saving your work → e-Portfolio
- For more practice → Self-study Pack, Unit 2

3

3.1 goals

- describe a book
- give a personal response

Language and literature

Life-changing books

SPEAKING and READING

1 a What genre do you think each book cover belongs to?

best-seller fiction humour autobiography
self-help guide current affairs adventure

b What do you think the books are about? How do you know?

c Read each book description. Which do you think would be worth reading? Why / Why not?

Broken heart? Finding it hard to get through the daily routine? With this easy, accessible program, your heart will be whole again and healed. With a wide range of exercises and insights, this book shows how you can face life again in less than a month – stronger and more positive than before.

Celebrated Japanese author, and runner of more than 20 marathons, Haruki Murakami details his love and experience of long-distance running from the 1980s onwards. Charming and intimate, his passion comes through in diary entries, essays and memories, providing good-natured advice on life.

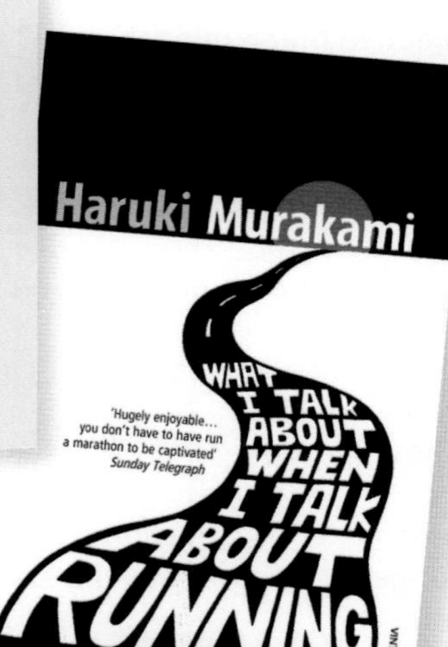

Haruki Murakami
'Hugely enjoyable… you don't have to have run a marathon to be captivated' Sunday Telegraph
WHAT I TALK ABOUT WHEN I TALK ABOUT RUNNING
VINTAGE

American soldier Billy Pilgrim is captured and sent to a German prisoner-of-war camp during World War II – a disused slaughterhouse named 'Slaughterhouse-Five'. Prisoners and guards alike take refuge in the camp cellar as the nearby city of Dresden is destroyed in bombing raids. One of the few survivors of the firestorm, Billy loses all sense of time, reliving experiences in his life – both real and imagined.

Zahra (aged 3) and Hawra (a few months old) have lost their family in a Baghdad missile strike. *Sunday Times* war correspondent Hala Jaber sets her heart on doing everything she can to help. In this beautiful account, Jaber (a Lebanese and a Muslim, but at the same time working for a London newspaper) tells her compelling Iraq story, with the unique insight of a writer able to understand both worlds.

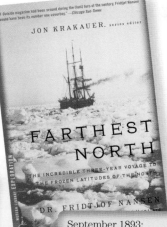

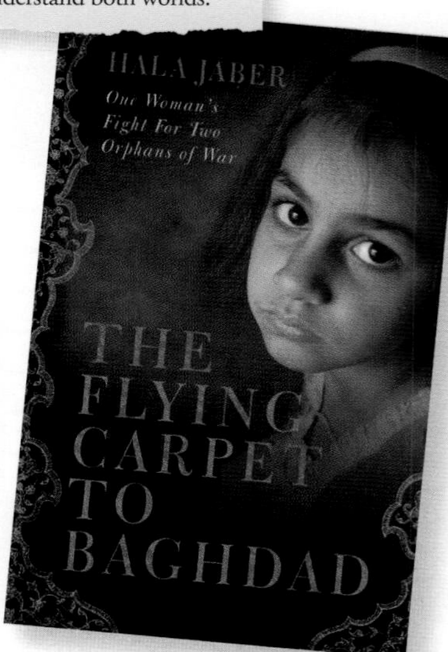

HALA JABER
One Woman's Fight For Two Orphans of War
THE FLYING CARPET TO BAGHDAD

September 1893: Norwegian adventurer Fridtjof Nansen embarks for the North Pole. Abandoning his ship, the *Fram*, he sets off by dog-sled with his companion Hjalmer Johansen. In a race against the pack ice, surviving encounters with walruses and polar bears, Nansen's three-year trek is one of the finest narratives of polar exploration.

It is January 1st. In the post arrives something interesting – a penguin! The next day, another penguin arrives. And then another … To start with, the new, uninvited guests are cute and funny – but who is sending them and why? As the number of penguins starts to grow, so do the family's problems, in this heart-warming story sure to become a children's classic.

LISTENING

Ian McDonald

2 a 1.17 Listen to Ian McDonald talking about *Farthest North*. Make notes on the main points.

b Compare notes. Do you have the same points?

c What do these statements from the interview mean?

1 I was a nerdish lad.
2 It was one of those very daring books.
3 It was quite a struggle to read.
4 It must have been quite a formative book for you.
5 It was about the way science was done rather than about science itself.

d Does Ian's description make you more, or less interested in the book? Why?

LANGUAGE FOCUS

Describe a book and its significance

3 a Here are some words used in the interview. What do you think is the difference between A and B?

A

B

b Can you remember how Ian used the words? Which go together?

c 1.17 Listen again to check.

SPEAKING

4 a Choose a book that has had an important effect on you. Make two 'word clouds' like in 3a.

1 Write words / expressions you could use to describe:
- the plot.
- a particular character.
- the atmosphere.
- the way it is written.

2 Write words / expressions you could use to talk about:
- the time in your life when you read it, and how you felt.
- the effect it has had on your life, or your outlook on life.

b Show your 'word clouds' to other students.

1 What can they work out about the book from your words?
2 Talk about each other's books. Ask questions to find out more.

5 Think of a book or an author you loved when you were younger. Is it true that 'the books that changed you when you were young are always going to be a disappointment when you are an adult'?

Learning a language

3.2 goals

- talk about languages and ways to learn them
- describe experiences of language learning

LISTENING

1 a **What different ways of learning a language do the photos suggest?**

b **Do people from some countries learn English more easily? Why / Why not?**

Norman from Germany

2 **1.18 Listen to a conversation with Norman.**

1 How and with whom did Norman learn conversational English?
2 According to him, why do Germans speak good English?
3 What are the incentives to learn English in Germany?

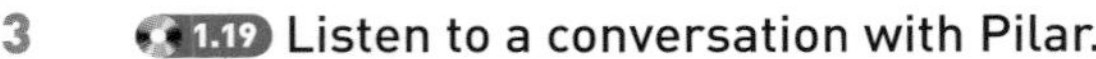

3 **1.19 Listen to a conversation with Pilar.**

1 What are the main differences between Pilar and Norman? How are they similar?
2 From what Pilar says, what do we know about:
   a her level of English when she first went to Britain?
   b the people she spent her time with?
   c her experience of learning French?

Pilar from Spain

LANGUAGE FOCUS
Language learning

4 a **Look at these sentences from the conversations. Complete the gaps.**

1 The school education there helped me to ______ the most important vocabulary in order to ______.
2 Conversational English, I mostly learned in the context of having had ______ native English speakers.
3 That helped me a lot to ______ a little bit more.
4 So, tell me about coming to the UK for the first time and ______ this culture and the language.
5 It was very difficult to even ______.
6 I ______ French some time ago, but no I didn't quite ______ the language.

b **1.20 Listen to check.**

c **Which expressions in 4a are about:**

1 learning a language?
2 having contact with a language?
3 speaking a language?

d **Talk together.**

1 List the foreign languages you know (including English). Then talk about how you learned them, and how well you speak them. Use expressions from 4a.
2 Do you think it is important to 'master' a language completely and sound like a native speaker? Or is it fine to retain your own accent and make a few mistakes, as long as you get your message across?

READING and SPEAKING

5 a Do you think these statements are true? Why / Why not?

1 Learning a new language can lead you to adopt a different identity.
2 It's difficult to translate directly from one language to another.
3 It's important to find your own 'voice' in a foreign language and express your own personality.

b Read three extracts from novels with language learning as their theme. How do they reflect the statements in 5a?

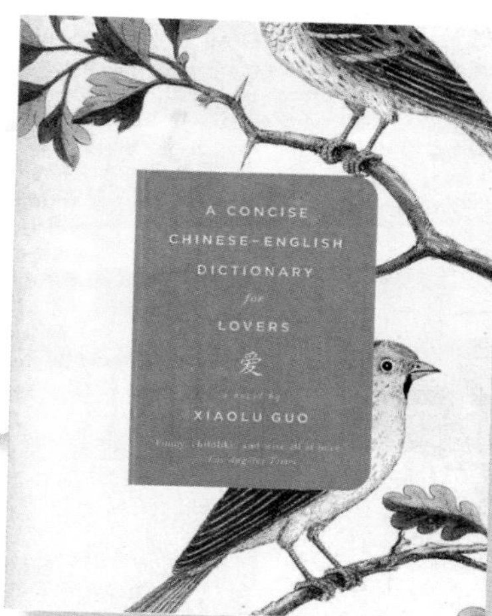

A

Chinese, we not having grammar. We saying things simple way. No verb-change usage, no tense differences, no gender changes. We bosses of our language. But, English language is boss of English user.

B

I could feel the French sticking in my throat, the new muscles in my mouth … I was full of French, it was holding me up, running through me, a voice in my head, a tickle in my ear, likely to be set off at any time. A counter language.

C

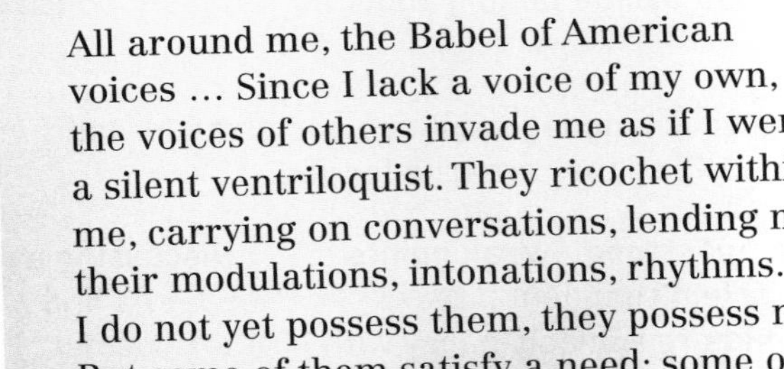

All around me, the Babel of American voices … Since I lack a voice of my own, the voices of others invade me as if I were a silent ventriloquist. They ricochet within me, carrying on conversations, lending me their modulations, intonations, rhythms. I do not yet possess them, they possess me. But some of them satisfy a need; some of them stick to my ribs … Eventually, the voices enter me; by assuming them, I gradually make them mine.

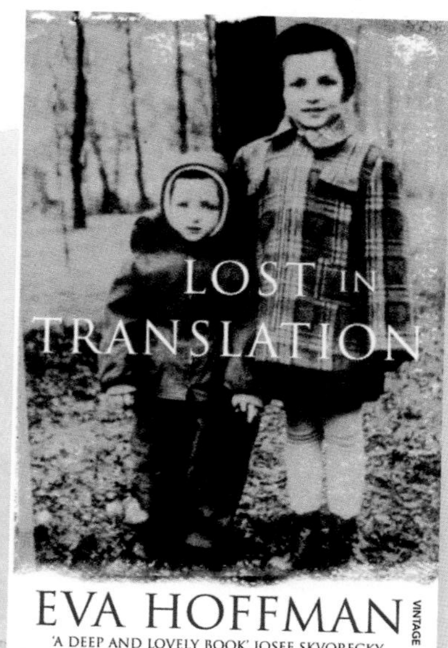

6 a Read the extracts again and identify where these points are made.

The new language:
1 obeys different rules and has a different form.
2 works in opposition to the speaker's mother tongue.
3 is absorbed little by little by the learner.
4 can be triggered at any moment.

Learning a new language:
5 can be a violent process.
6 involves issues of control.
7 requires adopting different sounds and speech patterns.

b Do you agree with the points? Do any reflect your experiences?

3.3 Target activity

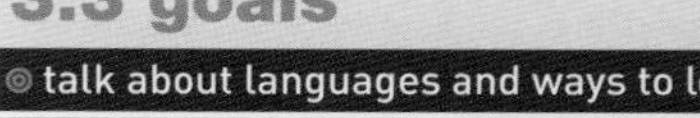

3.3 goals
talk about languages and ways to learn them
describe experiences of language learning
discuss plans and priorities

A plan to improve your English

A

Relax.
We'll give you the confidence to get by.

B

C

Do you know how silly your English sounds?

D

English gets you where you want to be.

TASK LISTENING

1 What message are these language-school adverts trying to communicate?

1 Are they positive or negative? Consider both the image and the message.
2 Which is the most convincing? Why?
3 What kind of person do you think the adverts are aimed at?
4 Which other messages would be important for someone studying English at an advanced level?

2 a Which areas of your English do you think you need to work on?

idiomatic expressions	writing	speaking fluently
pronunciation problems	exam practice	listening comprehension
grammatical accuracy	writing accurately	active vocabulary

b 1.21 Listen to Sybille talking about her English. Which of the areas in 2a does she talk about?

TASK LANGUAGE
Plans and priorities

3 a Think about your language abilities and plans for learning English. Complete expressions 1–7 so they are true for you.

Talking about strong / weak points	Discussing a plan
1 I (don't) feel confident … .	8 I'd find … a great help / really useful.
2 I'm quite / reasonably happy with my … , but … is another story.	9 I'd benefit from … .
3 My strong point / main problem is … .	10 … might be the answer / solution.
4 I have a hard time …	11 I think the best way to do this is …
Talking about priorities	12 … would be worth investigating.
5 My main aim / priority is to … .	13 … might be worthwhile / worth a try.
6 An important area for me is … .	14 I've considered …
7 Personally, I need to work / focus / concentrate on … .	15 I probably need more practice in / exposure to … .

b 1.21 Listen again. Which expressions did Sybille use?

TASK

4 a Work alone. Complete the questionnaire on page 127.

b Work in A/B pairs.

1 Discuss your abilities and needs.
2 Look at your partner's completed questionnaire and make suggestions.
3 Listen to your partner's response. Do you agree?

c Listen to feedback from other people in class. Do you share similar concerns?

Across cultures Attitudes to English

1 Read the background information on the Philippines. Then look at the advert promoting English there.

1 Which of these statements do you think are true?
   a Most young people in the Philippines aren't interested in learning English.
   b English is seen as a language of the upper classes.
   c The standard of English has improved in recent years.
   d Most young people are bilingual in English and Filipino.
   e English used to be more widely spoken in the Philippines than it is now.
   f Young people are aware of the importance of English as an international language.
2 What do you think the reasons for these attitudes might be?
3 In what way are these attitudes unusual?

Article | Discussion | Log in/create account

The Philippines, in South-east Asia, consists of over 7,000 islands. With an estimated population of 92 million people, it is the world's 12th most populous country.
Between 1565 and 1898, the Philippines were ruled by Spain. In 1898, the Spanish ceded the Philippines to the USA, which controlled the country until independence in 1946.
Since independence, there have been two official languages in the Philippines: English and Filipino (a version of Tagalog). Another 170 indigenous languages are also spoken.

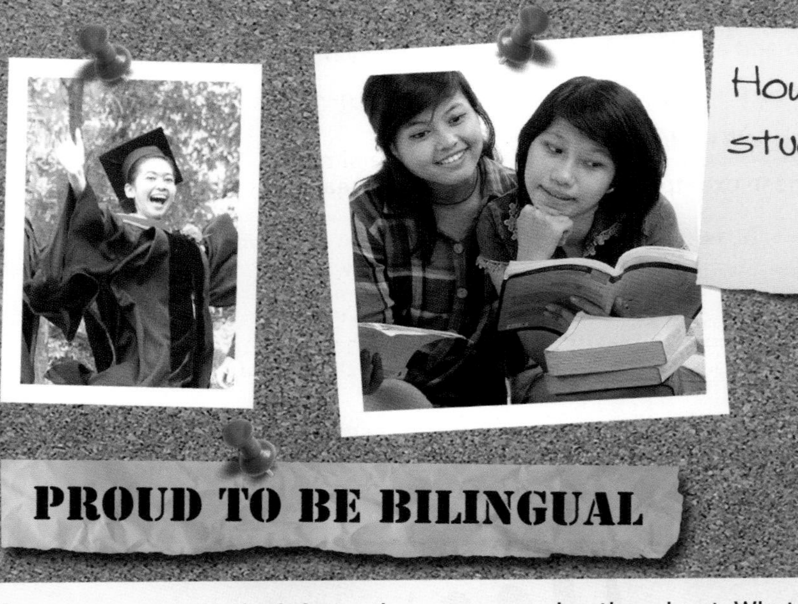

How can I study English?
Ticket to the future
988046
PROUD TO BE BILINGUAL

There is a cultural hindrance to the practice of English among the youth: many lack the self-confidence to speak English because they are afraid to make mistakes, and English is now perceived as elitist. In other words: it is perceived as yet another obstacle to social success and integration, rather than a means to achieve it. There is an urgent need to convince the youth to be proud to be bilingual.

In a globalised economy, **English is a Ticket to the Future.**

2 Look again at the information accompanying the advert. What verb is used when describing common attitudes to English?

3 Read these questions. Find four other verbs that have a similar meaning.

What is the status of English in your country? Is it:
- something that moves you up the social ladder?
- part of almost every university degree programme?
- considered essential for working in certain sectors?
- mainly a school subject?
- seen as a necessary evil?
- only popular with young people?
- viewed as a way of enriching your life?
- regarded as culturally threatening?

4 Talk together.

1 Discuss the questions in 3.
2 Do you think your attitude to English is typical of people in your country?
3 How many of your friends, family and colleagues speak it?
4 Has your attitude to English changed over the years?

Keywords *worth, worthwhile*

1 Look at these examples from the unit. What does worth mean in each? What grammatical forms is it used with?

```
1  Which do you think would be worth reading?
2  It was quite a struggle … but it was worth reading it.
3  I think it's worth a try.
```

2 a Continue these sentences with worth + a noun from the box. Sometimes there may be more than one possible answer. Does the noun take a definite or an indefinite article?

effort	wait	risk	try / shot	look	trouble / hassle	visit / trip

1. This takes a very long time to load but it's *worth the wait.*
2. I know steroids are dangerous, so is it …?
3. Though the food's expensive, there's something for everybody, so it's …
4. I don't expect to hear anything, but I thought it was …
5. Which leads to an inevitable question: is investing overseas … ?
6. The site is still under construction but it's …
7. It takes an hour to get there and back. It's not …

What is each sentence about? Are they more likely to be spoken or written?

b What words could you use before worth to add emphasis?

c Replace the noun in each sentence with a verb + *-ing*.

1 This takes a very long time to load but it's worth waiting for.

3 a What do you notice about worthwhile in these examples? What does it mean in each?

```
1  Watching films in the original version is really worthwhile, because you pick up the feeling of
   the language.
2  If you're going to buy greetings cards, it's better to give your money to a worthwhile cause,
   like Save the Children.
3  I could have studied for an MBA, but it wouldn't really be worth my while.
4  If you can afford it, it's probably worth your while to get a computer with a bigger hard drive.
```

b You are going to listen to four people talking about the things or people in these images. How might they use worthwhile?

1

2

3

4

c 1.22 Listen to check.

4 a Write examples of:

- a place to go out in your town.
- a film, play or TV programme.
- a tourist destination.
- an interesting food you have tried.

Would you recommend them or not? Think how you could talk about them using worth + noun, worth + *-ing*, or worthwhile.

b Give your examples to a partner. Ask each other about the things or places.

> What about the National Gallery? Would you say it's worthwhile?

EXPLORESpeaking

Goal

use strategies for communicating effectively

1 a Read about Xialou Guo's novel *A Concise Chinese-English Dictionary for Lovers*. What aspects of the book do you think sound interesting?

Z is a 23-year-old Chinese language student who has come to London to learn English. When the book begins she can barely ask for a cup of tea, but when language comes, so does love. As she gets to know British culture she also falls for an older English man who lives a resolutely bachelor life in Hackney. It's a million miles away from the small Chinese town she comes from, where her parents want nothing more for her than that she should follow them into the shoe business. Z learns about humour, companionship and passion, but she also learns the painful truth that language is also a barrier and the more you know about it, the less you understand.

Written in short chapters, each the definition of a word, this is a brilliantly clever book that pokes fun at England and China and explores the endless possibilities for misunderstanding between East and West, men and women.

b Read the start of the novel on page 126. What do you notice about the way it is written?

c 1.23 Listen to Sze talking about the novel and the kind of English it uses. What does she say about:

1 her first six months in the UK?
2 'broken' English?
3 the differences between Chinese and English?

2 1.24 Listen to these extracts. Match them to ways Sze communicates what she wants to say.

1 … when I came here, when I left China, everything was very new, very exciting for me.

2 The sentence become longer, more complicated, the character start to use past tense and then the future tense …

3 … and I guess, er, I mean that you do need to pay great attention to what is happening with language.

4 … it's wonderful to have these two sides to the novel, it's a wonderful achievement.

5 … when she writes a Chinese character, she actually, she makes an image of that word.

a She uses repetition to make her point more clearly. *4*
b She brings in a more personal angle to show the importance of a point.
c She paraphrases if she doesn't know the exact term.
d She uses fillers to give herself time to think.
e She emphasises certain words and varies tone to keep interest.

3 a 1.23 Look at the script on page 149 and listen again. Identify the parts where Sze best gets her message across.

b Which strategies do you think you use when you speak English? Do you think you use them consciously or unconsciously?

4 a Prepare to talk about one of these topics:

- an experience from which you learned something important. Why was it significant?
- an experience of being abroad. What did you find interesting, exciting or difficult?
- your experience of using English. What has been challenging, interesting or unexpected?

1 Make notes on the main things you will say.
2 Think about how you could use some of the strategies in 2.
3 Think of ways to 'stretch yourself' (try to go a bit beyond your comfortable limit in English).

b Talk with a partner. Listen to each other's topic and ask questions to find out more. Which strategies from 2 did you both use?

3 Look again

Grammar

Present verb forms

1 a Look at these examples from the unit. Underline the present verb forms.

1 … this is a brilliantly clever book that pokes fun at England and China and explores …
2 American soldier Billy Pilgrim is captured and sent to a German prisoner-of-war camp …
3 … the voices of others invade me as if I were a silent ventriloquist … Eventually, the voices enter me; by assuming them, I gradually make them mine.

b Match the examples to these uses:

a summarising the plots of books or films.
b writing a review.
c creating a sense of immediacy in past narratives.

2 Look at these examples. In what context might you find them? Are the highlighted verbs referring to the present, past or future?

1 Bad weather is set to continue.
2 Three years later, war between England and Argentina breaks out over the Falklands.
3 The bus leaves at 10.15, we've still got an hour.
4 David tells me that you have the date and everything. When is it to be?
5 We're all waiting for something to happen and then suddenly there was a terrible noise.
6 I hear you went to Bulgaria for your holiday.
7 I'm leaving on the 17th and then I'm coming back a week later.
8 I write to inform you that you have been chosen as one of the lucky winners.
9 You attach the file like this, then click here and send it.
10 Not again! I'm always losing my wallet.

3 a Some verbs can describe states and activities, but with a difference in meaning. What is the difference in these examples?

1 a I think I picked up most of my English at school.
  b I never know what he's thinking any more.
2 a I see what you're saying, but I don't agree.
  b We're seeing each other for dinner.
  c She's seeing some guy. I don't know if it will last.
3 a I expect you're happy with the result?
  b I expect they'll win tonight, they're playing at home.
  c She's expecting someone to arrive at two.
4 a I imagine she misses her family.
  b There's nothing there – you're just imagining things.

b Compare answers.

Adverbs

4 a Look at this example from the unit.

The stuff they did was unbelievably brave.

1 What adverbs can replace unbelievably?
2 What do you notice about its position in the sentence?
3 What other adverbs did Ian use?

b How would you classify unbelievably in terms of intensity?

5 Add an adverb in the correct position.

extremely fully practically highly generally

1 I'd say his views on language learning are questionable.
2 I'm aware of the time, thank you.
3 True fans will find the book disappointing.
4 They are happy at work, but say they don't get much money.
5 It's impossible to teach someone how to be a writer.

6 a Match the adverbs with the verbs.

vividly	enjoy
strongly	remember
thoroughly	agree
deeply	believe
entirely	regret

b Make sentences with the collocations you made.

I deeply regret not going to study in Australia.

c Read out only the last part of your sentences. Can your partner guess how they begin?

… not going to study in Australia.
I deeply regret …?

d Make sentences using combinations of these intensifying adverbs and the verbs in 6a.

definitely completely totally absolutely

I totally agree with you.

7 a What adverbs could be used as a response?

That's a fair comment, isn't it?
Yeah, ______.

b Take turns to make a comment and respond. Agree or disagree, using an adverb.

1 Footballers earn far too much money.
2 Most politicians are corrupt.
3 Do you remember your first day at school?
4 Isn't life wonderful?

Grammar reference, p141

Vocabulary

Expressions with *language*

8 a How many expressions with language can you remember from this unit?

Think about four categories:

A (phrasal) verbs + language	*take up a language*
B language used to modify a noun	*language teacher*
C adjective + language	*foreign language*
D other expressions + language	*to be immersed in language*

b Add words in the box to the gaps to make expressions with language. Which category in 8a does each expression belong to?

grasp preserve command master skills get by in common second barrier picked up exposure

1 He was a young American with an unusual ______ of Farsi, a language he ______ from an Iranian exchange student.
2 "Imagine how hard it would be without a good ______ of the language," she said.
3 In business circles, English is often the ______ language among people from different nationalities.
4 Seeing themselves on video, students are more motivated to improve their language ______ because they want to sound better and look better.
5 But the fact of the matter is, it takes a while to ______ a language, especially if you don't get much ______ to it.
6 The new US programme will help break down the language ______.
7 Many tribes today use modern technology to help ______ their language.
8 He speaks so well, nobody realises that's his ______ language, and he can ______ Italian too!

c Work in A/B pairs. Test each other.

1 A, say one of the expressions in 8b.
2 B, use it to say something from your own experience or knowledge.

Pick up a language.

I picked up a bit of Greek when I was on holiday, but I've forgotten most of it.

Idioms about speaking

9 a Look at this idiom from the unit.

```
So the way you get your message across must be
very, very different?
```

Match these idioms with their definitions. Which idioms do the cartoons show?

1 I was really tongue-tied.
2 He didn't let me get a word in edgeways.
3 He kept beating about the bush.
4 I couldn't string a sentence together.
5 Make your point as quickly as you can.

a talk around the topic, not get to the point
b give an opinion clearly
c speak articulately
d unable to have a chance to speak because someone else is speaking
e unable to speak because you're nervous

A

B

b 1.25 Listen to the idioms in context. What is each speaker talking about?

c 1.25 Listen again. How do speakers stress the key words?

Self-assessment

Can you do these things in English? Circle a number on each line. 1 = I can't do this, 5 = I can do this well.

describe a book	1 2 3 4 5
give a personal response	1 2 3 4 5
talk about languages and ways to learn them	1 2 3 4 5
describe experiences of language learning	1 2 3 4 5
discuss plans and priorities	1 2 3 4 5
use strategies for communicating effectively	1 2 3 4 5

• For Wordcards, reference and saving your work → e-Portfolio
• For more practice → Self-study Pack, Unit 3

4 World

4.1 goals

- interpret maps and facts
- make comparisons and talk about changes

Maps of the world

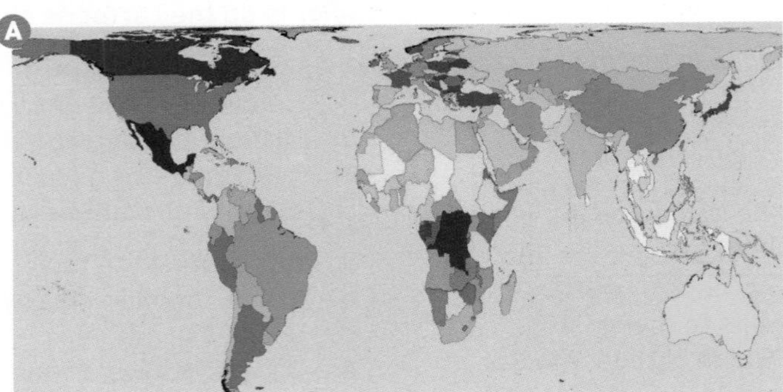

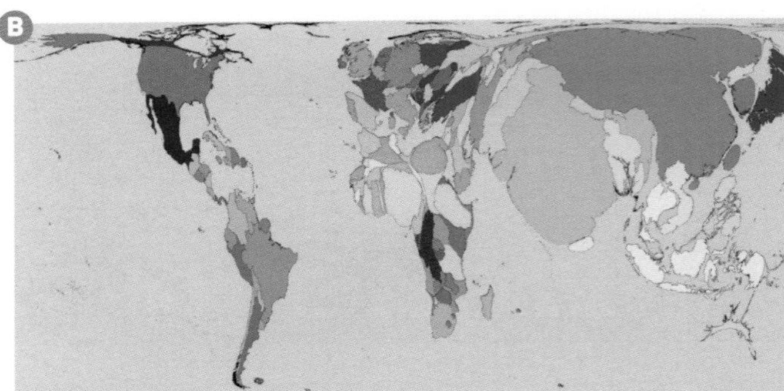

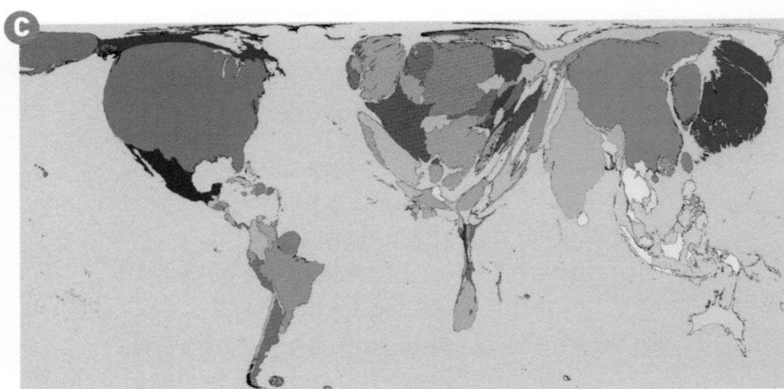

READING

1 a Cover the descriptions and compare map A (which shows land area) with B and C. What do you notice about the continents and individual countries in maps B and C? What do you think they show?

b Read the descriptions of maps B and C.

B

In Spring 2000, world population estimates reached 6 billion (that is, six thousand million). The distribution of the earth's population is shown in this map. The size of each country shows the proportion of the world's population living there.

For example, Canada is slightly bigger than the USA. But as the map shows, the USA has a much larger population. The map also shows that the countries of South and East Asia have by far the largest populations relative to their size.

This map shows the distribution of the world's wealth in 2002, based on the GDP (Gross Domestic Product) of each country. The region with the lowest wealth was Central Africa; its GDP was 0.8% that of the richest region, North America. There was a vast increase in the world's total wealth in the 40 years between 1960 and 2000: wealth per person more than doubled, and the world's GDP rose by about 250%. The most significant development was the growth of Japan, China, the Republic of Korea and Taiwan.

c Talk about maps B and C.

1 Which countries have the most distorted shapes? Which are barely visible?
2 How does your country look?
3 What conclusions can you draw about the world's population and wealth from these maps?

LANGUAGE FOCUS Differences and changes

2 a **Sentences 1–3 are about differences and changes. What words in the box could replace the highlighted words? Do they change the meaning?**

easily huge considerably significant dramatic significantly massive enormous far and away far marginally

1 There was a vast increase in wealth between 1960 and 1990.
2 The countries of Asia have by far the largest populations.
3 Canada is slightly bigger than the USA, but as the map shows, the USA has a much larger population.

b **Write one or two more sentences based on the maps, like those in 2a.**

c **Read out your sentences. Do other people agree?**

SPEAKING

3 a **Look at the maps again.**

1 Imagine a map showing population in 2050. How would it be different? What countries might be bigger or smaller?
2 Imagine a map showing wealth in the year 1500. How would it look? Think about:
- North America.
- Central and South America.
- India.
- China.
- Europe.
- the Middle East.

b **Work in A/B pairs. Student A, look on p127. Student B, look on p136. Tell your partner what your map shows. Then let him/her see the map.**

LANGUAGE FOCUS Interpreting meaning

4 **1.26 Listen to two people talking about the map on p136. What is the main point each speaker makes? Are any the same as your ideas?**

5 a **The speakers used various expressions to talk about what the maps mean. What did they say? Complete the sentences with expressions from the box.**

indicate about the significance of reveal much about is apparent doesn't necessarily mean means that as the maps show

Speaker A
1 One thing that ______ from these maps is how little has actually changed.
2 In fact ______, the difference between rich and poor has got bigger.

Speaker B
3 I'm actually not really sure what ______ the maps is.
4 What do they really ______ wealth?
5 It doesn't ______ lifestyle.
6 I suppose this ______ it wasn't producing much wealth.
7 That ______ that they were poor.

b **1.26 Listen again to check.**

SPEAKING

6 a **Work in groups. Imagine a map showing the world's wealth in 2050. What do you think it would look like? Sketch out possible ideas, and if you like, draw a rough 'map'.**

b **Present your ideas to the class. Interpret what your 'map' shows, using expressions from 2a.**

WRITING

7 **Write about a map.**

1 Imagine maps that would show:
- which countries produce the most greenhouse gases.
- which countries use the Internet most.
- which countries have the most and least violent crime.
2 Choose one, and write a short description. Which countries or regions would be biggest and smallest?

What the world eats

4.2 goals

- talk about diet and nutrition
- discuss changing trends

Australia: the Browns of River View
Food expenditure for one week: $376.45

Egypt: the Ahmed family of Cairo
Food expenditure for one week: $68.53

LANGUAGE FOCUS
Types of food

1 a Discuss these questions.

1 What seem to be the main differences in the food the two families eat?
2 Where do you think they do their shopping?
3 What kind of dishes do you think they make?

b Talk about other things that strike you as interesting about the photos.

2 a Which words in the box below collocate with:

- food?
- drinks?
- both?

Can you see examples of them in the photos?

nutritious bottled dried take-away locally produced sugar-free GM packaged fizzy canned raw diet refined processed soft convenience low-fat wholemeal

b Which words have a similar meaning?

c These words are commonly used to talk about food and diet. Which are *types* of food, and which are *contained* in food? Give examples.

pulses fibre cereals dairy products protein carbohydrate

d How much do you eat or drink of each type of food or drink in 2a and 2c?

3 a Work in groups. Group A, look on p130. Group B, look on p136. Discuss the questions.

b Tell the class about the family's diet.

SPEAKING

4 a Imagine a photo of your (or your family's) food for one week. Make notes about what it might show.

b Describe your 'photo' to other students. Which photo on this page is most similar?

Nutrition transition

READING

1 a You will read an article which accompanied the photos, describing how eating habits have changed in the world. What do you think it will say about these topics?

- new technologies
- food for convenience
- seasonal food
- processed foods
- malnutrition
- obesity

b Read and check.

Nutrition transition

Everyone eats. People around the world differ in many ways, but dinner unites us all. Throughout history, we humans have always found nourishing ways to use whatever food we could lay our hands on. The earliest diets were hunted and gathered from the foods that were available as a result of geography and climate. But as soon as people figured out how to trade foods, they did. As the photographs show, the current diets of most world populations have moved well beyond hunting and gathering. They have [1]evolved in response to changes in food production that began with the Industrial Revolution some 200 years ago. New means of preservation allow foods to be eaten long after they are grown and harvested (hence ketchup). New means of transportation – railroads, trucks and airplanes (as well as technologies such as refrigeration) – mean that foods grown in one place can be consumed 'fresh' many thousands of miles away. Thus, even in some place as remote as Bhutan, people eat oranges, surely grown well beyond the Himalayas. New processing technologies allow companies to make shelf-stable food products that can be transported and consumed much later (like pasta). New technologies have permitted the development of previously unknown food products like instant coffee and Cheese Whiz. New marketing methods can create worldwide demand for such products (chief among them, the almost ubiquitous Coca-Cola).

But the photographs have even more to tell us. As conflicts resolve and people in developing countries become better off, they acquire more stable resources and [2]change the way they eat. They inevitably [3]replace the grains and beans in their diets with foods obtained from animal sources. They buy more meat, more sweet foods and more processed foods: they eat more meals prepared by others. Soon they eat more food in general. They start gaining weight, become overweight, then [4]develop heart disease, diabetes, and the other chronic diseases so common in industrialised societies. Here we have the great irony of modern nutrition: at a time when hundreds of millions of people do not have enough to eat, hundreds of millions more are eating too much and are overweight or obese. Today, except in the very poorest countries, more people are overweight than underweight. Some socially conscious governments struggling to feed their hungry populations must also contend with the health problems of people who eat too much food. The phenomenon of going from not having enough food to overeating is now so common that it has been given its own name: the nutrition transition. To see nutrition transition in action, you need only compare the diets of families from Mali, Mongolia and the Philippines with those from France, Australia and the United States. Rates of obesity are [5]rising rapidly in all countries, but are highest in the most industrialised countries. To understand why, just examine the shopping lists and food displays.

2 a Match developments 1–5 with examples a–e. How are they connected?

1	preservation	a	Coca-Cola
2	transportation	b	instant coffee
3	processing technologies	c	oranges
4	manufacturing technologies	d	pasta
5	marketing methods	e	ketchup

b What is 'nutrition transition'?

LANGUAGE FOCUS
Changes and trends

3 a The highlighted verbs in the article are used to describe changes and developments. Which describe:

1 changes in diet?
2 obesity and heart disease?

b What are the noun forms of the highlighted verbs?

evolve → evolution

c Try using nouns instead of the verbs in the article. What other changes would be necessary? How would this affect the meaning?

SPEAKING

4 You are going to have a discussion about the way technology has changed food habits. Student A, look on p128. Student B, look on p135.

4.3 Target activity

Say how a town or country has changed

4.3 goals

- make comparisons and talk about changes
- discuss changing trends
- talk about result

TASK LISTENING

1 You are going to listen to Adrian talking about important events and changes in Britain. Look at the photos. What do you think he will say?

2 **a** 1.27 Listen. How do the photos illustrate what he says?

b What does Adrian say about the effect of joining the EU on:

- food? • cooking? • TV cookery programmes?

TASK LANGUAGE
Result

3 **a** Look at these expressions Adrian uses. What preposition comes next?

1 This had all kinds of consequences *for*
2 This had an impact ...
3 This gave rise ...
4 This led ...
5 This was a direct consequence ...

b Match the expressions in 3a with these endings. Is more than one answer possible?

a ... a whole new style of British cooking.
b ... people's attitude to food.
c ... the way people live.
d ... joining the EU.
e ... a new wave of TV chefs.

c 1.28 Listen to check.

TASK

4 **a** Prepare to talk about how things have changed where you live.

1 Think about changes to your town, region or country since you have known it. Write two or three important events that have taken place, such as:
- changes of government.
- new technology.
- new buildings or transport systems.
- new trends or fashions.

2 Make a list of how the changes have affected people's attitudes or lifestyles. How are things different now?

b Work with other students.

1 Listen to each other's opinion and ask questions to find out more.
2 If you come from the same place, do you agree?

Across cultures Restaurants

1 a What kind of restaurants can you see? What type of food do you think they serve there? How do you know?

A

B

C

b Match these restaurant names with the photos.

Ben's Chilli Bowl Jade Dragon Café Quentin

c Which was the easiest nationality to identify? Why? What does this suggest about some restaurant decor?

2 Talk about restaurants where you live which offer cuisines from different countries. Describe their decoration and atmosphere.

3 a What do you know about Mexican culture and cuisine?

b Read a blogger's review of a Mexican restaurant and underline the negative words.

1 What are the blogger's main complaints?
2 What do you picture when you read the highlighted expressions?

I had high hopes when they opened a new Mexican-owned restaurant on the next block from me. But sadly, it's comparable to the usual cardboard-tortilla fast-food outlets you get everywhere. When I first went there, I was served chips and salsa, like back home. That was a good start and, of course, I dove right in. But the chips were stale and the salsa tasted like candy! I asked my waiter if they had a hotter salsa, because the salsa was nothing but tomato ketchup with some chunks of onion in it. "We have to serve it like this, because the locals don't like the real thing," he said. I responded by telling him that if you're going to serve Mexican food, serve Mexican food.

I'm tired of Mexican-owned restaurants advertising their food as *auténtico*, only to be disappointed by how terrible our food tastes. Why don't the owners of the restaurants show off the beauty of our culture? Forget candy-flavoured salsa, and make a great-tasting one that not only makes our mouths water, but also makes us teary-eyed. But it's not just the food that they get wrong. Here, Mexican eateries play merengue, which is Caribbean. When they do play Mexican music, it's always the most stereotypical bands serenading you with deafening rancheras. Do they think everyone listens to that in Mexico? The waiters also dress in folkloric costumes which are real clichés, and serve margaritas which, contrary to popular belief, we don't drink that much at home!

4 Discuss these questions.

1 Do you have any idea how your cuisine might be represented abroad?
2 What do you think might be the stereotypical decor, etc.?
3 Do you think these are misconceptions about your country and could be damaging? Or do you think this gives a positive, attractive image of your country?

Keywords get, become

1 a In these examples, get is used to talk about changes that lead to a situation.

Now

Europe is wealthy compared to other countries.
The difference between rich and poor is bigger than before.
People are in the habit of eating well.
People are a bit more selfish.

Change leading to the situation

It got wealthier at the expense of other countries.
The difference between rich and poor has got bigger.
People have really got into the habit of eating well.
People have got a bit more selfish.

1 What kind of words can come after get?
2 In which examples could we also use become / became? Why / Why not?
3 Why do three of the examples use the present perfect?

b Think of an expression with get / got to continue these sentences.

1 Come and have some dinner before it ...
2 It was a long book, but finally I ...
3 I hated Japanese food at first, but after a time ...
4 Take a key so you don't ...
5 I usually keep up-to-date with my work, but this week ...

c Look at the examples in 1a and 1b again. Can you use any other verbs instead of get or become?

2 a Imagine you overheard these remarks. What do you think the people are talking about? In what context would you hear them?

1 ... it will get more humid ...
2 ... or it will get infected ...
3 ... it's easy to get overwhelmed on your first day ...
4 ... he got left behind on the last lap ...
5 ... I got carried away ...

b 1.29 Listen to check.

3 a In these examples, we use become rather than get. Why?

1 We will contact you as soon as a place becomes available.
2 It is only in the 20th century that nationalism became associated with the political right.
3 You need to be resident for ten years before you become eligible for citizenship.
4 It soon became apparent that a second runway would be needed.
5 It's given us good service for 10 years, but the parts have now become obsolete.
6 Her name quickly became well-known throughout the literary world.

b What are the sentences about? Where would you find them? Are they more likely to be spoken or written?

4 a Think of something that has recently become:

- more available.
- fashionable.
- apparent to you.
- well-known.
- obsolete.

b Compare your examples with other students.

5 Look at the photos. How many ways can you describe what has happened to the things and people, using get or become?

A

B

C

D
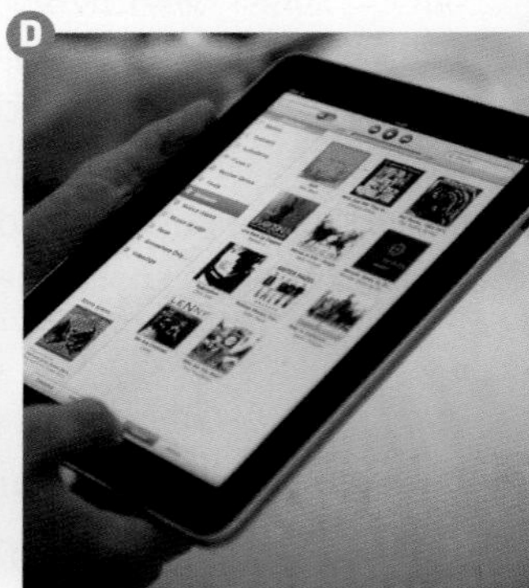

EXPLOREWriting

Goals

- write captions
- write economically

1 Read the website about Mumbai, India. Look at the photo and the descriptions.

1. What do they tell you about the city and the way people live?
2. Why are **transformed** and **elephant** good words to describe the changes taking place in India?
3. Why do you think people are **bewildered**?
4. What does the word **sprawling** suggest about the slums?

India, the second most populous nation in the world, is being transformed. We have heard about the rise of Asian tigers and the Chinese dragon – now here comes the elephant. India's economy is growing more than 9% a year, and the country is modernising so fast that old friends are bewildered by the changes. India is now the world's fourth largest economy. At the same time, more than a quarter of India's 1.1 billion people still live in slums and on less than $1 a day. Welcome to new India.

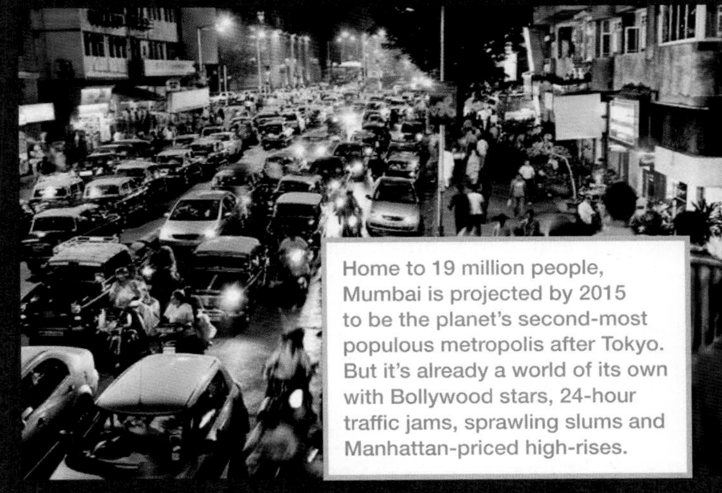

Home to 19 million people, Mumbai is projected by 2015 to be the planet's second-most populous metropolis after Tokyo. But it's already a world of its own with Bollywood stars, 24-hour traffic jams, sprawling slums and Manhattan-priced high-rises.

2 a Compare the caption with this more extended description. How are they different? Compare the number of:

- sentences.
- adjectives and two-word expressions.
- verbs.

> 19 million people live in Mumbai, and it is projected by 2015 to be the metropolis with the second-highest population in the world, after Tokyo. But it is already a world of its own. It has a film industry, 'Bollywood', with its own film stars. There are traffic jams 24 hours a day. It has slums which spread everywhere and also new apartment blocks which cost as much as some skyscrapers in Manhattan.

b Why is the language in the caption more effective?

3 a Read three more captions. Match them with photos A–C.

1. Chowpatty is Mumbai's most [1] *famous* beach. During the day, it is the [2] _______ of the happily unemployed who [3] _______ under the shade of its [4] _______ trees. But in the evening the atmosphere is more like a [5] _______ : kids [6] _______ on Ferris wheels or taking pony rides, astrologers and monkey shows.

2. The Sassoon Docks are the main fish loading and trading centre in South Mumbai. Hundreds of women [7] _______ around [8] _______ piles of tiny shrimp, shelling them one by one. Everywhere it is [9] _______ and smelly, yet somehow these women remain [10] _______ and clean in their [11] _______ orange, pink and turquoise saris.

3. The upper class [12] _______ with mineral water in a [13] _______ tapas bar. The booming concentration of business activity breeds a [14] _______, cosmopolitan outlook with [15] _______ restaurants and nightclubs.

A

B

C

b Choose a word for each gap. What effect is achieved by the way the captions are written?

famous grimy squat carnival enormous pristine snooze hangout sophisticated softly lit chill out exquisite fancy screaming stunted

4 Work in groups. Look on page 128 and follow the instructions.

Grammar

The future

1 Look at this example from the unit. Underline the different ways to talk about the future.

The world's population in the year 2050
"The choices that today's generation of young people aged 15–24 make about the size and spacing of their families are likely to determine whether Planet Earth will have 8, 9 or 11 billion people in the year 2050." (United Nations Population Fund, 2005)
By 2050 the earth's population is due to reach 9.07 billion. 62% of people will be living in Africa, Southern Asia and Eastern Asia – numerically this is the same as if all the world's current population lived just in these regions. In addition, another 3,000,000,000 are set to spread across the rest of the world.

2 a Which expressions in the table talk about:

1 something that will happen soon? *due to ...*
2 something that will certainly happen?

+ infinitive	+ noun or verb + *-ing*
is due to is sure to is set to is about to is bound to is certain to is to	on the point of on the verge of on the brink of

b How can you talk about the future when you are less certain?

it's likely to ...; it's unlikely to ...

3 Rewrite these sentences.

1 I'm sure there will be elections next year. (certain)
There are certain to be elections next year.
2 The schedule says that the president will arrive here at 5pm. (set)
3 Eating organic food will be a trend for some time. (bound)
4 The new pens will arrive very shortly. (point)
5 The trial shall take place on 23 May. (due)
6 I think I'm going to turn down that job. (verge)
7 Life might not be so different in 2050. (unlikely)

4 a Write three sentences about the future. Include information about something that:

- will happen soon.
- is certain to happen.
- is less certain to happen.

b Work with a partner. Compare sentences and ask questions to find out more about each other's opinion.

Comparisons involving different verbs and times

5 a How could these remarks continue?

"I was a bit disappointed by the Acropolis. It wasn't nearly as impressive as I ..."

"I have to work quite hard for exams this year. So I don't go out as much as I ..."

"New York has really changed. It's much safer than it ..."

b 1.30 Listen to check. Which words are repeated, and which aren't?

6 Change these sentences to comparatives. Are there different ways to express the same idea?

1 You do very little exercise. You ought to do more.
2 I was expecting it to be really dangerous, but it didn't seem to be dangerous at all.
3 The exam is usually not very difficult, but this year it was quite hard.
4 I had hoped to get a lot of work done today, but I've managed to do a bit.
5 Of course, I had expected her to be angry. As it turned out, she was absolutely furious.
6 I had imagined him to be in his late 40s, but he turned out to be nearly 60.
7 He promised to help a lot, but in fact he hardly helped at all.

7 How could you continue these sentences with a comparative form?

1 The film was much more exciting than ...
2 The president's speech wasn't as impressive ...
3 I'm sure the weather won't be as bad ...
4 Don't worry. When you meet him face-to-face, he's more friendly ...
5 She's over 80 now. She doesn't get around ...

Grammar reference, p141

Vocabulary

Changes

8 a In these sentences from *Nutrition transition* on p39, what other adjectives or adverbs could you use to replace gradual(ly) and rapid(ly)?

1 a People's diets have evolved gradually in response to changes in food production.
  b People's diets have undergone a gradual evolution in response to changes in food production.
2 a Obesity is rising rapidly in all countries.
  b There has been a rapid rise in obesity in all countries.

b Look at sentences a–h and discuss these questions.

1 What is each sentence about, and where might you read it? How do you know?
2 What noun means 'change' in the sentence? Does it mean a slow or a fast change?
3 Do you think the writer sees the change as being for the better or the worse?

a Nothing symbolises the remarkable transformation of the city from third-world capital to centre of global finance more than its glittering new shopping malls.
b He emphasised the importance of making a smooth transition to democracy.
c If you are interested in the historical evolution of the temples, stop off at Ajanta, where some caves are from the 2nd century BC.
d After a week of mass demonstrations that have paralysed the capital, the country is on the verge of total collapse.
e What we are witnessing is a technological revolution in the recording industry, one that is quietly taking power away from the big studios and putting it directly in the hands of artists.
f To protect your pearls from gradual deterioration, don't let hairspray or perfume touch them.
g Most patients treated with the drug showed a dramatic improvement within months.
h After being top of the league, United soon went into rapid decline.

c Notice the adjectives with each noun. What other adjectives could you use in the same context?

9 a Think of a change you know about. Choose one of these topics and write sentences giving your opinion.

- a place
- the environment / the world
- sport
- a person you know

Since the Wall fell, Berlin has undergone a remarkable transformation. In less than 30 years, it has developed from being a regional backwater to being one of Europe's most dynamic cities.

b Read out your sentences. Do other people agree?

Cause and effect

10 a In these sentences, which means:

- A caused B?
- B was caused by A?
- A influenced B?

1 British food became cosmopolitan. This gave rise to a whole new style of British cooking which was influenced by the Mediterranean.
2 This has had an impact on people's attitudes to food and cooking.
3 People have really started eating well. This was a direct consequence of joining the EU.

b These expressions could replace those highlighted in 10a. Could they be used in sentence 1, 2 or 3? Would they change the meaning?

led to *1*	generated	had an effect on
resulted in	brought about	influenced
resulted from	stemmed from	was caused by
triggered	had its origin in	had an influence on

11 Choose the best expression. Why is it better?

1 Celebrities have a huge effect / influence on young people. Look at the way people copy Paris Hilton, for example.
2 The conflict has its origins in / led to tribal feuds between nomadic herdsmen.
3 You want to be careful with this vaccination. It could trigger / bring about an allergic reaction.
4 It was mainly the irresponsible behaviour of the banks that had an effect on / brought about the crisis, so they should pay for it.
5 The problem stemmed from / resulted in the fact that she never received his emails.

12 a Complete these sentences so they are true for you.

1 My ______ stems from my family background.
2 ______ had a big impact on me.
3 ______ influenced me a lot, because …
4 ______ had an important effect on my future.

b Compare your sentences.

Self-assessment

Can you do these things in English? Circle a number on each line. 1 = I can't do this, 5 = I can do this well.

interpret maps and facts	1	2	3	4	5
make comparisons and talk about changes	1	2	3	4	5
talk about diet and nutrition	1	2	3	4	5
discuss changing trends	1	2	3	4	5
talk about result	1	2	3	4	5
write captions	1	2	3	4	5
write economically	1	2	3	4	5

- For Wordcards, reference and saving your work → e-Portfolio
- For more practice → Self-study Pack, Unit 4

5

Concepts of space

5.1 goals

- describe spaces in cities
- describe how spaces are used

Post-it city

A

B

C

D

READING

1 a The photos are from an exhibition called 'Post-it city'. Which cities do you think they are? Why?

- Hanoi, Vietnam
- Barcelona, Spain
- Warsaw, Poland
- Cairo, Egypt

b What does each photo show? What do they seem to have in common?

2 Read the captions and check. Which photos do they match with?

1

Once held around the edge of an abandoned football stadium, Jarmark used to be Europe's biggest open-air market. For many years, it brought a sense of community to traders and shoppers from different nationalities who otherwise would have been on the streets. It was closed in 2010, to be replaced by a new National Stadium, one of the venues for the Euro 2012 football tournament.

2

Every day in Hanoi, more than 2,000 women take to the streets selling a kind of noodle soup – *Phở Bó*, a mixture of soy, noodles, vegetables, pork or beef in a hot broth. Each of these soup-sellers carries a pole balanced across her shoulders: hanging from one side is a soup pot with chopsticks, plates and whatever else you might need for eating; on the other side, stacked in order, are tiny, coloured stools. This complex arrangement quickly becomes an improvised outdoor restaurant for up to ten people.

3

In an overcrowded city, living anywhere will do – even a cemetery could be called home. Described by politicians as a refuge for criminals, chosen by filmmakers and novelists as locations for stories of marginalisation, or declared as areas in need of protection by UNESCO, these makeshift homes remain a sign of real poverty.

4

Reclaimed as provisional allotments, these no-man's lands found along rivers and railway lines now serve a real purpose. Here, retired citizens build precarious sheds from waste and grow fruit and vegetables where they can. Making use of waste ground in an original way, the project gives these elderly people a function in life.

3 **Read the captions again. Which place:**

1 has now disappeared?
2 is viewed differently by different people?
3 gives a part of the population something to do?
4 is the result of a desperate situation?
5 is viewed the most positively?
6 brought different kinds of people together?
7 has to be set up again every morning?

LANGUAGE FOCUS
Describing spaces

4 **a** **Find adjectives in the captions that mean:**

a full of people.
b left empty.
c improvised.
d existing outside.
e unstable.
f used for a limited time.

b **Do the adjectives have a negative or neutral connotation in the captions? How does this affect the way we read them?**

5 **a** **Which of these adjectives can describe: spaces in cities? buildings? both?**

claustrophobic quaint restful run-down glitzy desolate imposing bustling vibrant futuristic picturesque stylish soulless seedy ramshackle

b **Which do you think have a positive or a negative connotation?**

c **Work with a partner. Choose a place or building in your town. Think how to describe it using one or more of the adjectives.**

d **Describe your place to the class. Can other people guess what it is?**

LISTENING

6 **a** **Match these words to make as many collocations as possible describing spaces and places.**

property	organism
urban	developers
public	dwellers
city	needs
basic	planning
living	space

b 2.1 **Listen to a lecture about 'Post-it city'.**

1 Which collocations do you hear?
2 What is the speaker's main point about: public spaces in general? 'alternative' urban spaces?
3 In what way are 'alternative' urban spaces like Post-it notes?
4 What is the lecturer's attitude to urban planning? What does he say that makes you think this?

c **Which adjectives did the speaker use to describe the way people use urban spaces? Are any the same as in the captions?**

d 2.1 **Listen again to check.**

SPEAKING

7 **Talk about spaces in the area where you live.**

1 Make a list of spaces which have been reclaimed or transformed, or areas which now serve an alternative purpose. Think about:
- squatters.
- teenagers.
- tourism.
- markets.
- music events.
- festivals.
- social groups.
- green spaces.
- building developments.

2 Do you agree with the changes? Listen to each other's opinions and ask questions to find out more.

Surveillance

5.2 goals

- talk about crime and surveillance
- comment on experiences

A

B

READING

1 a What do the images show?

b Talk together.

1 Where can you find surveillance cameras in your town? What do you think is their main purpose?
2 Do you think they have helped to reduce crime? If so, how?

2 a Read the article.

1 Where is the writer and why is he there?
2 Does he think CCTV cameras are useful, useless or sinister? What evidence can you find in the article to support this?
3 How does his attitude change in the second paragraph?
4 Who runs the operation? Why does that seem to be a good idea?

IN Manchester, I watch the man as he fumbles in his pocket, rolls a cigarette and lights it. He is young, thin, and seems nervous. He also seems oblivious to the camera through which I am watching him. He is outside, in the city centre; I am in front of a bank of screens, at the NCP car park. This is the control centre for Manchester's CCTV camera surveillance operation: five operators controlling over 250 cameras, covering public spaces throughout the greater Manchester area 24 hours a day. One of the operators had noticed something unusual about our man, but his suspicions, honed by hours of watching street activity, were soon allayed, and his attention turned elsewhere. At one end of the screens, an operator is observing the car park. A police officer is on shift for referrals for action. The operation has had its successes: nearly 50 football hooligans rampaging in the city centre before last year's UEFA cup final between Rangers and Zenit St Petersburg have been identified; mobile wireless cameras have assisted in a successful police operation against gangs in Moss Side.

It is not always so exciting. The operator showed me his computerised log of recent incidents: a man on a garage forecourt looking at the camera, a group of youths on bicycles, someone acting suspiciously here, a shoplifter being brought out of a shop there. The centre's manager is keen to stress that CCTV is there "to improve the quality of life, not just to catch criminals". The cameras are alert to fly tipping, traffic congestion, illegal street traders. "We want to be the fourth emergency service, watching out for the people of Manchester," the manager says. She also thinks this collection of functions and separation of powers between council and police is the proper model for CCTV, allowing checks and balances. Certainly, to the observer, the operation smacks more of the familiar British piecemeal pragmatism than any sinister desire for control.

b What do you think the highlighted words mean? How else can you express the same idea?

1 as he **fumbles** in his pocket
2 seems **oblivious** to the camera
3 his suspicions **were allayed**
4 **honed by** hours of watching
5 **rampaging** in the city
6 **smacks** more **of** ... pragmatism

3 Read two more paragraphs from the article on p129. Then answer the questions.

LANGUAGE FOCUS

Legal and illegal activities

4 a **These words are used to describe things people do in streets or in buildings. Explain what they mean.**

mugging burglary vandalism riots pick-pocketing squatting writing graffiti busking robbery protest marches shoplifting street trading hooliganism begging demonstrations sleeping rough gang warfare

b **Which words have a different verb form? Is there a noun for the people who do these activities?**

mugging → mug → mugger
writing graffiti → graffiti artist

c **Choose *five* of the activities you find interesting.**

1 In your country, which are legal, which are illegal, and which can be either?
2 Which do you think should be legal / illegal? Why?
3 Do you think any could (or should) be controlled by surveillance cameras?
4 Are any a particular problem where you live?

Security

LISTENING

1 **Look at the photos. What forms of security do they show? What is their purpose?**

A

B

C

D

2 **2.2 Listen to Jane, Uri, Patrick and Tina talking about security measures.**

1 What security measure do they talk about?
2 Are they in favour of them, against them, or do they have mixed feelings?

LANGUAGE FOCUS

Commenting on experiences

3 a **The speakers comment on things that happened to them. Try to complete the gaps.**

1 JANE I did think it was ______, as, you know, I wasn't really doing anything that dangerous.
2 JANE ______ any schoolchildren were actually crossing the road.
3 URI I think they serve ______.
4 URI Then they speed up again – it's ______.
5 PATRICK I think ______, but sometimes I think it's just a bit ______.
6 PATRICK But at no point did they actually ask to see my passport – it was ______. ______ getting priorities wrong!
7 TINA I do think they're ______, I mean, if you think about it, it does make it safer to buy things.
8 TINA There was a huge queue of people standing behind me – it was ______.

b **2.2 Listen again to check.**

SPEAKING

4 a **What do you think are the pros and cons of the four security measures?**

b **Comment on an experience you have had.**

1 Think about an experience you have had with security measures.
   - What happened?
   - How do you feel about the experience?
   - What comments would you like to make about it?
2 Talk about your experiences and how you feel about them. Listen to each other and ask questions to find out more.

5.3 Target activity

Plan a city square

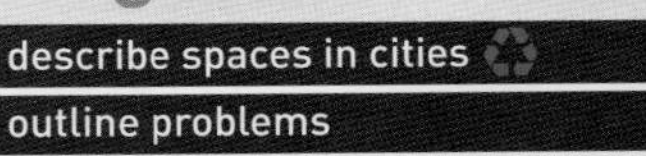

5.3 goals

- describe spaces in cities
- outline problems
- discuss and suggest solutions

View looking west

View looking east

TASK PREPARATION

1 a These photos show a square in Munich, Germany. Imagine living on this square. What would be the advantages and disadvantages?

b Read the report. Did it mention any of the things you talked about?

The square at Harras is situated on a major intersection of two main routes, one going south from the city centre and the other branching west towards the ring road and motorway. It is also the centre of the Munich district of Sendling and is the main shopping centre of the area. On the east and north-west sides of the square there are shops, offices and a library, with residential flats on the upper floors. On the south side is the main post office and other, smaller shops and flats. The centre of the square is kept free of traffic and is used as a bus station. There is also access to the underground from various points on the square, including the central area. At present, there is constant heavy traffic on all three roads which pass through the square, and they are separated from the buildings only by narrow pavements.

The main aim of the redevelopment is to improve the quality of life in and around the square, and to make it an attractive centre for Sendling which will be well used by residents and visitors to the area.

TASK LANGUAGE
Outlining problems

2 2.3 Listen to a town planner outlining the problems.

1. What does she say about:
   - the shops?
   - the square in the middle?
   - the traffic?
   - the buildings?
2. What needs to be done? Make a list of points she mentions. Then compare answers.

3 a Look at these two ways of outlining problems. Add words to the gaps.

a shortage of
inadequate
no access to
overcrowded
inaccessible
congested

There's / There are + noun	*is / are* + adjective
1 There's _a lack of_ communication between the different parts of the square.	6 The different parts of the square are _cut off_ from each other.
2 There's ______ the post office.	7 The post office is ______.
3 There's ______ parking spaces.	8 The parking spaces are ______.
4 There's no flow of traffic through the streets.	9 The streets are ______.
5 There are too many people in the square.	10 The square is ______.

b Which sentences apply to the square at Harras?

c Which sentences in 3a could you rephrase beginning with *There's a problem*? What words can come after *problem*?

TASK

4 a Try to find a solution for the square at Harras. Follow the instructions on p129.

b Present your ideas to the class.

c 2.4 Look on p138 and listen to the town planner's solution.

Across cultures Privacy

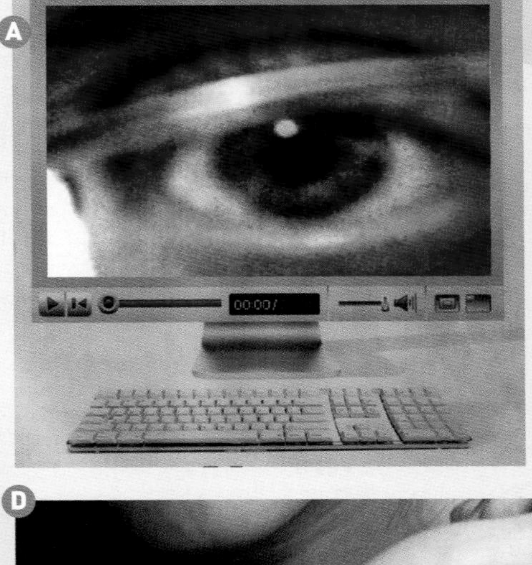

1 a These images were all posted on Flickr.com. Match them with these titles.

1 Invasion of privacy
2 Defining minimum privacy
3 Privacy is dead
4 Respecting beauty and privacy
5 A little privacy please!
6 Privacy vs. security

b How appropriate do you think each title is? Why / Why not?

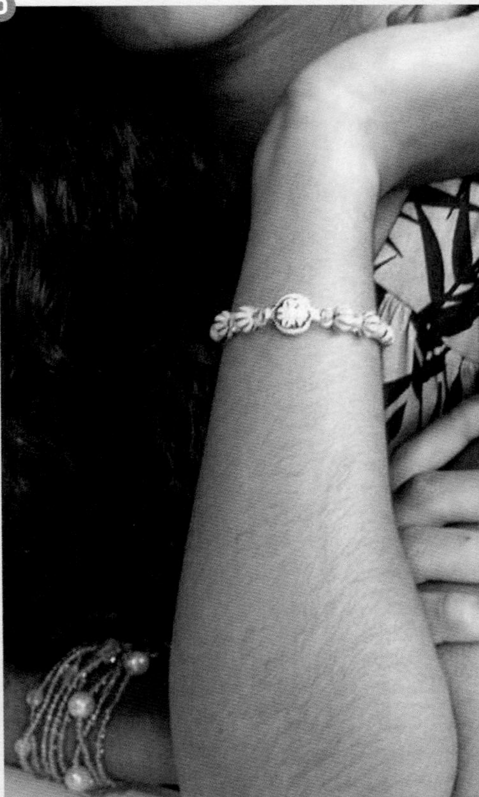

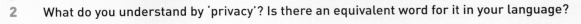

2 What do you understand by 'privacy'? Is there an equivalent word for it in your language?

3 2.5 Listen to David talking about privacy.

1 What is 'privacy' for him?
2 What can you tell about:
- his relationships and friends?
- his free time?
- his life up to now?

3 How was Egypt different from England? Is the image he conveys of England positive?

4 How important is privacy to you? Discuss these questions.

1 Do you work better with people around, or on your own?
2 If you went to a park or beach, would you try to find a place away from other people?
3 If you had a day completely on your own, would you enjoy it, or would you prefer to be with other people?
4 Would it bother you to share a hotel room with a friend?

5 Think of a country you know.

1 Is there *more* or *less* of a sense of privacy than in your country?
2 How does that show itself?
3 Why do some cultures attach more importance to privacy?

Keyword *need*

1 a Look at this example from the unit. What words could go in the gaps?

> In order to turn this square into an urban space of high quality it needs [1]_______, and it needs [2]_______ for the whole layout of the square. First of all, the road, the spaces taken up by the road need [3]_______, but enabling the flow of traffic for the same amount of vehicles and without causing traffic jams.

b 2.6 Listen to check.

c Notice how you can use need as a verb or a noun.

Verb	Noun
a The traffic needs to be completely re-organised. b We need more discussion before we can reach a decision. c The whole building urgently needs redecorating.	d There's an urgent need for more qualified staff. e It's OK – there's no need to panic. f Many people in the area are in desperate need of financial support.

1 What words and patterns follow need?
2 What adjectives / adverbs come before need? Can you think of any others?
3 Could you say each sentence differently, using need or another expression?

2 a These words / expressions often follow in need of. Which could be about: people? a building? a system?

a complete overhaul	medical treatment	a change
repair	a break	assistance
renovation	food and shelter	an upgrade

b Talk about these photos using expressions in 2a.

1

2

3

4

c 2.7 Listen to four news items. Which expressions from 2a do you hear? What is each item about?

3 a How could 1–6 continue? Add sentences with need (as a verb or noun).

1 The windows are rotting away. *They urgently need replacing.*
2 Don't worry about the loan.
3 Thousands of families have nowhere to live.
4 At the moment, the square doesn't fulfil its function.
5 The anti-smoking laws aren't very satisfactory.
6 I can hear you very clearly.

b Read out one of your answers. Can other people guess what the first sentence was?

4 a Work alone. Write down:

- a building that's badly in need of repair or renovation.
- something that needs reorganising or improving.
- a group of people who you think need more help.
- something there is an urgent need for.

b Compare your ideas with other people.

EXPLORESpeaking

Goal

◎ give a presentation with images

1 a These photos are from a slideshow presentation. What do you think it is about and who is it for?

b 2.8 Listen to Len Griffiths giving the presentation. At every 'beep' he shows a new slide. In what order do you think he shows the slides?

c What do we know from the presentation about:

1 Grenada?
2 the hotel?
3 the beach?
4 the food?

2 a Think about the way Len:

1 introduces the presentation.
2 moves from one topic to the next.
3 finishes the presentation.

Try to complete the gaps.

> **Introduction**
> Well, good afternoon. My name's Len Griffiths, I'm the manager of Petit Bacaye, and 1 _______ thank you very much for coming this afternoon.

> **Opening description**
> So, 2 _______ an idea what the hotel is like and what it's like to stay there. 3 _______ in a minute. But 4 _______ a general idea about where we are ...

> **Transition**
> OK, so 5 _______ Petit Bacaye itself, the hotel.

> **Conclusion**
> So, that's it, really. I 6 _______ what the hotel is like. 7 _______ any questions, 8 _______ answer them.

b 2.9 Listen to check.

3 a Look at these ways of presenting visual information. What other words could be used instead of the highlighted words?

Showing a view	Referring to a slide
This shows you ... Here's a view of ... Here's a closer view ... Let's just zoom in on ...	As you can see from this photo ... ... which you can see here. You can see that ...

b Choose one of the slides. Which expressions could you use to talk about it?

c Look at the script on p151. Did the speaker say the same as you?

4 Give a short presentation.

1 Imagine you spent some time at the Petit Bacaye hotel. Prepare to talk about your holiday using the photos on this page.
2 Think of other details you would like to explain.
3 Give your presentation to other students.

A

B

C

D
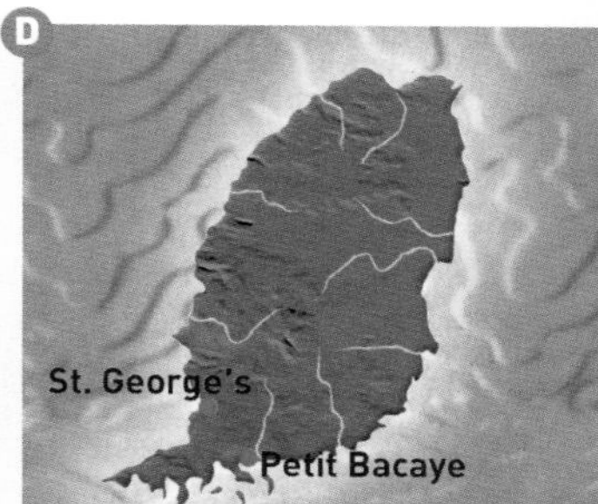

E

F

G

H

I

J

K

Grammar

Passive reporting verbs

1 a Look at these examples from the unit.

a	CCTV is reckoned to operate in around 500 British towns and cities, as against 50 in Italy, 11 in Austria, and one in Norway.
b	During the 1990s, roughly 75% of the Home Office crime-prevention budget is said to have been spent on installing CCTV.
c	It has also been shown that improving street lighting "is a rather more effective form of prevention".

1 The examples show two ways of using impersonal reporting verbs. What other verbs can be used in the same way? Make a list.

***it* + passive verb + *that* ...**
It is reckoned that ...
It is said that ...
It has been shown that ...
passive verb + *to* + infinitive
... is reckoned to ...
... is said to ...
... has been shown to ...

2 Which examples refer to:
- the present?
- the past?

How is this reflected in the grammatical structures used?

3 The expressions are typical of news reports or academic writing. How could you say them in a more conversational style?

b Rewrite these sentences. Use a suitable passive reporting verb.

1 People say that CCTV cameras in shops don't actually deter criminals.
2 People calculate that there are over 4 million CCTV cameras in the UK.
3 Many experts believe that the use of CCTV hasn't had a significant effect on crime.
4 They say that speed cameras have reduced road accidents.
5 Reports show that most security checks at airports are inefficient.
6 Many people feel that security checks at airports are reassuring.

c How are these impersonal constructions expressed in your language?

2 a Choose a photo and imagine a news item to go with it. Write one or two sentences using reporting verbs.

Milan are reported to have signed a new mid-fielder. It is believed to be the highest-paid transfer in the history of the club.

A

B

C

D

E

b Read out your sentences. Can other people guess the photo?

Grammar reference, p142

Vocabulary

Describing places

3 Look at this example from the unit. What two ways does the town planner use to describe the square? What other shapes could a town square be?

> The square itself is a very unusual shape. It is a triangular shape, and it is surrounded by some very fine buildings.

4 a What do the highlighted expressions mean? Which sentences best describe the photos?

A

B

C

D

1. The square is surrounded by fine old buildings, dating from the turn of the century.
2. The central mosque, dating from the 12th century, is the focal point of the city.
3. The road is bordered by shopping centres and retail outlets.
4. The main street is lined with restaurants.
5. The town is dominated by a citadel.
6. The neighbourhood is bounded by 35th Street and 7th Avenue.
7. There are rooms overlooking the square for about $10 a night.
8. Several small cafés look out over the river.
9. You can find good food at Viktor's, just off the main square.

b What do you imagine the other places to be like? Try to form a 'mental picture' and describe it to your partner.

5 a Think of a square, street or neighbourhood where you are now. Write a few sentences describing it.

b Read out your sentences. Can other students guess which place it is?

6 Think of a place which you think doesn't fulfil its function well and could be improved. Discuss:

1. what is wrong with it.
2. how it might be improved.

Solutions to problems

7 a 2.10 Listen to these extracts from presentations. Which person is talking about:

- a war?
- immigration?
- redesigning a city square?
- an industrial dispute?

b All these adjectives collocate with solution. Which speaker uses each expression?

diplomatic	global	practical	long-term
partial	proposed	interim	mutually agreeable

c Which expression in 7b means:

1. they don't fully solve the problem
partial solutions
2. it involves the whole world
3. we still need to find a better solution
4. it works
5. it avoids fighting
6. it's what we suggest
7. it will solve the problem for a long time
8. both sides agree to it

d What verbs collocate with solution?

come up with a solution

e 2.10 Listen again. What verbs did they use?

8 Discuss a problem.

1. Think of a world problem, a political issue or a problem in your area.
2. Prepare to talk about it. Make a few brief notes and try to use expressions from 7b.
3. Tell other students about the problem. Discuss possible solutions.

Self-assessment

Can you do these things in English? Circle a number on each line. 1 = I can't do this, 5 = I can do this well.

describe spaces in cities	1	2	3	4	5
describe how spaces are used	1	2	3	4	5
talk about crime and surveillance	1	2	3	4	5
comment on experiences	1	2	3	4	5
outline problems	1	2	3	4	5
discuss and suggest solutions	1	2	3	4	5
give a presentation with images	1	2	3	4	5

- For Wordcards, reference and saving your work → e-Portfolio
- For more practice → Self-study Pack, Unit 5

6

Appearances

6.1 goals

- describe appearance and changes to appearance
- discuss photos and images
- talk about aim and intention

The camera never lies?

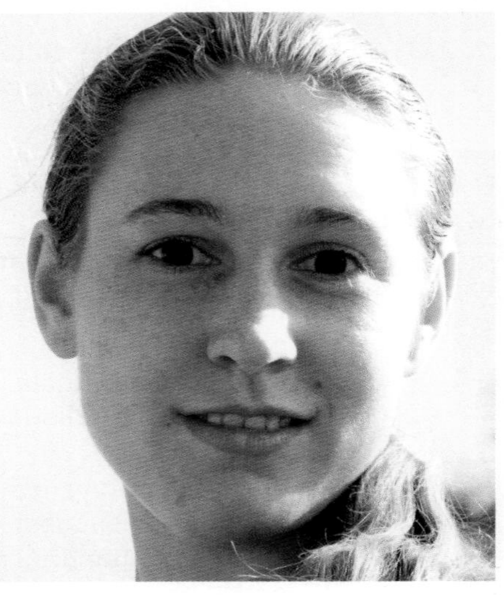

LISTENING

1 a The left-hand image has been changed in ten different ways. What changes do you think have been made? How?

b 2.11 Listen to check.

c Read the script on p151. What do you notice about the verbs?

1 What grammatical form do most of them have? Why do you think this is?
2 Find examples of verbs which are formed from adjectives.

READING

2 a Read an article about digital manipulation in the fashion industry. What do you think these highlighted words mean?

1 the arsenal of fashion photography
2 great bone structure
3 flawless on the page
4 with abandon
5 everything gets retouched to death
6 doesn't pretend to mirror real life
7 poor body image
8 void of any kind of humanity
9 readers are savvy enough

Thin, pretty and airbrushed

Clicking the shutter is just the beginning of model beauty

The arsenal of fashion photography has always included teenagers with great bone structure, chic clothes and a good make-up job. But with computer graphics, these models look even more flawless on the page. Since the advent of Photoshop, the fashion and advertising industries have been airbrushing pimples, removing wrinkles and shaving off thighs with abandon. "Everything gets retouched to death," says Eric Feinblatt, a photographer and professor at the Fashion Institute of Technology in Chelsea. "There's nothing you see on any fashion magazine cover that hasn't been manipulated."

Though the industry does not pretend to mirror real life, many are critical of the way that photo manipulation removes life from people's faces and hence contributes to poor body image. Michael LaMount, a freelance photographer in Los Angeles, objects to digital manipulation, because by removing lines, chins and shadows, retouchers are erasing people's individuality. "Once you start airbrushing, it becomes void of any kind of humanity," he explains.

But even the models know the point of the picture is to create an image, not a portrait. By the time a photo is taken, the model has already been heavily made up, her clothes pinned and tucked to her body. "How real is it anyway?" asks model Candy Frisbe.

Colleague Megan Shoemaker says readers are savvy enough to know fashion photographs do not represent real life. "I think that most people know that the images can be manipulated; consumers are aware," she says.

b Discuss the article.

1 Is the writer's opinion critical, positive or neutral?
2 Four people are quoted. What is each person's attitude to digital manipulation?
3 Who do you most agree with? Why?

LANGUAGE FOCUS
Altering physical features

3 a Find six words in the article that refer to physical features.

b What other physical features can be altered in photography? Make a list.

c Compare lists. Use these verbs to talk about them.

enhance lengthen shorten lighten darken reduce add remove alter

> Spots can be removed, cheek bones can be enhanced.

Fake photos

LANGUAGE FOCUS
Aim and intention

1 a These photos both have fake elements. What are they? How were they achieved?

Abraham Lincoln

Shark attacks helicopter

b Look at these expressions which describe the *aim* of the alterations. Complete them with words from the box.

to (x3) of as with in that

1 ... this composite may have been created so ______ ______ address that.
2 ... ______ order ______ give the impression of a shark attack ...
3 ... so ______ the claim would seem more genuine ...
4 ... hoping ______ convince people that the photo was real ...
5 ... ______ the aim ______ enhancing his stature ...

c Which photo do you think each expression describes?

READING and SPEAKING

2 Work in A/B pairs. Read about the photos in 1a. Student A, look at p127. Student B, look at p136.

3 a Read about these other fakes. Match the aims (a–d) to the descriptions (1–4), adding an expression from 1b. What changes do you need to make to the sentences?

1 In 2007, *National Geographic* showed a picture of the Giza pyramids, Egypt on its cover. The pyramids were moved closer together ...
2 In 1994, *Time* magazine showed American footballer OJ Simpson shortly after his arrest for murder. They changed his face to make it darker than it really was ...
3 A Reuters photographer covering an air raid on Beirut, Lebanon, used Photoshop to add extra smoke rising from the buildings ...
4 In 1994, the University of Wisconsin doctored a photograph on a brochure by inserting a black student in a crowd of white football fans ...

a look more dramatic
b fit the vertical format of the magazine
c emphasise the ethnic diversity of their students
d look more menacing

b To what extent do you think these changes are unethical, and why?

Genuine fakes

6.2 goals

- talk about fakes and forgery
- convince people and express doubt

LANGUAGE FOCUS
Fakes and forgery

1 a What do you understand by these expressions?

1 a forged birth certificate
2 an investment scam
3 a fake Rolex
4 credit card fraud
5 a con trick
6 counterfeit currency
7 cheat the system
8 a compulsive liar

b Look at the highlighted words. What verb, noun and adjective forms do they commonly have?

forge, forgery, forged

c Discuss these questions.

1 What other things can be forged?
2 What things are often fake?
3 In what ways do people often cheat the system?
4 Think of examples of a con trick or a scam. Have you (or people you know) ever been the victim of one?

READING

2 a One of these 'Picassos' is a fake.

1 Which one do you think it is?
2 If you were an art dealer, how would you find out?
3 How much do you think each painting is worth?

Maisons sur la Colline (Pablo Picasso, 1909)

Cadaqués (Pablo Picasso, 1910)

b Find out which painting is the fake on page 128.

3 a Read an article about John Myatt, who painted the fake 'Picasso' in 2a. Which of these statements do you think are true? Why / Why not?

1 John Myatt doesn't have a high opinion of his own painting style.
2 He took great care to make his fakes look as genuine as possible.
3 He wouldn't have succeeded without John Drewe's help.
4 It is surprisingly easy to deceive art experts.
5 His prison sentence was unduly harsh.
6 He deeply regrets what he did.
7 He always had a natural talent for painting fakes.

b What kind of person do you think John Myatt is? Why?

devious	daring	clever	modest	ashamed

The master forger

John Myatt was responsible for the biggest art con of the 20th century, and ended up going to jail for it. Now his story is being turned into a Hollywood movie – and a prestigious gallery is showing his 'genuine fakes'. He tells all to Mark Honigsbaum.

John Myatt is showing me some of his recent creations. "That's a Giacometti," he says, pointing to an abstract in swirling whites and greys entitled *Apples on a Stool* (1949). "I'm not sure it's quite finished yet." Next, Myatt walks me to another wall of The Air Gallery, in London's Mayfair, hung with a Modigliani, several Picassos and, in the centre, a large Ben Nicholson.

For a painter who is celebrating his first London opening, Myatt is disarmingly honest about both his working methods and his failings as an artist. But then, this is not the first time that Myatt's versions of works by Giacometti and Nicholson have found their way into the West End.

Between 1986 and 1994, Myatt churned out more than 200 new works by surrealists, cubists and impressionists, passing them off as originals with the help of an accomplice, John Drewe, an expert at generating false provenances. Despite the fact that many of Myatt's paintings were laughably amateurish (they were executed in emulsion, not oil), they fooled the experts and were auctioned for hundreds of thousands of pounds by Christie's and Sotheby's. It was, said Scotland Yard's art and antiques squad when they finally caught up with Myatt in 1995, "the biggest art fraud of the 20th century". Indeed, to this day, some 120 'Myatts' are still said to be in circulation.

Now, having served his time – Myatt was sentenced to 12 months in prison in 1999 but was released for good behaviour after four months – he feels he has nothing to apologise for.

Instead, he is seeking to forge a new career, so to speak, as a purveyor of what he calls 'genuine fakes'. These are works by the very same artists he used to imitate when he was a criminal – not only Giacomettis and Nicholsons, but Monets, Matisses and Renoirs. They even come with the artists' signatures. The only difference is that on the back of the canvas is a computer chip and the legend 'Genuine fake' written in indelible ink.

Myatt didn't set out to be a faker. As a young art student, he had high hopes of establishing his own artistic style. But whenever he turned his hand to landscapes or portraiture, he says the result was invariably "academic" and "dull". Instead, he taught evening classes and began selling the odd fake to friends and colleagues ...

c Can you think of verbs to replace these phrasal verbs from the article?

1 churned out more than 200 new works
2 passing them off as originals
3 didn't set out to be a faker
4 they finally caught up with Myatt

d How do these phrasal verbs add to the meaning? What 'mental image' do you associate with each?

e Look at this sentence. Why do you think the writer says 'so to speak'? At what other points in the text does the writer reveal his own attitude?

... he is seeking to forge a new career, so to speak ...

LISTENING

4 2.12 Listen to John Myatt talking about how he started forging paintings.

1 How did John Myatt start producing fake paintings?
2 How did he get to know John Drewe?
3 How did he start forging paintings illegally?
4 Why didn't he copy paintings?

SPEAKING

5 Role play.

1 Student A, you are an art dealer. You want to sell B this painting. Look on p130.
2 Student B, you like the painting, but you're not convinced it's genuine. Look on p138.

Interview someone and present a profile

6.3 goals

- describe appearance
- conduct a personal interview
- describe someone's life, achievements and attitudes

TASK READING

1 a What do you know about the Brazilian author Paulo Coelho?

b Read the interview.

1 What does the profile tell you about:
- Coelho's physical appearance?
- the way he presents himself?
- his personality?

2 Which parts of the interview:
- quote things he said?
- describe the setting?
- talk about his past life?
- discuss his achievements?
- refer to the promotion of his books?

3 What verb tenses are used for each of these purposes?
4 What order are these parts in? What effect is achieved by this?
5 What facts about his life and career surprised you? Why?

When Paulo Coelho was 17, his parents sent him to an asylum because they thought he was psychotic. Now he's the world's biggest-selling novelist – but, he says, some people still don't understand him.

Paulo Coelho is dressed entirely in black, as befits a spiritual sage whose books take as their subject the eternal human enigma. He is small, delicately proportioned and his soft grey hair has been grown into a rat's tail, of the kind one sometimes sees on Buddhist monks. He sits in the lobby of a plush London hotel – all clean minimalist lines and strangely placed mirrors – looking entirely at home, the black of his clothes contrasting decoratively with the beige upholstery.

"Every day I try to be in communication with the universe in an unconscious way," he smiles, staring at me with big, brown earnest eyes and speaking in heavily accented English.

Paulo has never had any problem communicating with other people. In fact, he's phenomenally successful at it. Since the publication of his first work, *The Pilgrimage*, in 1987, he has sold 65 million books, making him the best-selling author in the world – above John Grisham, Tom Clancy and the seemingly unassailable J.K. Rowling. He has been translated into 59 languages and collected an impressive portfolio of literary prizes – among them, the French Chevalier de l'Ordre des Arts et des Lettres, their most prestigious literary gong. His most famous book, *The Alchemist*, tells the story of an Andalusian shepherd boy in search of treasure in a far-off land, and has sold more than 30 million copies since its publication in 1988.

Despite, or perhaps because of his success, Paulo Coelho is a strong advocate of spreading his books through peer-to-peer file-sharing networks. After a fan had posted a Russian translation of one of his novels online, sales of his book jumped from 3,000 to one million in three years, with no additional promotion or publicity from his publishers. His blog Pirate Coelho provides free translations and downloadable versions of many of his books. Due to the openness regarding his content, author Jeff Jarvis named Coelho "the Googliest author" in the world.

TASK

2 **Work in A/B pairs. Prepare for an interview.**

1 Student A, you should be yourself in the interview. You can choose a 'setting' where you would like to be interviewed (at home? at work? in some other place that says something about you?). Decide what you will wear.
2 Student B, make notes on the setting and A's physical appearance.

3 **Conduct the interview.**

1 Student B, ask questions to find out some important things about A:
- A's past life.
- what A is doing, and what has led up to it.
- achievements.
- beliefs and attitudes.

2 Make notes, including one or two interesting quotes.

4 **Now change roles.**

5 **From your notes, present a profile of your partner.**

Across cultures Piracy

1 a Look at the images and the news headlines. What do you think they are about?

b Read the whole news items. Which do you think is the most or least serious offence? Why?

2 Which of these do you think should be allowed? Say why or why not, and under what circumstances.

1. Downloading films from the Internet.
2. File-sharing music on the Internet.
3. Making copies of DVDs.
4. Photocopying scientific or academic articles.
5. Selling pirate editions of published books.

3 a Which opinions do you agree with?

1. Authors put a lot of work and knowledge into writing a book. In effect, photocopying a book is stealing money from the person who wrote it.
2. The film and music industries make such huge profits that they can easily afford to lose royalties from people making illegal copies.
3. Illegal downloading actually helps unknown musicians: it enables more people to get to know their work, so they attract bigger audiences to their concerts.

b Discuss these questions.

1. How strictly is copyright enforced in your country?
2. What are the dangers of, for example, illegal downloading in your country?
3. Are you likely to get caught if you download something illegally?

A

Group jailed for illegal copying

Officials have arrested three women and two men, and have captured more than ten photocopies and 300 copied books in a crackdown on illegal copying.

B

Illegal downloaders threatened with Internet cancellation

The government today proposed new laws to stop illegal downloading of music and films. Those found swapping copyrighted material could have their Internet connection cut off.

C

Oil company faces copyright charges

A court in Washington has found one of the world's biggest oil companies guilty of encouraging its employees to photocopy research articles from scientific journals without paying royalty fees. The oil giant may be liable to pay damages to the owners of the material for breaching copyright.

Keywords *aim, purpose*

1 a Add these expressions with aim to the gaps.

is aiming for	aims to	is aimed at

Although the film with its 3-D effects and rather predictable plot [1] ______ a popular audience, it also touches on profound historical themes. Indeed, it can be seen as an indirect commentary on the destruction of Native American Indians by white settlers from Europe.

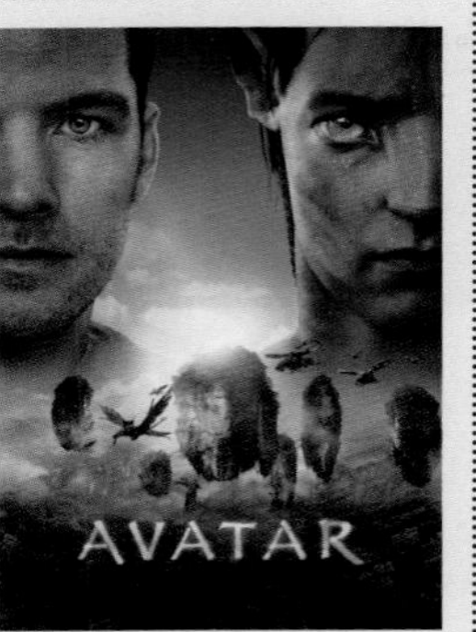

The course will run for two weeks, and [2] ______ teach basic skills in digital image manipulation. Students should have basic computer skills, but need no previous experience in graphic design.

23-year-old Anna Vovk, though still surrounded by controversy, [3] ______ a gold medal again this year.

"I'm in the clear and I'm confident about winning again this year," she told reporters.

b In the first two gaps, you could add these adverbs below. Where could you insert them? How would they change the meaning?

specifically	primarily	solely	mainly	clearly	apparently

c In this sentence from the unit, aim is used as a noun. Who and what is being talked about?

... carried out with the aim of enhancing the president's stature.

d Add an expression with aim.

1 ______ the law is to prohibit using mobile phones in vehicles.
2 Summer courses will be arranged, with ______ bringing new students up to the required level in English.

2 a How do you think these sentences might continue?

1 We need to be there by six, so we're aiming ...
2 *Women's Pages* is a broadly focused, popular magazine aimed ...
3 The average theatre-goer is aged between 55 and 85, but our new play is aiming ...
4 The tour started with a visit to Beijing this weekend, aimed ...
5 She made the mistake of marrying a man whose sole aim in life ...

b 2.13 Listen to check. Were your answers similar?

3 a These sentences all contain the word purpose. Which do you think is:

a part of a brochure?
b part of a report?
c part of a conversation?
d part of a lecture?
e part of an opening speech?
f part of a news report?

1 Thank you all for coming this afternoon. The purpose behind this meeting is really twofold.
2 The purpose of this paper is to analyse trends in the mining sector.
3 Actually, we're getting quite worried about him – he just doesn't seem to have any purpose in life.
4 They are believed to be enriching uranium for the purpose of developing nuclear weapons.
5 The primary purpose of the club is to encourage young people to do sport.
6 As Straczinski says in *The Essence of Art*, art exists for the purpose of putting real events into perspective.

b How could you express the sentences in 3a using aim?

The purpose behind this meeting is ... → The aim of this meeting is ...

4 Talk about your future aims.

1 Think of things that you aim to do in the future (work, studies, family and leisure).
2 Make notes, using expressions from this page.
3 Discuss your aims.

6 EXPLOREWriting

Goals
- use written and spoken styles appropriately
- appreciate written and spoken genres

1 What kinds of writing and speaking do the images represent? What kind of style would you need to adopt in each case? How do you think spoken and written styles vary, in general?

2 a Look at the two extracts from the John Myatt interview, and the same information expressed in written form (e.g. an autobiography). How are the spoken and written versions different? Think about:

1. the number of main verbs.
2. the use of expressions like you know, really, sort of, anyway.
3. the number of times and is used
4. the underlined expressions.
5. the use of reported speech and questions.

Spoken version

It started about 1983, 1984, when I was a single parent, I had two very small children. I was a school teacher at the time, but my wife had left home and she wasn't coming back, and there were two very young ones to take care of. So I was trying to find a way of working from home, and, you know, keeping the family together really. And one of the things that cropped up was this idea of putting an advert in the back of *Private Eye* magazine, which is a sort of satirical magazine we have in England. And it just said 'Genuine fakes. Paintings from 150 to 250 pounds'.

But if you had a study by Leonardo da Vinci on the wall of your house, you know, and it was a tiny bit of ripped paper and it was all beaten up and all that, well, it's much more credible if not necessarily believable. Anyway, to cut a long story short, he said to me would I be interested in having half of the 25,000? And I said yes, and I took the money, and proceeded, really, to go into a career of art fakery with this man over the next six or seven years.

Written version

It started in about 1983 or 1984, when I was a single parent with two very small children. I was a school teacher at the time, but my wife had left home for good and I needed to take care of two young children, so I was trying to find a way of working from home and keeping the family together. One idea I had was to put an advert in the back of *Private Eye*, an English satirical magazine, saying 'Genuine fakes. Paintings from 150 to 250 pounds'.

But if you had a study by Leonardo da Vinci on the wall of your house, in the form of a tiny piece of torn paper in very bad condition, it would be much more credible, if not necessarily entirely believable. So briefly, he asked me if I would be interested in having half of the 25,000. I accepted, took the money, and proceeded to go into the business of art fakery with this man over the next six or seven years.

b Compare answers. Do you agree?

3 a Look at the notes you made for your partner's profile on p60. Write out these facts in three separate paragraphs in a fairly formal style, as if writing part of a biography.

b How would the same information be conveyed in a spoken, conversational style?

1. Think about the features in 2a.
2. In how many ways can the text become 'spoken'?

4 It has been said that the gap between spoken and written English is getting smaller. Why do you think this might be? Is the same happening in your language?

Grammar

Present perfect simple and progressive

1 a **Look at these examples from the unit. Match them with uses a–c of the present perfect simple.**

> 1 The lips have been reddened, so now they're a brighter red.
> 2 Customs officials have arrested three men and two women.
> 3 *The Alchemist* has sold more than 30 million copies.

a to describe a recent event, without saying when it happened
b to describe a recent change (something is different now from before)
c to describe events happening over a period up to now

b **Look at these examples of the present perfect progressive. Match them to uses a and b.**

> 1 Since the advent of Photoshop, the fashion and advertising industries have been airbrushing pimples, removing wrinkles and shaving off thighs with abandon.
> 2 I've been waiting for this day for so long – and now it's come.

a to refer to an activity or feeling continuing up to now, but which has now stopped
b to refer to an activity that started in the past and is still continuing

c **Look at examples a–d.**

1 Has the activity / feeling stopped, or is it continuing?
2 How might each sentence continue?

a I've been waiting for you for ages. Where ... ?
b I've been trying to get hold of her, but ...
c It's been snowing for ages, but thankfully ...
d Over the last hour, I've been discussing ...

d **Complete these sentences so they are true for you.**

I've been meaning to write to you since our meeting, but ...

1 I've been meaning to ...
2 I've been hoping ...
3 I've been wondering what ...
4 I've been planning to ...

Grammar reference, p142

Present participle expressions

2 **We often use participles to describe *appearance*. Look at these examples from the unit. Notice that there are two patterns:**

1 **same subject**
He sits in the lobby of a plush London hotel. He looks entirely at home.
→ He sits in the lobby of a plush London hotel, looking entirely at home.

2 **different subject**
He sits in the lobby of a plush London hotel. The black of his clothes contrasts decoratively with the beige upholstery.
→ He sits in the lobby of a plush London hotel, the black of his clothes contrasting decoratively with the beige upholstery.

3 a **Here are some examples of descriptive expressions from novels. What do you think they are about? Match them with the topics in the box.**

1 ... sparkling with excitement
2 ... glowing dimly through the fog
3 ... leaning on the counter, chatting to the clerk
4 ... gazing at a computer screen
5 ... strolling along the beach

a man at an airport	the lights of a farmhouse
people by the sea	a woman's eyes
people in an office	

b **What 'mental picture' do you see for each example? Compare ideas.**

c **2.14 Listen to the original contexts. Do they change your 'mental picture' in any way?**

4 a **Look at these sentence beginnings, and try to imagine a 'mental picture' for each one. Add a participle expression to describe what the person was doing, or what they looked like. Use either of the two patterns in 2.**

1 He lay on the beach, ...
2 She cantered along the path, ...
3 He was sitting on a park bench, ...
4 He paused, ...
5 She stood by the window, ...

b **Compare what you have written with the sentences on p130.**

5 **Work in pairs.**

1 Write a descriptive expression like in 3a on a piece of paper. Pass it to another pair.
2 Write what you think might come before the participle expression. Pass it to another pair.
3 Add another sentence, either before or after. Pass it to another pair.
4 Read out your sentences.

Vocabulary

New crimes

6 How many 'new crimes' (crimes which did not exist 50–100 years ago) can you remember from this unit?

7 a What crimes are these images associated with?

A

B

C

D

b Match these 'new crimes' with pieces of advice 1–4 and images A–D.

phishing	hacking	card theft	identity fraud

1 Be sure that no one else can see the PIN number that you key in. Thieves can copy card details that way and clone cards.
2 Be suspicious of all unsolicited emails you receive, even if they appear to originate from a reliable source such as a bank.
3 Always think before you give away your personal details, and dispose of documents with any personal information on them securely.
4 Keep firewalls, anti-virus software and anti-spyware programmes up-to-date to help protect your computer.

c Match 1–4 with a–d to make sentences written by victims of the crimes in 7b.

1 Just wanted to apologise for the random email you received from me.
2 I checked my credit card statement and saw a purchase that I hadn't made.
3 The email said 'verify' or 'update' your account, but I knew what it was.
4 I don't know who knew I had that property.

a Fraudsters who cheat the system and want to take on your identity, I guess.
b It was one of those phishing scams, and I was just being conned.
c I didn't send it – it appears my email account was hacked into.
d It turns out somebody had cloned my card.

Verbs with *-en* and *en-*

8 a Look at these sentences from the unit. You can use verbs ending with -en or beginning with en- to talk about changes.

1 The teeth have been whitened.
(= made whiter)
2 The lips have been reddened.
(= made redder)
3 The skin has been enhanced.
(= made better, clearer)

b What do these verbs mean? How are they formed?

blacken strengthen lengthen widen
soften enlarge enliven darken weaken
shorten deepen harden endanger enclose
lighten toughen thicken straighten

c Which adjectives could you use to talk about:

- a road? • a bridge? • a room? • a skirt?
- a canal? • a sauce? • a photo?
- your health? • your feet?

9 a Think of contexts for these sentences.

1 They tried to blacken my name.
2 They're an endangered species.
3 I enclose my CV.
4 It strengthened our determination.
5 Can you enlarge the picture?
6 He tried to soften the blow.

b 2.15 Listen to check.

10 a Choose two verbs from 8a or 8b. Write true sentences about something (or someone) that has changed recently, but do not give a context.

b Read your sentences to another student. Can they guess what you are talking about?

Self-assessment

Can you do these things in English? Circle a number on each line. 1 = I can't do this, 5 = I can do this well.

describe appearance and changes to appearance	1	2	3	4	5
discuss photos and images	1	2	3	4	5
talk about aim and intention	1	2	3	4	5
talk about fakes and forgery	1	2	3	4	5
convince people and express doubt	1	2	3	4	5
conduct a personal interview	1	2	3	4	5
describe someone's life, achievements and attitudes	1	2	3	4	5
use written and spoken styles appropriately	1	2	3	4	5
appreciate written and spoken genres	1	2	3	4	5

• For Wordcards, reference and saving your work → e-Portfolio
• For more practice → Self-study Pack, Unit 6

7 Health

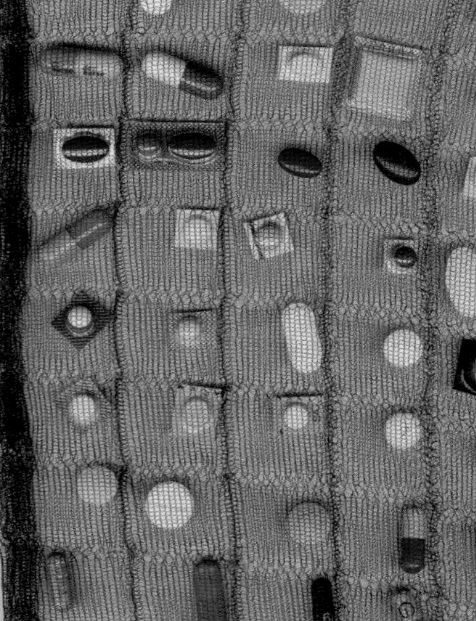

Cradle to grave

READING

1 a The photos show an art installation at the British Museum, London. What do you think the installation is? Try to describe it from the photos.

b Read the description and check.

1 What kind of medicines are, and are not included in the installation?
2 What do we know about: the man's life? the woman's life?
3 What do you think the exhibition says about our approach to health?

Cradle to grave by Pharmacopoeia

Cradle to grave explores our approach to health in Britain today. The piece consists of a lifetime supply of prescribed drugs knitted into two lengths of fabric, illustrating the medical stories of one woman and one man.

Each length contains over 14,000 drugs, the estimated average prescribed to every person in Britain in their lifetime. This does not include pills we might buy over the counter, which would require about 40,000 pills each.

Some of the treatments are common to both: each starts at birth with an injection of vitamin K and immunisations, and both take antibiotics and painkillers at various times. Other treatments are more specific. The woman has a relatively healthy life, but suffers from arthritis and diabetes in middle age. The man has asthma and hay fever when young, but enjoys good health until his 50s. He finally stops smoking after a bad chest infection when he is 70. He is treated for high blood pressure for the last 10 years of his life and has a heart attack and dies of a stroke in his 70s. He takes as many pills in the last 10 years of his life as in the first 66.

Cradle to grave also contains family photographs and other personal objects and documents. The captions, written by the owners, trace typical events in people's lives. These show that maintaining a sense of well-being is more complex than just treating episodes of illness.

LANGUAGE FOCUS
Health problems and treatment

2 a Read the description again. Find eight words / expressions which refer to *illnesses*. Find six which refer to *treatments*.

b 2.16 Which words in 2a are similar in your language? Listen to the recording. Are they pronounced differently?

c Discuss these questions.

1 Which of these health problems are common in your country? Which are less common? What about the forms of treatment?
2 How would the installation change if it represented the lives of people from: your own country? another part of the world?

Audio guide

LISTENING

1 a 2.17 **You will hear an audio guide to the exhibition. What *additional* information do you hear about these topics? Listen and make brief notes, then compare answers.**

1 the people who created the installation
2 the people whose lives it shows
3 the textiles
4 the pills
5 the photographs

b Here are some of the things the audio guide mentions. Who or what do they relate to? Put them in order of 'age'.

syringes a lilac footprint a Christmas tree a kitchen cupboard a gas and air mask a coffin a silver blade rolled-up fabric an ashtray

c 2.17 **Listen again to check.**

2 a Do you think the audio guide focuses mainly on:

- the installation as a work of art?
- its significance?
- how it was produced?

b Read the script on page 152. What features of language and style support your view?

LANGUAGE FOCUS
Descriptive participles

3 a The audio guide uses passive forms and participles to describe the installation. Look at the sentences. Add words from both boxes in the gaps.

sewn interspersed arranged wrapped intermingled	in (x2) with (x2) into

1 The piece comprises a lifetime's supply of prescribed drugs, ______ ______ two lengths of textile.
2 There are large and small tablets ______ ______ foil.
3 The tablets forms solid blocks of one colour, ______ ______ vivid geometric patterns.
4 Photographs in black and white and colour are ______ ______ order of the subjects' ages.
5 ______ ______ the photographs are personal objects that relate to the course of the man's or woman's life.

b Check in the script on page 153.

4 Add expressions from 3a to make these sentences more descriptively precise.

1 She sat close to the fire with a blanket round her.
2 The old houses in the street have newer houses between them.
3 They discovered that he had an ID card in the lining of his jacket.
4 Many third-generation immigrant families are now mixed with other groups.
5 The main standing stones of Stonehenge are in a circle.

SPEAKING

5 a Discuss these questions.

1 The 'Cradle to Grave' installation obviously involved a lot of work. Do you think it is worth spending time and money on art of this kind? Why? / Why not?
2 Why do you think the British Museum in London decided to show the installation? Is a museum an appropriate place for it? Why? / Why not?

b Describe an exhibition or show you have seen.

1 Think of an exhibition or show that you have seen and remember well. What made it memorable? Make notes describing it as precisely as you can.
2 What was your opinion of the exhibition / show? What comments would you like to make about it?
3 Work with other students. Listen to each other's descriptions. Do you think the exhibitions you heard about were worth seeing?

Mind over matter

7.2 goals

- describe a process or experiment
- discuss implications and significance

SPEAKING and LISTENING

1 Discuss these questions.

1 Do you consume much caffeine? In what form? Are you dependent on it?
2 What physical and mental effects do you think caffeine has on you? Does it:
- help you concentrate?
- improve your cognitive abilities?
- make you more alert?
- improve your motor skills?
- improve your reaction times?
- make you jittery?

3 What is the 'placebo effect'? What connection do you think it has with caffeine?

2 2.18 Listen to an interview about Professor Irving Kirsch.

1 Why do you think coffee was chosen for the experiment?
2 What were the four main stages of the experiment?
3 What does the experiment seem to show?
4 Are you convinced or surprised by it? If so, why?

3 The interview was from a TV report. How do these images relate to what was said?

A

B

C

LANGUAGE FOCUS Describing processes and experiments

4 a These words were used in the documentary to talk about Professor Kirsch's research. Which words go together in pairs?

devise ability measured correlation experiment prove co-ordination task performance effect skills report concentrate placebo significant perform assess test

Professor Kirsch devised an experiment.

b Summarise the experiment, using as many words from the box as possible.

The 'nocebo' effect

READING

1 What do you think the images show? How are they connected with these words?

witch doctor spell doll curse protection voodoo evil eye

2 a Read the article. Which of these points do you think it is making?

1 Just believing you are ill can make you ill.
2 The 'nocebo' effect is like the placebo effect, but with a negative result.
3 Doctors should be very careful what they tell patients.
4 Doctors are the witch doctors of the modern world.
5 We don't really know how the 'nocebo' effect works.

Beware witch doctors

Late one night, 80 years ago, in a small Alabama cemetery, Vance Vanders had a run-in with the local witch doctor, who wafted a bottle of unpleasant-smelling liquid in front of his face, and told him he was about to die and that no-one could save him.

Back home, Vanders took to his bed and began to deteriorate. Some weeks later, emaciated and near death, he was admitted to the local hospital, where doctors were unable to find a cause for his symptoms or slow his decline. Only then did his wife tell one of the doctors, Drayton Doherty, of the 'hex'.

Doherty thought long and hard. The next morning, he called Vanders' family to his bedside. He told them that the previous night he had lured the witch doctor back to the cemetery where he had forced him to explain how the curse worked. The medicine man had, he said, rubbed lizard eggs into Vanders' stomach, which were now inside him.

Doherty then summoned a nurse who had, by prior arrangement, filled a large syringe with a powerful emetic. With great ceremony, he inspected the instrument and injected it into Vanders' arm. A few minutes later, he began to be sick. In the midst of it all, unnoticed by everyone in the room, Doherty produced his *pièce de resistance* – a green lizard he had stashed in his black bag. "Look what has come out of you, Vance," he cried. "The voodoo curse is lifted."

Vance did a double take, lurched backwards to the head of the bed, then drifted into a deep sleep. When he awoke the next day he was alert and ravenous. He quickly regained his strength and was discharged a week later.

The facts of this case were corroborated by four medical professionals. Perhaps the most remarkable thing about it is that Vanders survived. There are numerous documented instances from many parts of the globe of people dying after being cursed.

Cases such as this may be extreme examples of a far more widespread phenomenon. Many patients who suffer harmful side effects, for instance, may only do so because they have been told to expect them. What's more, people who believe they have a high risk of certain diseases are more likely to get them than people with the same risk factors who believe they have a low risk. It seems that modern witch doctors wear white coats and carry stethoscopes.

The idea that believing you are ill can make you ill may seem far-fetched, yet rigorous trials have established beyond doubt that the converse is true – that the power of suggestion can improve health. This is the well-known placebo effect. Placebos cannot produce miracles, but they do produce measurable physical effects.

The placebo effect has an evil twin: the 'nocebo' effect, in which dummy pills and negative expectations can produce harmful effects. The term 'nocebo' (which means 'I will harm') was not coined until the 1960s, and the phenomenon has been far less studied than the placebo effect.

What we do know suggests the impact of nocebo is far-reaching. "The voodoo curse, if it exists, may represent an extreme form of the nocebo phenomenon," says anthropologist Robert Hahn from Atlanta, Georgia.

b Underline any *five* words in the article that are new and that seem useful to you.

1 Compare them with another student. Did you make a similar choice?
2 Would you need to use these words or just be able to recognise them? Why?

c In the article, the writer explores the implications and significance of what happened. Find examples which express that something:

1 is certain.
2 is surprising.
3 is possible or probable.
4 seems unlikely.

SPEAKING

3 a Can people convince themselves that they are suffering something when they are not? Rank these scenarios from 1 (= very unlikely) to 10 (= very likely).

a You read about damaging effects of mobile phones. Soon, you notice that you get a headache when using your phone.
b Someone tells you it is risky to swim after eating. You ignore the advice and immediately develop serious stomach pains as a result.
c Halfway through eating seafood, you notice it smells odd, and you think you might have food poisoning. Quickly, you start to feel sick.

b Have you (or people you know) had similar experiences to these? Do you think they are examples of the 'nocebo' effect, or were other factors involved?

Global issues

7.3 goals

- discuss implications and significance
- discuss an issue

TASK LISTENING

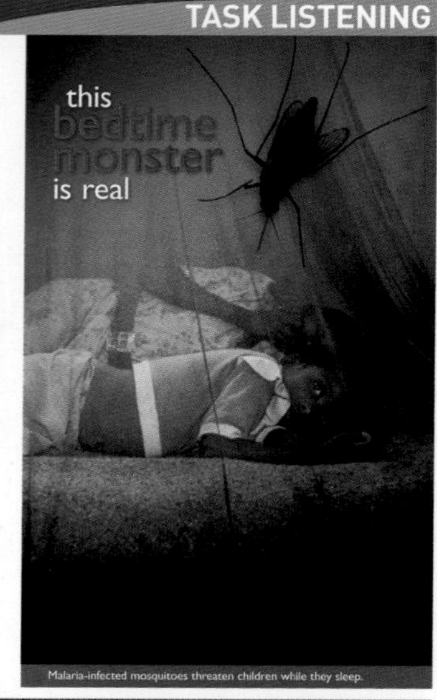
this
bedtime
monster
is real
Malaria-infected mosquitoes threaten children while they sleep.

1 What do you think is the message of the anti-malaria campaign advert?

2 Discuss these questions about malaria. Then check on p131.

1. In what parts of the world is it a problem?
2. How dangerous is it?
3. What kind of disease is it? How can you catch it? What are the symptoms?
4. How can it be treated? How can you protect yourself against it?
5. What is being done about malaria? What needs to be done?

3 a 2.19 **Listen to a doctor talking about malaria. What does he say about:**

1. misconceptions?
2. people at risk?
3. current treatment?
4. what needs to be done?

b **What does he see as the most important issue connected with malaria?**

TASK LANGUAGE
Discussing issues

4 a 2.19 **The doctor uses expressions to talk about problems and solutions. Listen again. What words go in the gaps? Use these words to help you.**

a health issue	the only long-term solution	don't necessarily
a question of	factor in this	attitudes are changing
the main problem	a lot to do with	a big issue

1. Another ______ is the lack of available medicines.
2. Malaria is partly ______ but it's partly an economic one.
3. This is ______ providing education.
4. They ______ know how malaria is caused.
5. It's also got ______ providing infrastructure.
6. Corruption is ______ .
7. ______ is the problem of resistance.
8. ______ involves developing a vaccine.
9. There are signs that ______ .

b 2.20 **Listen to check.**

TASK PREPARATION

5 a **The doctor says that malaria is an** economic issue **and also a** political issue**. What does he mean by this?**

b **Look at some other types of** issue**. Match them with the examples.**

health	cultural	social	moral	global	environmental
conservation	political	economic	educational		

1. childhood literacy
2. the destruction of rainforests
3. using English as a world language
4. banning smoking in public places
5. the spread of fast-food chains

TASK

6 a **Together, choose *one* interesting and important issue from 5b.**

b **In groups discuss the issue. Decide the main points to discuss, and what you think about them. Then discuss the main problems and possible solutions.**

7 **Choose one person from each group to sit on a 'panel'.**

1. Members of the panel: in turn, give your group's opinion.
2. The others: make comments or ask questions after each person has spoken.

Across cultures Health campaigns

1 a 2.21 **You will hear Percy, a research scientist from Ghana, talking about using mosquito nets to prevent malaria.**

1 What's the problem with mosquito nets?
2 What do people in villages often do? Why?
3 What new idea does he talk about? How does it work? Why is it better?

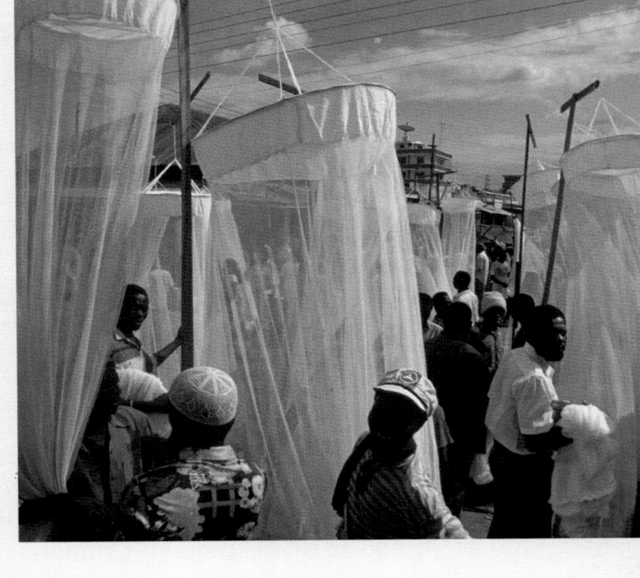

b 2.21 **Listen again and complete the gaps.**

1 Average homes have ______ ventilation.
2 Mosquito nets are quite ______ to sleep in.
3 That's where ______ comes in.
4 There are a lot of programmes which ______ sponsors.
5 Mosquito nets are ______ in the villages.
6 People don't ______ properly.
7 People leave them ______ loosely.
8 This is a permanent net ______ all the walls.
9 You don't have to ______ every night.
10 You get better ______.

c **From what you have heard, do you think Percy is a native speaker of English, a bilingual speaker, or has learned English as a foreign language? Why?**

A

telenet
KEEP COMMUNICATING
GIVE AN AIRSHAKE
1
2
10 cm
3
Learn how to airshake on airshake.be

B

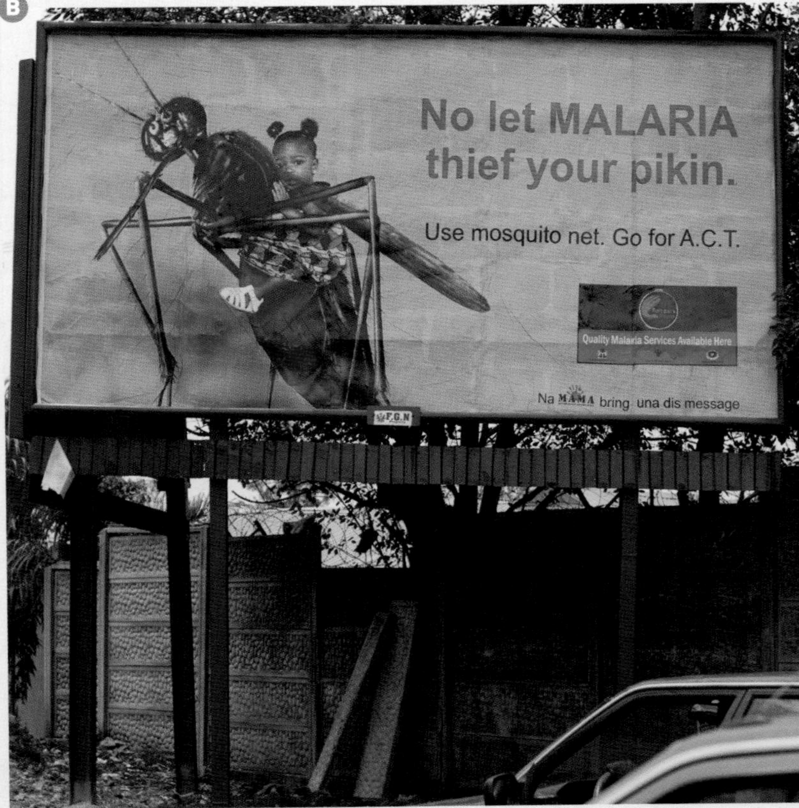

No let MALARIA thief your pikin.
Use mosquito net. Go for A.C.T.
Quality Malaria Services Available Here
Na MAMA bring una dis message

2 **Look at these campaign posters to raise awareness about swine flu and malaria. What message are they trying to make? What steps do they suggest taking to alleviate the problem?**

b **Which poster do you think would be the most effective where you live? Why?**

c **Discuss these questions.**

1 Which health problems in your country are in the public eye?
2 How does the population find out about them?
3 Is there enough information?
4 What kind of campaigns are established to make the population aware of these health issues? Do you think they are effective?

Keywords *consist, include*

1 a Look at the examples. Which highlighted verbs mean:

1 this is the whole of it?
2 this is only part of it?
3 it has this inside it?

1 Each length contains over 14,000 pills, tablets, lozenges and capsules, the estimated average number prescribed to every person in Britain during their lifetime.
2 The piece consists of a lifetime supply of prescribed drugs knitted into two lengths of fabric.
3 So the experiment involved testing people's responses before and after drinking ...
4 These activities tested the volunteers' co-ordination. That included the ability to concentrate, remember strings of numbers.
5 People generally use traditional treatments, comprised of herbal remedies.

b Look at these sentences from the unit. Which verb do you think was used in each case? Why?

1 This does not include / contain pills we might buy over the counter, which would require about 40,000 pills each.
2 The 'Cradle to Grave' installation included / involved a lot of work.
3 'Cradle to Grave' contains / comprises family photographs and other personal objects.

2 a Look at these newspaper extracts. How do you think they continue? Think about the kind of information that would be needed in each case.

1 The majority of people who attend motor racing events are male. This is starting to irk the car companies that organise them, as women comprise ...
2 For decades, travel between America and Europe involved ...
3 Near the centre of Old Havana lies the Casa de los Arabes, a Moorish-style, 17th-century building that now comprises ...
4 Minneapolis-St. Paul International Airport was in the midst of a construction programme that includes ...
5 For Britons trying to enter the US, the situation is about to get worse. From the end of October, all British subjects will need a visa or a passport containing ...

b 2.22 Listen to check. What are the news reports about?

3 a Write complete sentences from these notes. Use verbs from 1a.

1 Hobbies: cycling, rowing, skiing *My hobbies include cycling, rowing and skiing.*
2 UK: England, Scotland, Wales, N. Ireland
3 Return flight New York – Paris, $695: in-flight meals, insurance, taxes
4 Threats to wildlife in Danube Delta: drainage, new building projects, pollution
5 My job with PR company: sending out press releases, organising events, contacting journalists
6 'Placebo effect' experiment: giving coffee to volunteers (no caffeine), conducting co-ordination tests
7 Chess: two players, a 64-square board, 16 pieces (king, queen, bishops, rooks, knights, pawns)

b 2.23 Listen to check. Were the answers similar to yours?

c Look at the photos. Imagine you are 'selling' these products.

1 How would you do it?
2 What could they contain or include which would make them more appealing to consumers?

d What verbs would you use in your own language to express the same ideas? How similar are they?

EXPLORESpeaking

Goals

- take turns in a discussion
- give opinions in an extended conversation

1 Look at the cartoon.

1. What's the point of the joke?
2. Why are children often asked to 'take turns'? In what contexts?
3. In what other situations do you need to take turns in life? Why?
4. What is the opposite of taking turns in conversation?

2 a Read these conversations. What are the people talking about?

1

A Well, I think it's been quite successful, because, you know, it's done what it set out to do. It's made cafés and restaurants places where you, I can, well, we can all now go without having to breathe in everyone else's smoke ...

B (*Find a way to interrupt and stop A talking*) [1] _______. What about the terrible effect it's had on small businesses. Right? I mean, some of these places have actually had to close down because of it. Now how is that, how does that help non-smokers?

C (*Support what B said*) [2] _______. There's just no point in having all these nice clean bars if there's nobody going into them.

2

A I think it hasn't worked. Quite honestly. People have started buying drinks to take home just so they can smoke, so bars and cafés have gone out of business.

B (*You disagree with A*) [3] _______. I mean, how many bars have actually gone out of business?

C (*Support what A said*) [4] _______. Not many bars have, have actually had to close, but a lot of places are struggling. Especially ones that don't have any outdoor space for smokers.

3

A Well, I'm on the side of smokers on this one. I, they quite rightly see it as an infringement of their personal liberty. You know, their freedom to smoke if they want to.

B (*You think A is missing the point*) [5] _______. I mean, I see it as a health issue, I don't want to be forced to breathe other people's smoke, so it's not really about personal liberty.

C (*You strongly disagree with B*) [6] _______. No-one's forcing you to breathe their smoke, you can always go and sit in a different room, really.

B Why should I have to?

4

A The way I see it, the solution would be to provide separate rooms for smokers, right? Not just ban smoking altogether. Why couldn't we let smokers smoke if they want and non-smokers could have their own room?

B (*You think A is over-simplifying*) [7] _______. I guess it's fine if you have a big restaurant with separate rooms, but what about just a small café?

C (*You strongly agree with B*) [8] _______. It's discrimination against small businesses – so the big businesses, well they're fine, and the small ones, they're the ones that are having to close.

When we were kids, my brother and I would take turns hitting each other.
Oh, isn't that lovely. It's so nice when children take turns.

b In groups, look at the strategies for interrupting, agreeing and disagreeing (in *italics*). For each one:

1. make a list of possible things the person might say in the gaps.
2. in each case, which remark would achieve the speaker's aim most successfully? Why?
3. try out each conversation, and see how your chosen remark sounds.

c 2.24 Listen to the conversations.

1. Were the speakers' remarks similar to yours?
2. Who was better at making their point?
3. Why do the speakers interrupt each other? Would you do this in everyday conversation?

3 Work in groups. Choose an issue from p70 or your own topic. Try out conversations. Practise each conversation more than once, until you can 'take turns' fluently.

Conversation 1
A, give an opinion about the topic.
B, interrupt A. Comment on what A said.
C, support what A or B said.

Conversation 2
B, give an opinion about the topic.
C, say B is missing the point or is exaggerating. Give your opinion.
A, strongly agree with B or with C.

Conversation 3
C, give an opinion about the topic.
A, strongly disagree with C.
B, support what C or A said.

4 Work in the same groups.

1. Have an unrehearsed discussion about a different topic.
2. Other students: how successful was the conversation?

7 Look again

Grammar

Passives and participles

1 **Look at these examples from the unit. You can often use passives and participles to describe the appearance, position or arrangement of things.**

1. They **are laid** side by side in a long glass case.
2. **Laid out** in groups, the tablets form solid blocks of one colour, **interspersed** with vivid geometric patterns.
3. The end of the fabric **is rolled up** and empty.

Notice that you can use a passive form, or just a participle. Find other examples in the script on page 152.

2 a **What do you think each example below is about?**

a ... stuck on the windscreen ...
b ... stacked against the walls ...
c ... pinned on a white cupboard ...
d ... spread out along the valley ...

b **Match each example with an image and write a complete sentence.**

1

2
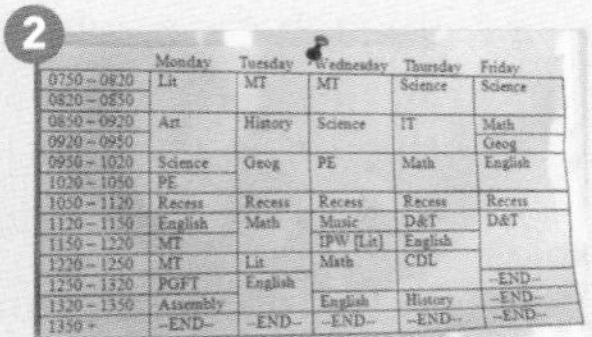

3

4

c 2.25 **Listen to check.**

d **Think of synonyms you could use in each case.**

stacked → piled

3 **Make participles from these verbs. Add them to the sentences to make them more precise.**

gather	arrange	stick	bury	hide	park

parked
1. The car is ∧ at the back of the hotel.
2. It's dangerous to walk on the beach as there are mines in the sand.
3. The sign is partly behind a tree, so you can't see it very clearly.
4. We may be a bit late. We're in a traffic jam.
5. In chess, each player's pieces are in two rows.
6. There are huge crowds of protesters in front of the bank.

4 a **Write a sentence including a participle as in 3. Then write it again, leaving out the participle.**

b **Show your sentence to another student. Can they guess what the missing participle is?**

Referencing and substitution

5 a **Look at these examples from the unit. Do you remember what they refer to?**

1. ... though it doesn't kill as many as it once **did**.
2. Some of the treatments are common to **both**.
3. **This** has been tried in certain countries and has been proven to significantly reduce malaria cases there.
4. **One** that could show that what people believed could affect their bodies?
5. Only **then** did his wife tell one of the doctors, Drayton Doherty, of the hex.

b **Match extracts 1–6 with a–f.**

a Well, malaria is in fact preventable by simply providing mosquito nets.
b Some weeks later, emaciated and near death, he was admitted to the local hospital, where doctors were unable to find a cause for his symptoms or slow his decline.
c So how did Professor Kirsch devise this test?
d The first thing to say is that malaria is a very dangerous disease,
e ... illustrating the medical stories of one woman and one man.

6 a **Which of the highlighted pronouns in 5a refer back to previously stated ideas?**

b **Which other words substitute and avoid repetition of previously used information?**

7 a **Look at this conversation. Rewrite it, so that no words are repeated.**

A So what did the doctor say?
B He said I might have to have an operation.
A Oh, I hope you don't have to have an operation ... for your sake.
B I hope I don't have to have an operation, too!
A Well, if you don't have an operation, what's the other option?
B I don't know, I think convalescence is much longer. I have to go to the clinic tomorrow and wait in the clinic all morning for tests and then he'll tell me the results of the tests.

b **Compare your conversations.**

Grammar reference, p143

Vocabulary

Tests

8 a Think about the caffeine experiment. What kinds of test did the participants do? Here are some other kinds of test.

1 In what situation might you do each one?
2 What would be its purpose?
3 How many are related to health?

a placement test	an eye test	a literacy test
a driving test	an IQ test	a typing test
a hearing test	a DNA test	a personality test

b We can say do a test, have a test or take a test.

1 Which of the tests in 8a are more likely to be used with do / take? Which are more likely to be used with have? Why?
2 Can you think of other verbs that could be used with the expressions in 8a?

c Which of these tests have you done (or had) in your life? Tell your partner what happened.

All-purpose nouns

9 On p70, the doctor referred to problems and solutions, nouns which can serve many purposes in different contexts. Look at this news extract and underline five 'all-purpose' nouns.

The three party leaders' speeches have received much attention in this election campaign, but one of their most interesting qualities is the debt they owe to the ancient Greeks and Romans. For the Romans, politics was all about oratory. For the Greeks, big questions such as whether or not to go to war were decided by discussion and debate. Oratory, therefore, was very sophisticated, and closely scrutinised. There have been many surprising aspects to this election, but one thing is clear: the leaders' skill in public speaking has been an important concern – and may possibly become the most important factor – in the end result.

10 a Choose the best all-purpose noun.

1 As far as personality traits go, Carl has one characteristic / feature that I particularly dislike.
2 Why don't you change your approach / attitude and tackle the problem from this angle?
3 The process / manner of counting votes is extremely time-consuming.
4 The issue / context of whether to publish the news or not should have been decided beforehand.
5 Easy navigation is one of the key elements / devices in successful website design.

b What other nouns could be used?

topic	quality	technique	system	feature

Health problems and treatments

11 a How many different words referring to illnesses and treatments can you remember?

b Look at the sentences. Who or what could the pronouns in *italics* refer to?

a doctor	a surgeon	a patient	medicine
a wound / an injury		an illness / a disease	

1 *It*'s taking a long time to heal.
2 *She*'s still convalescing.
3 I'm sure *he*'ll recover OK.
4 *I* decided to operate on *him*.
5 *He* will need to undergo heart surgery.
6 Unfortunately there's no way to cure *it*.
7 *I* treated *her* for shock.
8 *She* prescribed me *something* called Antiflaxin.

c Answer these questions about the highlighted verbs in 11b.

1 How many mean 'improve' or 'get better'?
2 Which is followed by a preposition?
3 Which have equivalent noun forms? What are they?
4 How could you rephrase the sentences using these nouns instead of verbs?

12 a 2.26 Listen to three short conversations. How many words from 11 did you hear? What other words related to health problems and treatments were there?

b 2.26 Listen again.

1 What illness / medical condition are the people talking about in each case? How do you know?
2 Have the patients recovered? If not, what symptoms do they still have?

Self-assessment

Can you do these things in English? Circle a number on each line. 1 = I can't do this, 5 = I can do this well.

talk about health problems and treatment	1	2	3	4	5
describe and comment on an exhibition or a show	1	2	3	4	5
describe a process or experiment	1	2	3	4	5
discuss implications and significance	1	2	3	4	5
discuss an issue	1	2	3	4	5
take turns in a discussion	1	2	3	4	5
give opinions in an extended conversation	1	2	3	4	5

- For Wordcards, reference and saving your work → e-Portfolio
- For more practice → Self-study Pack, Unit 7

8

Brand awareness

8.1 goals

- discuss brands
- describe effects and influences
- talk about the image and qualities of products

Brands

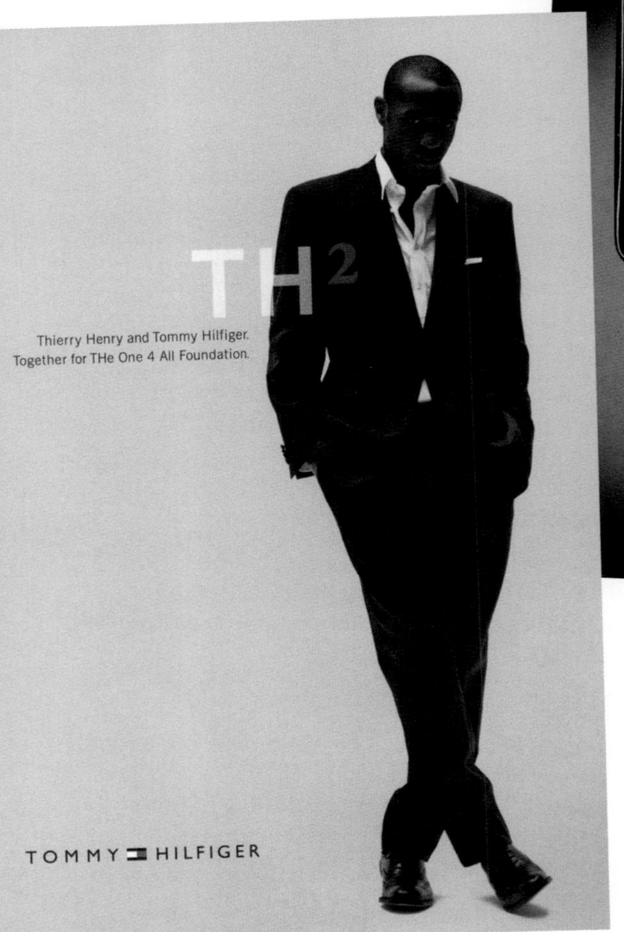

TH2
Thierry Henry and Tommy Hilfiger.
Together for THe One 4 All Foundation.
TOMMY HILFIGER

LISTENING

1 a Discuss these questions.

1 How 'brand conscious' do you think you are? Think about:
- clothes.
- shoes.
- cars.
- household appliances.
- drinks.
- electronic goods.

2 How much importance do you attach to the brand? Why do you think it is or isn't important?
3 Would you avoid particular brands? If so, why?
4 For which kinds of product would you worry about the brand you buy? Why?

b Talk about the adverts.

1 What 'image' do you think they are selling?
2 Are they effective?
3 What do the models themselves add to the message?

2 2.27 Listen to Lydia talking about brands.

1 How 'brand conscious' is she?
2 What does she say about:
  - top designer labels?
  - individuality and belonging?
3 How is the interviewer's point of view different?
4 What kind of person do you imagine Lydia is? Why?

LANGUAGE FOCUS
Effects and influences

3 **a** **The interview contains expressions for saying what effect things have. What did the two people say? Add one or two words from the box in each gap. Make other changes if necessary.**

enhance difference have effect make define influence people

1 If I wear a Boss suit, it doesn't ______ to my personality.
2 It will ______ see you in a different way.
3 Your appearance will ______ by the cut of the garment.
4 Brands ______ also your attitude towards life.
5 If you have something that ______ a positive ______ on you, then your whole personality is more positive.
6 I'm ______ by brands at all. I don't care about them.

b 2.28 Listen to check.

c **Do you agree with the statements in 3a? Think of examples from your own experience.**

Brand images

LANGUAGE FOCUS
Image and qualities

1 **a** **Three people say what words they associate with three international brands. What kind of product are they? What brands do you think they are?**

B
success
innovative
reliability perfection
sound quality

C
fast dynamic
fun speedy
retro good design
small

b 2.29 Listen to check.

c **Which words in 1a are nouns? Which are adjectives?**

d 2.29 **Listen again. Write two more words or expressions each speaker uses. Which are about:**

- the product?
- lifestyle?

2 **a** **Think of a well-known brand (internationally or in your country). Make a list of words associated with it, like those in 1a.**

b **Read out your list. Can other people guess the brand?**

SPEAKING

3 **a** **Think of advertisements for soft drinks in your country. What images and qualities do they usually present to encourage customers?**

b **Work in groups. Look at the advertisements for Pepsi on p132. Follow the instructions.**

Viral ads

8.2 goals
- talk about advertising and marketing
- describe an advert

READING

1 Cover the article. Do you know what a viral ad is?
- If not, what do you imagine it might be?
- If you do, tell other people about viral ads you know.

2 a Read the article. Why are marketing companies excited about viral ad campaigns?

Adverts so good people choose to watch them? Send them to their friends, even? We report on what makes viral ads infectious.

The Internet has revolutionised a plethora of pastimes: the way people communicate, find dates, commit crimes, you name it. But the business of selling stuff and of building brands continues to see one of the most radical transformations.

At the cutting edge is the viral campaign: the short video clip that is so compelling that much of an advertiser's work is done for them when their prospective customers forward it to their contacts, quickly building up an audience of millions.

A whole new industry has sprung up, dedicated to unravelling what makes viral ads infectious. GoViral, for instance, specialises in launching viral campaigns – in part by 'seeding' clips on the Internet, where they are picked up by the online populace.

What once was much a matter of luck is slowly being transformed into a science. Jimmy Maymann, GoViral's chairman, has built a system, "which every campaign is taken through prior to launch in order to ensure virality".

The ideal viral campaign is edgy, surprising, original and emotional – and taps into popular culture, says Maymann. His system attempts to quantify these elements. It's easy to see why businesses would want to embrace viral marketing. Not only is it supposed to create stellar growth rates, but it can also reduce the marketing budget to approximately zero. Against this too-good-to-be-true backdrop, though, is the reality: viral marketing only works when the user is in control and actually endorses the viral message, rather than merely acting as a carrier.

b Discuss these questions.

1 The article says viral ads are 'infectious'. Why is this a good description? What other things can be infectious?
2 Cover the article. Can you remember any other adjectives to describe viral ads? Why do you think these qualities are important?
3 Look at these highlighted words from the article. What do they mean? What mental image do they suggest?
   a dedicated to unravelling
   b a new industry has sprung up
   c 'seeding' clips on the Internet
   d taps into popular culture
   e prior to launch
   f businesses want to embrace viral marketing
   g stellar growth rates

c In what sense is the user 'in control' of a viral ad?

LANGUAGE FOCUS
Marketing words

3 Discuss these questions. The highlighted words are all connected with marketing.

1 Think of a large company in your country.
   - How does it promote its products?
   - Does it have a particular slogan?
   - Do they use a particular kind of marketing campaign or sales pitch?
   - How effective are they?
   - Who is their target audience?
   - Do they have the biggest market share?
   - Who are their competitors?
   - What brand image do they present?
2 'There is no such thing as negative publicity.' Do you think this is true?

A video clip

LISTENING

1 What product(s) do you think this video clip shows?

2 a 2.30 **Listen to someone talking about the video.**

1 Why was it so successful?
2 How is it different from a conventional advert?
3 Look at the features of a good viral ad mentioned in the article. Which (if any) of them apply to this video?

b The speaker uses these words. What does he say?

planned – fizzes – geyser – firework display – globally – user-generated eruption videos – hype – lethal – publicity

c 2.30 **Listen again to check.**

3 **Imagine you are telling someone about the clip. Describe what happens and why it became 'viral'. Use the words in 2b.**

4 **Look at the quote. How do you think it applies to the viral video you heard about?**

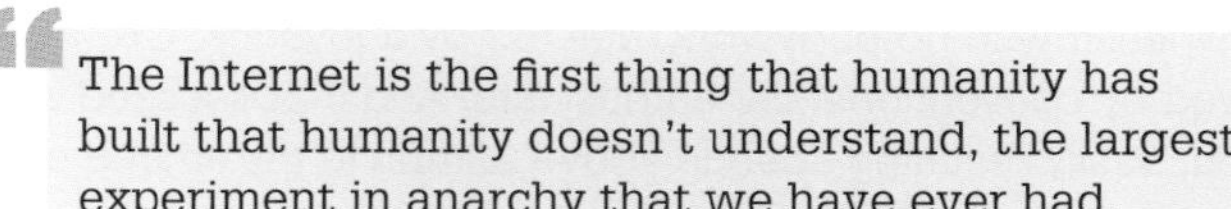

> The Internet is the first thing that humanity has built that humanity doesn't understand, the largest experiment in anarchy that we have ever had.
>
> **Eric Schmidt, CEO of Google**

SPEAKING

5 **Think about an advert that you have seen. It could be:**

- an advert on a hoarding or in a magazine.
- an online video clip.
- a TV or film advert.

1 Prepare to talk about it. Think about:
   - how to describe it.
   - whether you think it's successful, and why.
   - what its message is.
   - why you like or don't like it.
   - what audience it was intended for.
2 Tell other people about the advert.

Sell a product

8.3 goals
talk about the image and qualities of products
talk about advertising and marketing
pass on detailed information

TASK READING

1 The photo shows the AIRpod, an air-powered car.

1 How do you think it works?
2 What other kinds of 'eco-car' are possible? What do you know about them?

2 a Read the article. Check your answers to 1.

b According to Guy Negré, what are the advantages of air-powered cars?

Environment > Travel and transport

On the road with the AIRpod air-powered car

How would you react to someone who tried to sell you a car that runs on fresh air? Perhaps you would think he was peddling potentially planet-saving technology. More likely, you would dismiss him as a conman or a fantasist. Yet, that is precisely the pitch being made by French auto engineer Guy Negré, a good-humoured man in his mid-60s who claims to have developed a state-of-the-art car powered by compressed air: one that produces a fraction of the carbon emissions of a standard engine, reaches speeds of more than 30mph, travels 65 miles on a one-minute recharge and, best of all, costs just over £3,000.

Negré is quick to point out the drawbacks of existing eco-car technology. "Whatever people may tell you about hybrids, they are only marginally less polluting than the most efficient combustion engines," he says. "Hydrogen power is expensive and impractical. Fuel cells are expensive and unproven and electric cars are reliant on expensive, unreliable battery technology."

Given the number of false green-auto dawns, you might wonder why air-powered cars should be any different. While Negré's air cars have similar carbon emissions to electric cars (it all depends how the electricity to power the pumps that fill their air tanks is generated), he argues that air power is a superior technology. "Compared to electric cars, air-powered cars cost a fraction of the price to buy, they don't need expensive batteries to be replaced every five years or so, and crucially they take only a fraction of the time to recharge."

I confess I was so sceptical that I reserved judgment until I had driven one of his cars. The version I drove was an early prototype, a three-wheeler with no bodywork, steered by a joystick. OK, it didn't deliver the smoothly upholstered power so beloved by conventional car enthusiasts. And it possessed all the glamour of a souped-up lawnmower. But it worked, easily reaching speeds above 25mph in the limited space of the factory car park, which doubled as my test track.

TASK LANGUAGE
Describing technology

3 a Make a list of adjectives in the article which refer to cars or technology. Which are: positive? negative? neutral?

b What other adjectives could describe the AIRpod?

compact, fun, ...

TASK

4 a Student A, look on p132. Student B, look on p135. Read more about the AIRpod.

b Work in A/B pairs. Prepare a marketing campaign based on what you read.

1 Choose your target audience (e.g. young people, families, people who want a second car, city dwellers).
2 Think of 'brand images' and slogans.
3 Plan a brochure, highlighting the car's main selling points. Or, think of visual ideas for a TV, cinema or Internet advert.

5 Present your campaign ideas to the class.

Across cultures Megabrands

1 a You will read writer Naomi Klein's views about the growth of 'megabrands' and how they may be shaping cultures.

1 What do you think a 'megabrand' is?
2 In what way do successful companies sell ideas as well as products?

b Read her views and discuss these questions.

1 What is the main development in marketing brands that Naomi Klein describes?
2 What are the 'lifestyle ideas' that these companies sell?
• Coca-Cola • Walt Disney • Nike
3 She says the measure of a successful brand more and more is not whether it's truly a mark of quality on a product, but how well it stretches. What does she mean by this? Can you think of examples?

2 Discuss these questions.

1 Which of the brands Naomi Klein mentions are well-known in your country?
Which of them have you bought yourself?
2 Do you think large companies can influence people's culture? Do you think they are generally beneficial or harmful in their effect on people's lifestyle?

3 a Work alone.

Some people object to the influence of global companies and the way they operate, and campaign to boycott their products. What reasons do they give for this, and do you agree with them? Mark your position on the line.

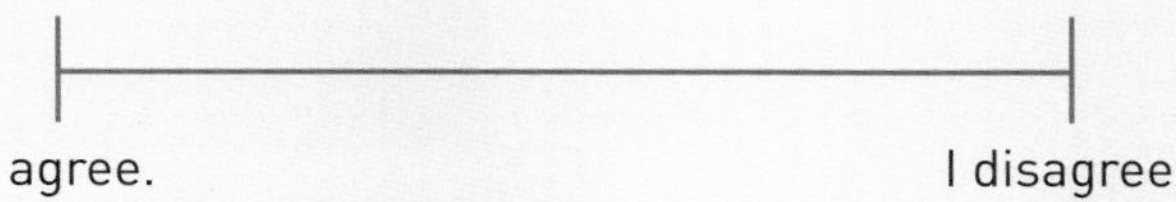

b Find other students who have a similar view to yours. Find out if you think exactly the same, and discuss the reasons for your opinion.

c Now talk to students who have a different opinion. Discuss your ideas.

The process of branding in its simplest form is just the process of marking a product with a consistent logo, image, mascot, that sends a message to the consumer – a message of consistency, a message of quality. How did we get from this fairly simple role of the brand to these brand tribes that we have now, where we almost follow brands like we would follow rock stars? We organise ourselves into brand tribes, we are a Nike type of person or a Tommy Hilfiger type of person. How did that happen?
There were a handful of brands that understood that marketing could play a larger role than simply branding their product as a mark of quality. They understood that they could sell ideas, that they could sell lifestyles. Coca-Cola, Disney, McDonalds – these core American brands became powerful precisely because they understood that they were selling ideas instead of products, that they were selling an idea about family. Coca-Cola was selling the youth lifestyle – in the 60s they started selling peace and love – they were selling something way more profound than their fairly generic product, which was this black fizzy liquid. Walt Disney understood that he was selling the American dream, he was selling a nostalgic vision of the small-time American town that people felt sad about – they felt it had disappeared. The CEO of Nike, Phil Knight, says that he had a kind of an epiphany in the mid 80s where he realised that he didn't want to compete in a commodity marketplace any more, that he did not want to be a sneaker company, or, as he said, a fashion company. He wanted to be a sports company. And that their core image or their core idea was not about their sneakers being better than Reeboks but was an idea about the nature of sports, and that pure athletic ability – the raw ability of truly superstar athletes like Tiger Woods and Michael Jordan – is a metaphor for the American dream, and so he decided to sell that idea. The measure of a successful brand more and more is not whether it's truly a mark of quality on a product, but how well it stretches. If it's a successful cola, can it also be a line of clothing? If it's a line of clothing, can it also be a house paint? So you have this stratosphere of warring megabrands that want to be everywhere and be everything. ”

Keywords *effect, affect*

1 **Look at these examples.**

1 Many experts believe that the use of CCTV hasn't had any significant effect on crime. Unit 5
2 The film, with its 3D effects and rather predictable plot, is aimed at a popular audience. Unit 6
3 He showed that this could significantly affect people's co-ordination skills. Unit 7
4 If you have something that has a positive effect on you, then your whole personality is more positive. Unit 8

1 Change this sentence using effect.
 • Did the advert affect you? *Did the advert ...*
2 What prepositions can follow effect?
 Complete the gaps.
 • We need to reduce the effects ______ advertising ______ the general public.
3 Continue this sentence with the adjective form of effect.
 • The marketing campaign was very ...

2 a **Look at these news report extracts. Add the correct forms of the verbs in the box plus effect.**

take produce come into reduce

1 Tough new laws will ______ ______ ______ next year.
2 Much of this advertising takes time to ______ ______ – it's subliminal.
3 Any change in lifestyle, however slight, can ______ a negative ______ on your sense of well-being.
4 Taking certain other prescription drugs can ______ the ______ of the medication.

b 2.31 **Listen to check. What are the news reports about?**

3 a **Look at the example.**

• The news had a significant effect on her life.

These other adjectives could replace significant. Which of them would change the meaning?

major positive profound dramatic great devastating lasting important

b **Which words could be used as adverbs with affect?**

The news significantly affected her life.

4 a **What things have:**

1 a calming effect on you?
2 a cumulative effect?
3 an energising effect on you?
4 a detrimental effect on your health?
5 a beneficial effect on your neighbourhood?
6 a disproportionate effect on poor people?
7 an adverse effect on the environment?
8 a devastating effect?
9 an immediate effect on you?
10 a far-reaching effect on the future of the world?

b **Work in pairs. Using expressions from 2 and 3, talk about:**

• something that had a major effect on your life.
• someone who affected you positively.
• something or someone you think is effective.

5 **Match these expressions with the images. What do they mean and when would they be used?**

a snowball effect a ripple effect a domino effect a boomerang effect the butterfly effect the greenhouse effect the placebo effect

A

B

C
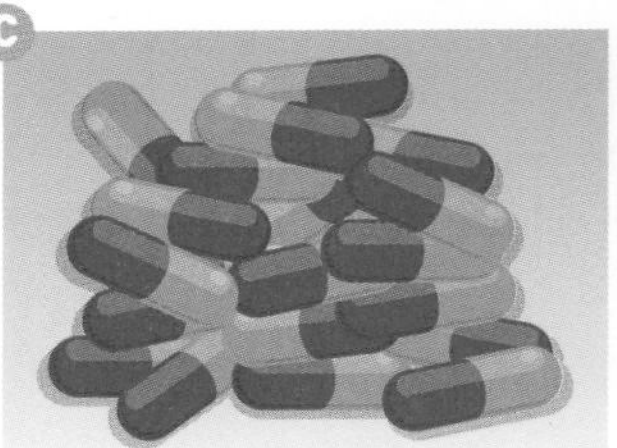
D

E

F
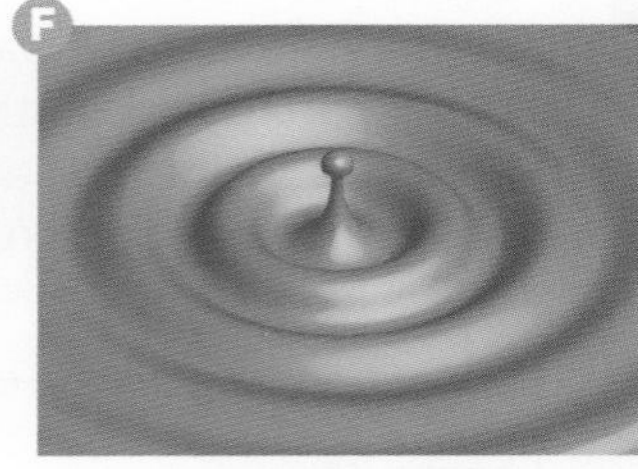
G
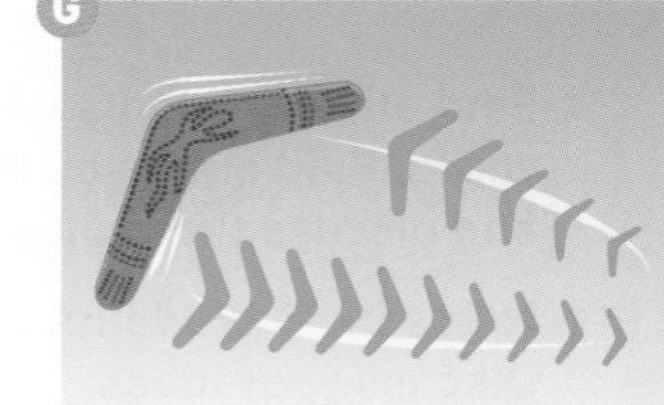

EXPLOREWriting

Goal

use advertising language

1 a Read the advert for London's Tate Modern Art Gallery as a venue for dining, events and entertainment. Then match the pictures of the three rooms with their captions.

TATE

Entertain at the top of one of London's most iconic and best-loved buildings with the City's stunning skyline as backdrop. The Tate Modern Restaurant, East Room or Members' Room all capture an unforgettable vista of London.

1

Boasting a specially commissioned mural, currently James Aldridge's *Cold Mouth Prayer*, The Tate Modern Restaurant offers guests the opportunity to be entertained alongside a magnificent piece of art, while also enjoying unrivalled evening views of the London skyline and the River Thames.

2

With unparalleled views of the London skyline and the River Thames, The East Room is a dramatic and versatile space which can be enjoyed during the day and evening.

Surrounded by sheer glass walls, daytime events are bathed in natural light, while an intimate setting is evoked for evening events against the spectacle of London by night.

3

The impressive Members' Room, with exclusive balconies on both its north and south sides, provides uninterrupted views of the London skyline and the River Thames. The balconies also offer a unique opportunity for outdoor evening receptions.

A

B

C

b Which room would you choose for these events? Give reasons.

1 a lunch for 40 guests
2 a summer evening reception for 150 guests
3 a celebration dinner for 200 guests

2 a What do you understand by the highlighted words? What would be more common ways of expressing the same ideas? Why do you think the writer chose to use these words?

1 an iconic building
2 a backdrop
3 a vista
4 boasting a mural
5 sheer glass walls
6 bathed in natural light
7 unrivalled views

b Discuss these questions.

1 Are there more verbs in the texts, or more adjectives? Why do you think that is?
2 Look at the verbs. How many are active verb forms, and how many are passive? Why do you think that is? What do you notice about the active verbs?
3 How many adjectives can you find that mean 'very good' or 'very beautiful'?

c What impression is the writer trying to give of an evening spent at this venue?

3 Work in groups.

1 Choose a place you know or have been to, which might be suitable for a reception, a meal or a party.
2 Plan a description like those above.
   - What features would you emphasise?
   - Which of the adjectives in your list could you use to describe it?
   - Think of sentences you could write using the verbs offer or provide.
3 Write the description in pairs or small groups.
4 Try to 'sell' your venue to other people. Were they convinced by your promotion idea?

Grammar

Measuring differences

1 a Look at this sentence about the AIRpod.

```
Compared to electric cars, air-powered cars
cost a fraction of the price to buy, they don't
need expensive batteries to be replaced every
five years or so and crucially they take only a
fraction of the time to recharge.
```

The recharging time of air-powered cars is two minutes. The recharging time of electric cars is about five hours. How else could you express this difference? Use these expressions. You may need to change the order of the sentence.

much less	several hours	about 150 times

b Think about how the comparisons might continue. Which could use:

- than?
- as?
- of?
- that?

c How can you measure these differences? Express the comparison in as many different single sentences as you can.

1 Vegetable oil costs €2 a litre. Extra virgin olive oil costs €8.
2 Our old flat had 3 rooms. Our new flat has 6.
3 We used to live about 2 km from the university. Now we live about 4.5 km away.
4 She looks 35. She is 45.
5 The painting was actually worth $50,000. He managed to buy it for $5,000.
6 There were 60,000 burglaries from homes in London last year. Only 5,000 of the homes had burglar alarms.
7 The average British schoolchild spends 22 hours a week at school and 30 hours a week watching TV.

whatever

2 a Look at these examples. What does whatever mean in each?

```
1  It's your perfect travel companion,
   whatever your journey.
2  Thousands of people contributed their own
   eruption videos, with groups of bottles
   together, or people running about, or on
   bikes, or whatever ...
3  Whatever people may tell you about hybrids,
   they are only marginally less polluting
   than the most efficient combustion engines.
```

b These sentences include whatever, or an expression with whatever. Match them with a–f.

1 Maintaining a balance sheet is absolutely essential, whatever business you're in.
2 I had a talk with him which left no doubt whatever in my mind.
3 Whatever do you want to do that job for? It's so badly paid.
4 A What would you like to drink?
B Oh, whatever...
5 A Come on! You know I'm right...!
B Oh, all right then. Whatever you say...
6 Web 2.0, whatever that is, was mentioned a lot.

a at all
b I don't know it
c it doesn't matter
d it's your decision
e anything, I don't mind
f I've no idea why

c 2.32 Listen to the remarks, paying attention to the intonation. Are the speakers:

- being emphatic?
- expressing lack of interest?
- showing disbelief?
- agreeing unwillingly?

3 a The words whatever, wherever, whoever are commonly used in marketing language. Look at these phrases from advertising slogans. What type of product do you think they might go with?

whatever the weather	whatever the occasion
whatever the time	whoever you're with
wherever you go	whatever you like

A

B

C

D

b Choose a photo. Write a caption for it, including one of the phrases in 3a.

c Say your sentences to other people. Can they guess which photo you chose?

Grammar reference, p143

Vocabulary

Multi-word expressions

4 a **Look at these sentences from the unit. What part of speech are the highlighted expressions? How else could you express the same idea?**

> 1 Against this too-good-to-be-true backdrop, though, is the reality: viral marketing only works when the user is in control.
> 2 Guy Negré claims to have developed a state-of-the-art car powered by compressed air.

b **Compare these examples. How are the expressions different? Why?**

1 He got a phone call out of the blue, asking him to give a TV interview.
2 Predictably, their out-of-the-blue marriage only lasted 20 months.

c **What do the highlighted expressions mean?**

1 Until Wednesday we are giving away a pair of tickets a day to allow 16 readers a once-in-a lifetime opportunity to watch what promises to be the game of the season.
2 One indication of changing attitudes is all the do-it-yourself stores and how-to classes springing up across the country as people adapt to hard times.
3 Keep ready-to-eat foods away from raw products or other contaminated products.
4 Successful applicants will have a can-do attitude to their job and be prepared to work long hours.
5 The prime minister will set out to silence his critics in a do-or-die conference speech.
6 It's likely to be this year's must-have gadget for teenagers.

5 a **Look at these other multi-word expressions. Match the adjectives with the nouns. In what context might you hear them being used?**

no-win	call
wake-up	experience
peer-to-peer	situation
hands-on	network

b 2.33 **Listen to check.**

6 **Think of two or three questions to ask other people, using any of the expressions in 4 or 5.**

Influence and effect

7 a **Look at this example from the unit.**

> But you see it as a positive influence on people, do you?

1 What prepositions can appear after influence?
2 What verbs commonly combine with influence?

b **Complete the gaps using a verb from the box.**

exert	use	fall under	lose	have

1 Gospel music ______ a major influence on other musical styles, especially soul music.
2 Ramsey will be remembered as a leader who ______ his influence to improve schools.
3 We don't realise to what extent we ______ ______ the influence of advertising, especially subliminal ads.
4 I hate those articles like 'How to ______ influence over others and get what you want'.
5 The newspaper used to be hugely important in shaping public opinion, but has ______ a lot of influence in recent years.

c **Transform sentences 1–5 using influential. You may need to change or add words.**

Gospel music was very influential, affecting other musical styles ...

8 **Choose the best adjective. In what cases could both be used?**

1 The campaign was very influential / effective in persuading people to buy the product.
2 Each year, the magazine awards prizes for the country's most influential / effective people.
3 Is the threat of punishment an influential / effective crime deterrent?
4 Any diet will only be truly influential / effective along with exercise.

9 a **Complete these sentences in any way you like with influence or affect.**

1 The film had a very powerful message. I ...
2 The news of the earthquake was terrible. His relatives ...
3 That blunder was all important to the election campaign. It ...
4 The fire destroyed everything. Even the ...

b **Write three sentences about someone or something you have been influenced by.**

Self-assessment

Can you do these things in English? Circle a number on each line. 1 = I can't do this, 5 = I can do this well.

discuss brands	1	2	3	4	5
describe effects and influences	1	2	3	4	5
talk about the image and qualities of products	1	2	3	4	5
talk about advertising and marketing	1	2	3	4	5
describe an advert	1	2	3	4	5
pass on detailed information	1	2	3	4	5
use advertising language	1	2	3	4	5

- For Wordcards, reference and saving your work → e-Portfolio
- For more practice → Self-study Pack, Unit 8

9 Icons

9.1 goals
- speculate about images and objects
- interpret and respond to a story

Apples

Two young men (Crispin van den Broeck)

SPEAKING

1 a When you hear the word 'apple', what comes to mind? Write down any associations you have. Then compare with other students.

b Now, *picture* an apple in your mind. What kind of apple do you see (think about size, texture, colour, taste, type)? Think of adjectives to describe it.

2 Look carefully at the painting. What elements do you notice? Do you think it represents or symbolises anything?

LISTENING

3 a 3.1 Listen to four people interpreting the painting. Which details in the painting do they mention and which do they leave out?

b 3.1 Listen again and complete the sentences according to the speakers' analysis.

1. Generally speaking, the apple represents ...
2. The two men could be ...
3. There are a number of other details such as ...
4. The overall analysis suggests that the painting is ...

LANGUAGE FOCUS
Interpreting and defining

4 a The speakers used various expressions to talk about the painting. What did they say?

1. Also, the apple ______ to have a symbolic value ...
2. It's ______ what the painter intended.
3. What ______ me are the expressions on their faces.
4. It ______ they know each other very well.
5. It's ______ whether he's offering it or ...
6. It ______ there's a whole lot more going on here.
7. The owl and crow ______ symbols of death.
8. The painting ______ that behind the happiness of youth lies ...

b 3.2 Listen to check.

c What other expressions could be used to replace those in 4a?

It appears that they know each other.
→ They appear to know each other. *→ It looks as if they know each other.*

SPEAKING

5 Work in groups. Look at the images on p131.

Family story

READING

1 **Look at the city in the photo. What connection does it have with apples?**

2 a **Read this extract from a family anecdote.**

My sisters and I loved to listen to a simple story about an immigrant's mistake in our own family. My grandfather's first cousin, who my sisters and I called Uncle David, left Norway when he was 22 years old to make his way alone to America. He arrived at Ellis Island in August 1902. He spent his first day in New York City and was flabbergasted by the chaos, colour and crowds. Somewhere in the city, he saw a man selling apples, the most gorgeous, red, perfect apples he had ever seen. He had almost no money, but he lusted after one of those apples, and, overcome by desire, he splurged and bought one. The story goes that he lifted the apple to his mouth, bit into it and spat it out in disgust. It was a tomato. Uncle David had never seen or heard of a tomato. ”

b **Ask and answer.**

1 What does this anecdote say about our hopes and expectations?
2 Why is it significant that the story happens in New York?
3 Why do you think the narrator loved to listen to this story?
4 Why do you think this anecdote has a universal significance?

c **Read the next part of the anecdote and check your answers.**

My sisters and I roared with laughter at this story. It encapsulates so neatly the lesson of expectation and reality that it could serve as a parable. The fact that tomatoes are good is beside the point. If you're thinking you're getting an apple, then it's no use getting a tomato instead. That New York should be nicknamed the Big Apple, that an apple is the fruit of humankind's first error and the expulsion from paradise, that America and paradise have been linked and confused ever since Europeans first hit its shores, makes the story reverberate as myth. ”

d **Read both parts again more carefully.**

1 How does the writer give the impression that she is telling a story?
2 When does she begin the 'analysis'? How does she do this?
3 When does she address the reader directly? Why do you think she does so?
4 What stylistic touches give the story more impact (e.g. alliteration)?
5 Do you agree with the writer's opinion?

SPEAKING

3 a **You are going to tell the story from memory. Write down ten words from the first part which you think are important.**

b **Tell the story.**

1 Cover the anecdote and reconstruct it only using the words you wrote.
2 Work in groups. Take turns to tell the story. Listen carefully. Which elements do each of you mention and leave out?
3 Choose the story you think was most successful and tell it a second time to the whole class.

4 **Tell an anecdote about your family.**

1 Think of a story you can tell about:
   - your parents when they were young.
   - your grandparents or great grandparents.
   - an important event in the history of your family.
2 Tell it to another student.
3 Can your partner see any special or symbolic significance in your story?

Iconic

9.2 goals

- discuss icons
- identify critical language in a text

SPEAKING and READING

1 a Look at the magazine cover. Who does it show? In what sense do you think she was an icon?

b What other icons do you think appear in the person's face?

2 a Look at the article and the images on the opposite page. In what way do you think they are iconic?

b Read the article and check.

c Do these statements summarise the writer's argument in each paragraph? If not, correct them.

Paragraph 1 Words easily become over-used and so lose their true meaning.
Paragraph 2 Nowadays, everything can be termed 'iconic' because the word no longer means what it did.
Paragraph 3 People have a tendency to honour or worship others.
Paragraph 4 Almost any artefact can become iconic.
Paragraph 5 Famous people often reach iconic status when they are still alive.

d What do you think the writer means by these expressions?

1. a lexicon of invasive usages
   words used in ways which could be considered overused and inappropriate
2. the jargon of the linguistically unfeeling
3. marginally literate word-operatives
4. the props of their desperate trade
5. the sense acquired through recent abuse
6. stadium-rock stage sets

LANGUAGE FOCUS
Critical language

3 a Read the first two paragraphs again. What is the writer's attitude to the topic?

b The writer uses many words with negative connotations. Make a list, then think of a more neutral alternative. What connotations do the negative words have?

c Replace the highlighted neutral words with negative words from the box. How does the choice of word change the meaning?

brusque a rip-off irritating mobbed packed inescapable dismissive dismal seething overpriced contemptuous hemmed in dreary crawling ubiquitous smothered invasive minimal

1. At the exit, the rock star was surrounded by fans asking for autographs.
2. The mobile phone has become a common feature of modern life.
3. He sent me a short reply by email.
4. We didn't enjoy our holiday much. The place where we stayed was expensive, it was crowded with tourists, and the weather was cloudy.

d Compare answers. Which words do you think are most critical?

ICONIC: THE OVERUSED ADJECTIVE

[1] Every era suffers a lexicon of invasive usages. Words are as subject to fashion as politics and popular music – today's tiresome coinage is tomorrow's ubiquitous cliché. It is the jargon of the linguistically unfeeling whose job is to smother page upon page with words. And there are more pages than ever, and more screens, and thus more marginally literate word-operatives struggling to smother them. Where would these people be without the following clichés, the props of their desperate trade: *genius, guru, legend, cool, multi-cultural, post-modern*? Where, above all, would they be without the word *iconic*?

[2] Here are some nouns that have been prefixed by this most dismal of vogue words: *iconic art, iconic brand, iconic building, iconic film star, iconic cocktail, iconic shampoo*. This suggests that there is nothing that cannot be deemed iconic. Iconic, that is, in the sense acquired through recent abuse, not in its original meaning. According to one dictionary, 'iconic' in this newer sense means "very famous or popular, especially being considered to represent particular opinions or a particular time".

[3] Implicit in the modern use of 'iconic' is the perhaps unconscious aspiration to invest things and people with properties which render them miraculous and superhuman, magical and godlike. It is an expression of humankind's tendency towards worship of objects and other humans. That tendency lives on in the stadium-rock stage sets for alternative gods such as The Rolling Stones.

[4] Conditions for an artefact to become truly iconic may be the fact that: 1) it is recognised at once (think of the Taj Mahal or a Vespa); 2) it has an unchanging quality (again like the Taj Mahal or the Mona Lisa); and 3) it embodies strong values, like the US flag. The Coca-Cola bottle has it all!

[5] Iconic status is less common in humans, unless, of course, they are dead. However, recent attempts have been made to make the living equally iconic. Los Angeles street artist Shepard Fairey provided us with an example for our age. He was the creator of the Obama *Hope* poster – surely the most celebrated image of a political leader in recent memory.

A
B

C

D

E

F

SPEAKING

4 a Make a list of five people or five things that you think are 'iconic'. Think about:

- buildings.
- people.
- products.
- songs or pieces of music.
- objects.

b Discuss your list.

1. Explain your choices.
2. Talk about someone or something that is considered iconic, but you think does not fulfil the conditions mentioned in the article.

Madonna. She's supposed to be an icon of pop music, but I think she'll be forgotten in about 10 years.

9.3 Target activity

Icons for today

9.3 goals
- discuss icons
- talk about what something represents
- present arguments and counter-arguments

TASK LISTENING

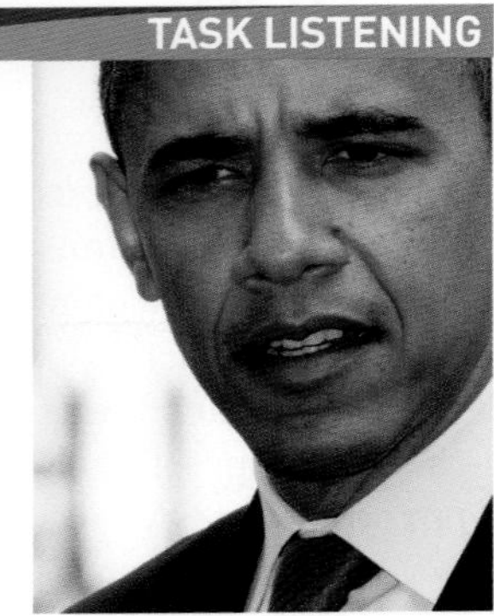

1 a Look at the poster of Barack Obama, which was used in his election campaign of 2009.

1 How is it different from other images of politicians?
2 How is it different from:
- the photo?
- the way Obama looks now?

b 3.3 Listen to a journalist talking about the poster.

1 What did the artist want to say about Obama in this poster?
2 What kind of public did the artist want to attract?
3 What was his chief objective?
4 What did he do with the money made from the poster?
5 What was his attitude to people who copied the image? Why?

TASK LANGUAGE

Saying what things and people represent

2 a Look at these extracts. What verbs go in the gaps?

1 He felt that he should make something that ______ Obama as having vision and the ability to lead ...
2 He felt that he wanted something that he felt was going to ______ the counterculture.
3 All the knockoffs and parodies say how much the image has ______ and become a reference point.

b Check in the script on p156. For each sentence, think of another verb or expression that would have the same meaning.

3 a Which icons in the unit do these statements refer to?

1 She **epitomises** the glamour and vulnerability of celebrity culture.
2 To some people it **stands for** freedom and democracy, but many people associate it with power.
3 It's **a symbol of** timeless beauty and artistic perfection.
4 She **conveys** a sense of subtle, inaccessible beauty.
5 They **embody** the rebelliousness of rock and roll.
6 It **encapsulates** the West's image of the Orient.
7 It **represents** mobility and efficient design.

b Think of three examples of iconic things or people.

1 Write sentences about them using verbs from 2a and 3a.
2 Can other students guess which icons the sentences refer to?

TASK

4 a 3.4 You are going to choose a set of iconic images for our time. Listen to a group of people discussing whether the Obama poster should be included.

1 What arguments do they give in favour of and against including the image?
2 What conclusion do they come to?
3 Which viewpoint do you share?

b What expressions did the people use to:

1 push their own point of view?
2 question or disagree?
3 agree?
4 suggest an alternative?

c Look at the script on p156 to check.

5 Work in groups. Group A, look on p131. Group B, look on p137.

9 EXPLORE

Across cultures Loan words

1 **The word icon is 'borrowed' from the Greek language.**

1. What English words are used in your language? Can you think of any new ones?
2. What words from other languages does your mother tongue borrow from?

Hotel room soap wrapper, Spain

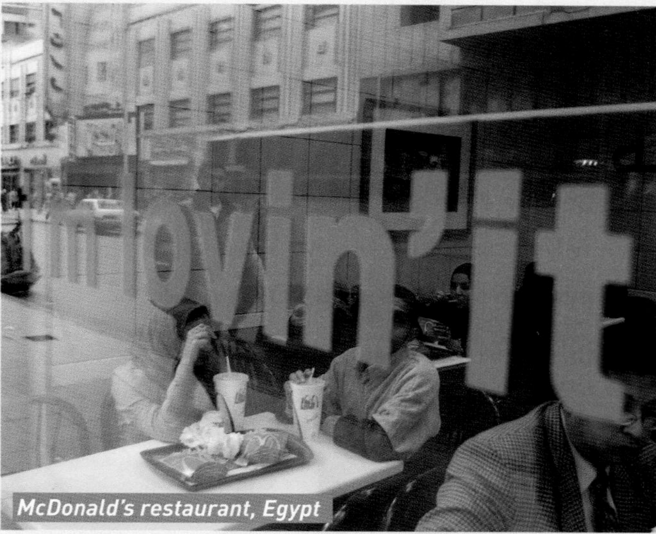

McDonald's restaurant, Egypt

2 **A lot of English is used in advertising. Why do you think this is? Look at these images. Why and how is English being used here?**

3 **a** **Are any of these words used in your language? If so, what kind of people use them?**

training	cool	supermarket	image	manager	handy	email	marketing

b 3.5 **Listen to Norman and Olga talking about some English words that are used in their language.**

1. Where are the people from?
2. In which contexts are English loan words most often found in their countries?
3. What is each speaker's attitude to this?
4. Which words in 3a do they mention?

c **Are there any loan words in your language which have been given a new local meaning (like 'icon' or 'handy')?**

d **Look at this photo which shows the word 'Internet' being used in Poland.**

1. What do you think of this mixing of languages?
2. Do you think that a language should stay 'pure' without any influence from others?

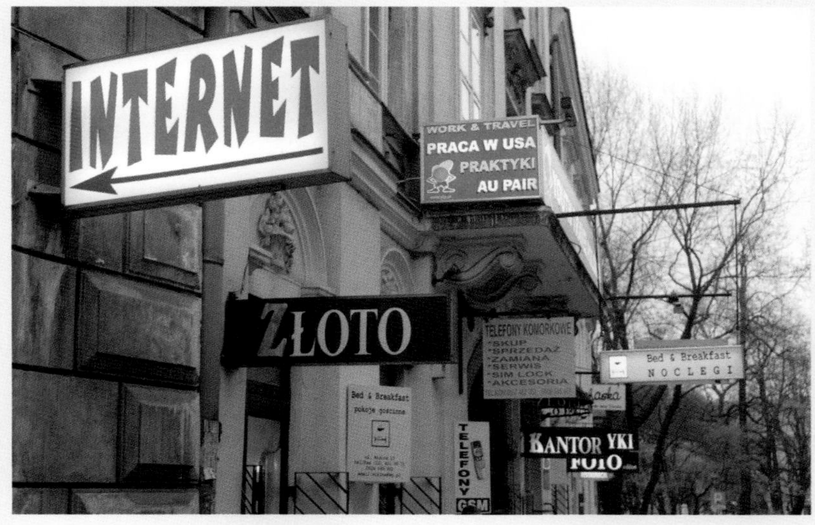

Keywords describing what things represent

1 a Think about the verbs represent, depict and convey. What do they normally describe?

b Choose the best verb.

1 A good photograph can often convey / represent far more than words.
2 Brando portrayed / represented the character of Kowalski brilliantly.
3 It was the first time the film was depicted / shown on television.
4 She was conveyed / depicted as a woman whose luck had run out.
5 The colour red commonly represents / portrays danger.

c How many of the verbs in 1b can be used to talk about the *meaning* of pictures or images? Complete the gap in this sentence.

- The painting ______ the leader of the party as a lonely figure.

d In which sentence in 1b could you use the verb stand for?

2 a Complete these sentences with verbs from 1. Sometimes, there may be more than one correct answer. In which sentences could the verb symbolise also be used?

1 The initials and logo ______ the 'Campaign for Nuclear Disarmament'.

2 Wearing this ______ my love for New York.

3 It ______ a very strong message about change.

4 This ______ a cyclist's campaign to fight cancer.

b Complete these sentences with a form of depict or convey and a noun from the box. Sometimes, there may be more than one correct answer.

message   life   the world   a sense of   information   scenes

1 Two new biographies ______ his ______ in unprecedented detail.
2 The director hopes that the film ______ a more positive ______ than at first sight.
3 His unhappy background explains how the painter came to ______ ______ in this way.
4 It features some attractive examples of bas-reliefs which ______ ______ from the Hindu Ramayana epic.
5 Few novelists ______ ______ place as well as Howard Frank Mosher.
6 He speaks quickly, packing his sentences with facts, ______ ______ in the fewest syllables possible.

3 Think of an image, book, person or film that represents something important to you. Describe it using verbs on this page.

EXPLORESpeaking

Goals
- give criticism
- respond to criticism

1 a How do you think the magazine cover:

1 attracts the reader's attention?
2 illustrates the idea of a 'weak' currency?

b 3.6 Read and listen to this conversation about the cover image. Who do you think the people are and what are they discussing in particular?

A So what do you think of the design?
B I like the basic idea, but in general I don't think you quite capture the seriousness of the topic.
A What do you mean?
B Well, I think this image is a bit too light and cartoony, it doesn't really convey what the article's about.
A Well, I beg to differ. I think it is clear, you know, it shows the dollar going down in flames. I didn't want to make it too boring. It seems to me that we need to grab people's attention, so to speak, you know, make them realise it's important.
B I'm not sure ... I just think we need something that's a bit more serious, that's all. But let's see what the others think.

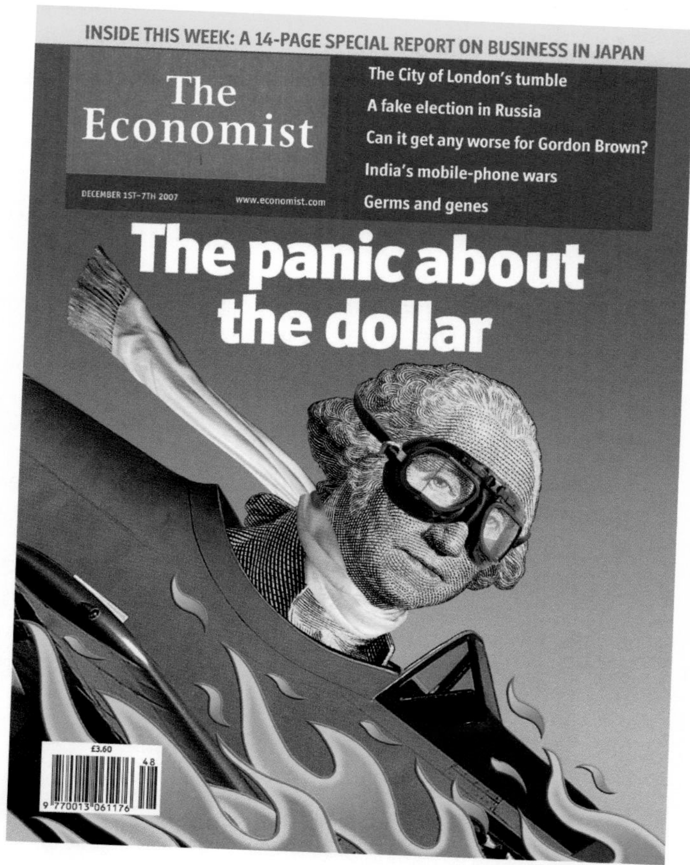
INSIDE THIS WEEK: A 14-PAGE SPECIAL REPORT ON BUSINESS IN JAPAN
The Economist
DECEMBER 1ST-7TH 2007
www.economist.com
The City of London's tumble
A fake election in Russia
Can it get any worse for Gordon Brown?
India's mobile-phone wars
Germs and genes
The panic about the dollar
£3.60

c Identify expressions used to give criticism and respond to criticism.

d Find examples of how the criticism is softened and then followed by an explanation.

2 a Rank these examples of *giving criticism* from least to most critical.

a "It's not actually what I had in mind."
b "What on earth is this? Is it yours?"
c "This is totally wrong, you'll have to redo it."
d "I think it would have been better to take a different approach."
e "I expected something different."
f "It doesn't seem quite right. It's missing something, really."
g "I think it's really nice, but there are a few things that don't quite work."

b Compare answers.

1 Do you have different opinions?
2 Which criticisms do you think are too harsh? How could they be softened?

3 a Rank these examples of *responding* to criticism according to how strongly the speaker rejects it.

a "OK, I'll redo it straight away."
b "It's not my fault the brief was a bit vague."
c "Could you be more specific?"
d "Yes, I know I can do better. I've been under a lot of stress."
e "What do you think needs changing?"
f "What's wrong with it, then?"
g "OK, maybe it needs a bit more thought."

b Compare answers.

1 Which response do you think is too aggressive?
2 Which do you think are good examples of deflecting criticism?

4 Role play.

1 Together, choose one of these situations.
- You work for *Food World* magazine. Create a cover design to reflect the new lead article: "Invasion of the Italians. Italian cooking is everywhere, from the humblest pizza to elaborate seafood dishes. We trace the way Italians have influenced our eating."
- You work for *Financial Matters* magazine. Sales have been declining. Think of a plan to increase readership (e.g. celebrity interviews, free gifts, appealing to a younger audience, etc.).
- You work for *Elegant Fashion* magazine. It is going to run a series called 'The top ten style icons'. Decide on ten people who will appear on this list (including some who could be interviewed).

2 Work in groups: A, B and C. In your group, develop a few ideas and make brief notes.
3 Form new groups so each group has one A, one B and one C. In turns, tell the others your ideas and respond appropriately. Be critical, but find ways to soften your criticism.
4 Choose the ideas you think are the best.

9 Look again

Grammar

It's no ...

1 a Look at these examples from the unit. It's no + adjective/noun can be used as a subject and be followed by that or by an -ing form.

> 1 It's no coincidence that in Latin, 'apple' and 'death' are almost the same word.
> 2 If you think you're getting an apple, then it's no use getting a tomato instead.

b Complete these examples with expressions from the box. There may be more than one correct answer. What do you think the context might be for each sentence?

it's no good	it's no wonder / surprise
it's no use	it's no trouble / big deal / problem
it's no secret	it's no coincidence
it's no different	

1. So, ______ that on the first day of trading, stocks of real estate investment trusts surged.
2. But now she's gone and ______ wanting her back because she's not coming.
3. ______ that tobacco advertising has targeted teens.
4. It's how you're born, and ______ from being born short, tall or anything else.
5. Because ______ just going in there and throwing products at them, it doesn't work.
6. ______ for me to get his phone number – I'll get it tonight.

c Discuss these questions.

1. Which expressions in the box are followed by:
   - verb + *ing*?
   - *that* + clause?
   - *to* + infinitive?
2. Which expressions have a similar meaning?

d Look at this example. To make it's no good more emphatic, just is added. What other words can add emphasis to these expressions?

> I've tried dieting, but it's just no good.

Modifying a sentence

2 Look at these sentences from the unit.

> 1 Barack Obama's image has become an icon. (for better or worse)
> 2 They would check him out further and see his merits the way I see them. (hopefully)
> 3 He made something that he felt was going to transcend the counterculture. (actually; maybe)
> 4 And all is forgiven if Obama gets elected. (really)
> 5 What you did seems well-suited for grassroots campaigning. (in a way)
> 6 So I'm very happy people care. (in that sense)

1. Where do you think the expressions in brackets should go in the sentence? Could they go in more than one place? How would it affect the meaning?
2. What does each expression 'do' to the sentence? Which:
   - adds a comment to the sentence?
   - adds emphasis to the sentence?

3 a Add the expressions in brackets from 2 to these sentences. How many are possible each time?

1. That was a terrible mistake!
2. It would be better to do something different.
3. I don't think that was the right decision.
4. She'll be earning next year, so she'll be more independent.

b Work with a partner.

1. Choose a sentence in 2 with the expression you added.
2. Think of a situation where it might be said.
3. Develop it into a short dialogue, adding extra sentences.
4. Practise until you can say it without reading the sentences.
5. Perform your dialogue to other students. Can they guess the situation?

Grammar reference, p144

Vocabulary

Uses of *suppose*

4 a Look at these examples. What does suppose mean in each? What do you notice about the form of the verb?

1 I suppose the best thing is aspirin. Unit 7
2 The apple was supposed to have a symbolic value in Greek mythology. Unit 9
3 What's it supposed to mean then? Unit 9
4 She's supposed to be an icon of pop music, but I think she'll be forgotten in about 10 years. Unit 9

b Replace each suppose with a synonym.

1 Suppose / Supposing (that) it's bad weather, what will we do then?
2 A little salt is supposed to be good for you, isn't it?
3 A Will Tim be at the party?
B I suppose so, yeah.
4 The plane's supposed to be here by now.
5 I suppose you wouldn't be able to pick me up, would you?
6 We can only suppose that they made a mistake.

c Match each sentence in 4b with meanings a–f.

a Could you do this? *5*
b That's what I think.
c People think this is what happened.
d It says that on the schedule.
e This might happen.
f People say this is true.

d Use suppose negatively in each sentence in 4b. What changes are necessary?

e In which sentences could you use supposedly? How would the sentence need to change?

5 a Look at the photos. Think of a remark that could go with each. Use an expression with suppose from 4b.

b Work with a partner. Build a short conversation from one of your sentences. Use an expression with suppose.

c 3.7 Listen to five conversations. Where are the people and what are they doing? How similar were the conversations to yours?

6 a Think of things which are commonly said about your country, its food, culture or people. Write sentences with suppose.

We're supposed to be dark and have black hair.

b Talk about your sentences. Do you consider them to be true or not?

We're supposed to be dark and have black hair. But actually, there are lots of blond people in Spain.

1

2

3

4

5

Self-assessment

Can you do these things in English? Circle a number on each line. 1 = I can't do this, 5 = I can do this well.

speculate about images and objects	1	2	3	4	5
interpret and respond to a story	1	2	3	4	5
discuss icons	1	2	3	4	5
identify critical language in a text	1	2	3	4	5
talk about what something represents	1	2	3	4	5
present arguments and counter-arguments	1	2	3	4	5
give criticism	1	2	3	4	5
respond to criticism	1	2	3	4	5

- For Wordcards, reference and saving your work → e-Portfolio
- For more practice → Self-study Pack, Unit 9

10

10.1 goals

- describe groups and membership
- describe feelings about belonging

A sense of belonging

Groups

SPEAKING

1 Look at the groups of people.

1 Where are they? What do you think they are doing?
2 What kind of groups are they? What do they have in common?
3 What connections and differences are there between the images?

A

B

C

D

2 a What different groups do people belong to?

b What kinds of groups do *you* belong to?

1 Make a list. Think about:
- organised groups.
- social groups.
- clubs.
- professional groups.
- informal groups.

2 Show your list to a partner. Which group is the most important to you?

LISTENING

3 3.8 **Listen to Grover talk about his sense of belonging to a group.**

1 What group did Grover belong to?
2 What exactly is *esprit de corps*?
3 Why didn't this affect him as personally as other people?
4 What three positive things does he say about being in this organisation?
5 Why is there a temptation to stay in this group?

Grover

LANGUAGE FOCUS

Belonging to a group

4 a **Complete these extracts with the expressions in the box.**

a sense of loyalty   part of a larger group   bonded with   get territorial   belonging to

1 I felt as if I was ______ .
2 You develop ______ to these people.
3 What was your experience of being in the army and ______ this organisation?
4 You can't ______ about things.
5 There was a strong temptation to rejoin the army, and that's how they get you, you know, because you are so ______ your group.

b 3.9 **Listen to check.**

Joining a group

LANGUAGE FOCUS

Talk about membership

1 a **The expressions in A are all used to talk about joining groups.**

1 Which expressions in B could they match with?
2 Which expressions have almost the same meaning?

A	B
1 I joined ...	a ... a lot of people.
2 I got involved in ...	b ... the Scottish National Party.
3 I teamed up with ...	c ... a few colleagues from work.
4 I got to know ...	d ... a drawing class.
5 I signed up for ...	e ... a training course.
6 I enrolled in ...	f ... politics.
7 I became a member of ...	
8 I collaborated with ...	

b 3.10 **Listen to check. What is each person talking about?**

LISTENING and SPEAKING

2 3.11 **Listen to Pilar talk about belonging to a group.**

1 What group does she refer to? How do you know?
2 How does she feel about belonging to it?
3 Which expressions from 1a does Pilar use?

3 **Choose one of the groups you listed earlier.**

1 Don't say what the group is, but tell a partner how you joined it and how you feel about being a member.
2 Can your partner guess what the group is?

Football

10.2 goals

- give opinions emphatically
- explore strategies for analysing authentic texts

READING

1 a How do you think these football photos are connected to the topic of *belonging*?

b You will read four extracts, each related to a photo. What do you think they will say?

2 a Read the extracts quickly.

1. Where is each extract from (a magazine, a novel ...)? How do you know?
2. Who is speaking in each: a fan? a journalist? a footballer? an expert / academic?
3. Who is being addressed?

A

Playing football and attending football matches ... It turned you into a member of a new community – all brothers together for an hour and a half, for not only had you escaped from the clanking machinery of this lesser life, from work, from wages, rent, doles, sick pay, insurance cards, nagging wives, ailing children, bad bosses, idle workmen, but you had escaped with most of your mates and your neighbours, with half the town, cheering together, thumping one another on the shoulders, swapping judgements like Lords of the Earth, having pushed your way through a turnstile into another and altogether more splendid life.

B

Exactly when chaos comes into our life, is when we must never lose hope, we never must lose faith in holy love and wisdom. If we have faith, small that it is, one day it goes to help us to transform our life. My life is an example of this! And one of the ways to show my gratitude is to extend and to share, when I can, my luck, with those who need it. Because I believe that this way, we will be able to create a happier, more just society. As my art is in my feet and not in my hands, it is with great honour that I associate the power of soccer to this noble, social cause.

C

Is there any cultural practice more global than football? No single world religion can match its geographical scope. The use of English and the vocabularies of science and mathematics must run football close for universality, but they remain the lingua franca of the world's élites, not of its masses. McDonalds? MTV? Only the most anodyne products of America's cultural industries can claim to reach as wide as football's, and then only for a fleeting moment in those parts of the world that can afford them. Football is available to anyone who can make a rag ball and find another pair of feet to pass to. Football has not merely been consumed by the world's societies, it has been embraced, embedded and then transformed by them...

D

Jafar Panahi's film *Offside* is so ensconced in the here-and-now that it was actually filmed in real time during the event it dramatises – the Iran–Bahrain qualifying match for the 2006 World Cup. And Panahi insists on using real people, too: "When I write a script I look around for people who can do the job best. For the girl supporters, they were mainly university students – and I found them through friends and colleagues and my contacts at universities. As for their interest in football, yes, they are genuinely interested and passionate about football. They wanted to go to the matches." Panahi went on: "I was very conscious of not trying to play with people's emotions; we were not trying to create tear-jerking scenes. So it engages people's intellectual side."

b **In which extract is football seen as:**

1 a way to challenge stereotypes?
2 a form of escape?
3 having an important social function?
4 a way of bonding people?
5 a subject for an artistic project?
6 a phenomenon of universal and mass appeal?

c **What techniques do the writers use to add variety and immediacy to their texts? Find examples.**

questions to get reader's attention	lists of nouns	
inversion for emphasis	exclamations	rhetorical questions
richly descriptive language	use of direct quotations	

d **Which extract would you like to carry on reading? Why?**

LANGUAGE FOCUS
Being emphatic

3 **a** **Look at these sentences from the extracts. If you read them aloud, which words would you emphasise?**

1 For not only had you escaped from the clanking machinery of this lesser life, but you had escaped with most of your mates and neighbours.
2 No single world religion can match its geographical scope.
3 Football has not merely been consumed by the world's societies, it has been embraced by them.
4 Exactly when chaos comes into our life, is when we must never lose hope.
5 As for their interest in football, yes, they are genuinely interested and passionate about football. They wanted to go to the matches.

b **3.12 Listen to check.**

c **Look at the sentences again.**

1 What conventional word order has changed in sentence 1?
2 What words / expressions could replace: no, merely, exactly, yes?
3 Are these ways of emphasising more common in spoken or written language? Why?
4 How could you communicate the sentences in a less emphatic way?

SPEAKING

4 **a** **Work alone. Do you agree with these statements?**

1 Football is the most popular sport in my country.
2 Football helps break through barriers and is a way of bringing people together.
3 The same number of women as men like football.
4 Nowadays, football is about love and money equally.

Not only is football the most popular sport in my country, it's also the most popular topic of conversation.

b **Change the statements so they reflect your opinion. Add emphasis, if you feel strongly enough.**

c **Talk about your opinions. Do other people agree?**

Prepare a campaign

10.3 goals

- persuade others to take action

TASK PREPARATION

1 a How do you think the photos are connected with *homelessness*?

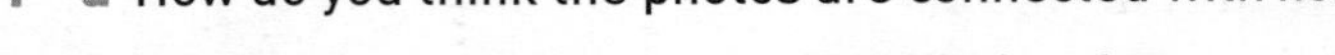

b Match the summaries on p133 with the photos.

1. Which campaign would be the most effective? Why?
2. What do you think causes people to become homeless?
3. What do people in your country do to prevent homelessness?

2 a Imagine you wanted to support the Homeless World Cup. How could you help?

b Read this campaign message from the Homeless World Cup website.

1. What answers does it give to 2a?
2. What is the difference between being a partner, a volunteer and a fan?

A BALL CAN CHANGE THE WORLD

Make a difference.

Become a partner
Become a partner and make a profound impact, engage employees and align with a powerful positive message for the world.

Volunteer
We are looking for 500 special people to help make the next Homeless World Cup the best ever. Bring your spirit of co-operation, your skills and talents and create an unforgettable event for everyone involved.

Become a fan
Sign up for the Homeless World Cup Fan Club and unite to make the tournament happen to give thousands of players around the world the chance to stand proud, represent their country and change the world forever. Support football with the power to change the world.

Make a donation
Help the Homeless World Cup Foundation grow the ambition to reach one million players with the benefits of football. Make a donation now! Thank you.

Raise money
Do something to raise money for the grass-roots projects making the benefits of football available to people who are homeless all year round.

Spread the word
Join the Homeless World Cup on Facebook, Myspace, Bebo, YouTube and Twitter to post your comments, photos and videos.

3 a Find examples of these features in the campaign message.

1. imperatives
2. the present progressive
3. exaggeration
4. compliments to the reader
5. positive adjectives and collocations
6. slogans and catchy expressions
7. pledges and claims
8. alliteration

b Which expressions from p97 are used here?

TASK

4 a Work in groups. Choose a charity which you think is worthwhile.

1. Plan the campaign message. Think about:
   - what you want to get across.
   - the target audience.
   - ways to get people involved.
   - expressions, slogans and visuals.
2. Together, write the campaign message. Include ideas for images and attractive presentation and use features from 3a.
3. Plan how to present your campaign, and how to persuade others to contribute.

b Give your campaign message to another group and give them time to read it.

c Choose one person in your group to:

- present your campaign and answer any questions.
- try to persuade other groups to contribute to the campaign.

d Decide which other campaigns you will support, and how. Tell the class.

10 EXPLORE

Across cultures Football rivalries

1 **Do you know these rival football club shields? Match them to the team names and their cities.**

Galatasary / Fenerbahçe
River Plate / Boca Juniors
AC Milan / Internazionale

2 **3.13 Listen to a radio programme about football rivalries.**

1 What is the cause of the rivalry in each case?
2 Why is the rivalry so strong?
3 What do all three rivalries have in common?

3 **Look at the script on page 157. How many words connected with sports can you find?**

4 a Talk together.

1 Where you live, what are the greatest sporting rivalries?
2 Do the teams or players have nicknames?
3 Why do you think that rivalry is so strong? Was the original cause historical, political, social or economic?
4 What are their matches like?

b What do you think is happening in the photo? Write a brief caption. Then compare with other students.

Keyword *together*

1 What does together mean in sentences 1–6? What do you think the people are talking about?

at the same time as a whole side by side
in a relationship against each other round each other

1 You can wait a long time and then two arrive together.
2 I knew they were close but I didn't know they were together.
3 Tie the two ends together well, otherwise it might break.
4 Put your hands together for our special guest!
5 The two together must be worth a fortune.
6 All of us must fight together against this menace.

2 a What do you think are the most common verbs that collocate with together? Complete the gaps with a verb + together.

1 It's a good thing we ______ tonight. It might be our last chance.
2 We must begin to ______ as a team – that way we're stronger.
3 ______ your things now, we're leaving.
4 Do you think the shirt and tie ______?
5 He's been helping Mark ______ a business plan.

b What other verb could you use in each sentence to express a similar idea?

It's a good thing we met tonight ...

3 a Put is the verb which most commonly collocates with together. Think of a synonym for each of these examples.

1 Our panel of experts put together a list of top ten foods to eat.
2 The movie is being put together by a group of independent film-makers.
3 She had put together a proposal for a book about Thomas Jefferson's boyhood.
4 I'm going to put together the best staff to improve the office.

b What do you think these highlighted expressions mean?

1 They won more medals at the Barcelona than the last four Olympics put together.
2 We're planning a little get-together for next Saturday.
3 I really admire her – she's such a together person.
4 I put two and two together and saw that I wasn't welcome.
5 I wanted to go to Nepal but I just didn't get it together.

4 a Complete these questions with a verb + together.

1 Who is married in your family? How long have they ______?
2 Have ever had to ______ a report or a proposal for your work? What was it about?
3 When you go on holiday, how long does it take you to ______ the things you need to take?
4 Why do you think countries find it so hard to ______ to fight global warming?
5 Look at the photos. Do you think the colours ______? Why / Why not?

b Ask and answer the questions.

A

B

C

EXPLOREWriting

Goals

- describe an organisation
- present something in the best possible light

1 a Look at this campaign poster for Shelter, a UK charity. How does the image transmit its message?

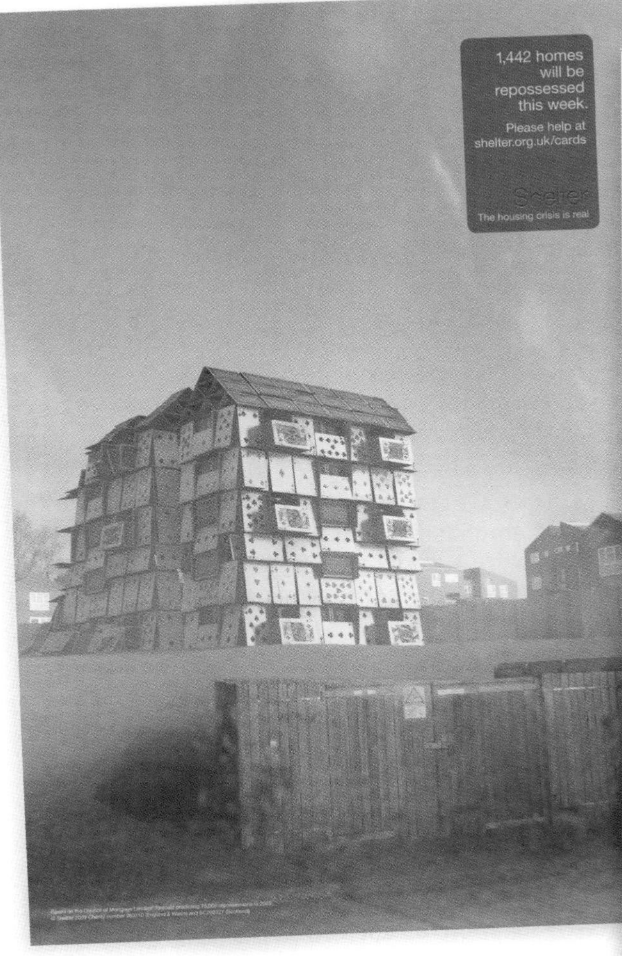

1,442 homes will be repossessed this week.
Please help at shelter.org.uk/cards
Shelter
The housing crisis is real

b What do you think the charity fights for, apart from combating homelessness?

Shelter

1 ______

Shelter is a charity that works to alleviate the distress caused by homelessness and bad housing.

We do this by giving advice, information and advocacy to people in housing need, and by campaigning for lasting political change to end the housing crisis for good.

2 ______

Shelter cannot house you, but we can give confidential help to people with all kinds of housing problems.

3 ______

Shelter tackles the root causes of bad housing by lobbying government and local authorities for new laws and policies, and more investment, to improve the lives of homeless and badly housed people.

Our influential campaigns bring aspects of bad housing to the attention of the media and the public, who help us fight for solutions.

As a leading expert on housing in Britain, we develop practical solutions to address the housing crisis.

4 ______

We're proud to join forces with like-minded organisations, to share our ideas, and develop creative ways of tackling housing need.

2 a Read the extract from the Shelter website. How does it answer 1b?

b Add these subheadings to the gaps.

Fighting for change   About us   Help and advice   Informing professionals

c What do you think is the best overall heading for this extract?

Our values   Who we are   Equality and diversity   How we make a difference

3 a How does the webpage express these ideas? Why? Consider individual words / expressions as well as verb forms.

1. Homeless people are helped by Shelter.
2. Confidential help is given to those people with housing problems.
3. We fight the main causes of bad housing.
4. The media and the public find out about us through our campaigns.
5. The housing crisis is dealt with using practical solutions.

b The webpage was written to cast the organisation in the best possible light. How is this done? Think about:

- the general content.
- the language items chosen.

c Find verbs in the website extract which talk about:

1. helping and solving problems.
2. fighting something.

d Why do you think there are so many of these verbs? Which other verbs do you think could be used in texts of this type?

4 Write a 'Who we are' description of the charity organisation you chose on p100.

Grammar

Inversion

1 a Look at this example from the unit.

> Not only had you escaped from the clanking machinery of this lesser life, but you had escaped with most of your mates and neighbours.

1. The sentence starts with an adverbial phrase. How does this affect the word order?
2. You could also say: *You hadn't only escaped ... but ...* How would that change the meaning?

b Here are some more adverbial phrases that can start a clause or sentence. Which words in A can combine with words in B?

A	B
not very at no in no only	way until rarely now recently once time

2 a Complete the gaps with expressions from 1b.

1. I should add that ______ have I, or anyone on my behalf, received a complaint.
2. ______ does the crisis threaten their business.
3. Seven years I've known him and ______ has he let me down.
4. Usually you audition for things so many times. ______ do you get the dream call.
5. ______ have we discovered what the real problem was.

b Which are formal and which are informal in register?

c Which words would you stress for emphasis?

d 3.14 Listen to check.

3 Rewrite these sentences with adverbial phrases.

1. The business started slowly, but now we are making a profit. *Only ...*
2. He didn't pick up the phone to see how I was. *At ...*
3. It hardly ever rains here in July. *Very ...*
4. I didn't realise my bag was gone until we were leaving the bar. *Not ...*
5. It's pouring with rain, and it's also freezing! *Not ...*

4 a No way is common in conversations. What do you think it means here? What are the people talking about?

1. No way will United win the league. They haven't got a chance.
2. No way did he write that himself. He copied it from the Internet.
3. It's great for a holiday, but no way would I want to live there.

b 3.15 Listen and mark the words where the emphasis is placed in each sentence.

5 a Write true sentences beginning with an adverbial phrase about:

- something that rarely or never happens.
- something that only happened recently.
- something you believe is impossible or a ridiculous idea.

b Listen to each other's sentences and ask questions to find out more.

6 a What do these pictures show? Write a brief caption for each with no way.

b Compare your captions.

Grammar reference, p144

Vocabulary

Collective nouns for people

7 a How many different kinds of groups can you remember from the unit?

b Sentences a–g talk about other groups of people.

1. Who do you think is talking in each sentence, and about what?
2. Which of the highlighted nouns describes a small group? Which describes a large group?
3. Which have a negative connotation? Which could be both negative or neutral?
4. What other words could replace the highlighted nouns?

a Well, the hordes of admirers are difficult to put up with sometimes.
b The suspect's court hearing today will be on a live video link from prison, so police do not have to confront an angry mob.
c While you were just "hanging out with the gang" I was wondering if you were alive or dead!
d *The Hunting Party* – a camera crew (Gere, Howard, Eisenberg) goes looking for a Bosnian warlord in this darkly comic thriller.
e They've had to learn to adjust to a high school where, if you're not in a clique, you're nobody.
f All of a sudden, they became a top-40-type group appealing to the younger crowd.
g Aberdeen's top scorer, Stavrum, has been linked with a move to German team St Pauli.

8 a Which nouns in 7b can also be used with the ones in the box? Make as many collocations as you can. Use these patterns:

1 noun + noun. *mob rule*
2 noun + of + noun. *hordes of children*

tourists violence member rule flight capacity children leader

b Make these sentences more precise by replacing group with an alternative.

1. He was hanging out with the wrong group.
2. They were a professional group and sorted out our problems easily.
3. These are the towns where they can recruit new group members.
4. If you go to the beach resorts in the summer you'll find groups of tourists.
5. I was ill on the flight but the cabin group were very helpful.
6. Group violence is a cause of inner-city crime.

9 Writing game.

1. Write a sentence that could be part of a story, including a collective noun for people. Pass your sentence to another pair.
2. Continue the story with another sentence. Pass your sentences to another pair. Continue with four or five more sentences.
3. Read out your story.

Collective adjectives

10 a We can use adjectives as nouns to talk about certain groups of people:

- homeless people → the homeless.
- elderly people → the elderly.

Complete these sentences with the and an adjective from the box.

rich poor elderly homeless needy disabled

1. He knows that it's wrong to park in spaces for ______.
2. The goal is to prevent ______ from dying of exposure.
3. The gap between ______ and ______ is steadily increasing.
4. The risk of infection is greater in ______.
5. It's ______ rather than the greedy that have to be protected.

b How do you express the ideas in your language?

c Talk together.

1. How are these groups of people talked about in your society?
2. Do you think attitudes towards them have changed over the last 50 years? If so, how?

Self-assessment

Can you do these things in English? Circle a number on each line. 1 = I can't do this, 5 = I can do this well.

◎ describe groups and membership	1	2	3	4	5
◎ describe feelings about belonging	1	2	3	4	5
◎ give opinions emphatically	1	2	3	4	5
◎ explore strategies for analysing authentic texts	1	2	3	4	5
◎ persuade others to take action	1	2	3	4	5
◎ describe an organisation	1	2	3	4	5
◎ present something in the best possible light	1	2	3	4	5

- For Wordcards, reference and saving your work → e-Portfolio
- For more practice → Self-study Pack, Unit 10

11

Climate

11.1 goals

- talk about climate change
- describe inventions and how they work
- discuss proposals

Radical ways to save the planet

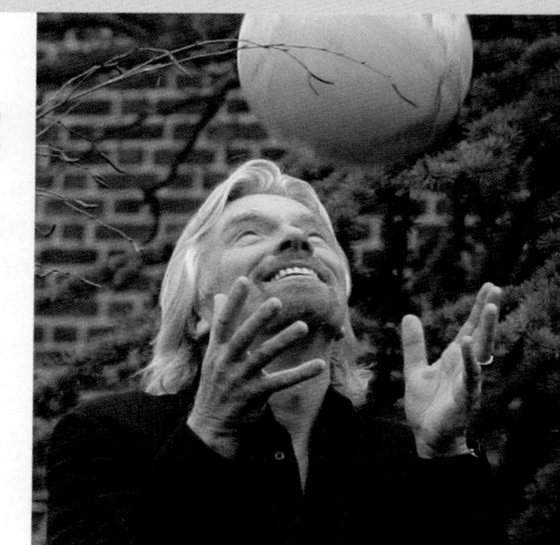

LISTENING

1 a What do you know about the billionaire Richard Branson? Why do you think this photo was taken?

b 3.16 Listen to the news story.

1. How much did Richard Branson offer, and for what?
2. Why do you think he did this? What do you think of the idea?

LANGUAGE FOCUS
Climate change

2 a The 'word cloud' shows some key words from the broadcast.

carbon dioxide, global warming, 1 billion tonnes, humans, temperatures, 25 million dollars, atmosphere, climate change, 90%, Richard Branson, century, six degrees, United Nations, billionaire, greenhouse gases

1. Which are directly connected with climate change?
2. Write sentences to show connections between the words in the word cloud. How many can you think of?
   Carbon dioxide is a greenhouse gas.
3. Try to use all the words to reconstruct what the reporter said.

b 3.16 Listen again. Were any words used differently?

READING and SPEAKING

3 a These images show five ideas which could be used to fight global warming. What different ideas do you think they show?

b **The article describes four of the ideas. Which involves:**

- reducing CO_2 levels?
- absorbing the sun's heat?
- deflecting the sun's rays?

Climate change is being experienced everywhere in the world, and just reducing carbon emissions may not be enough. Some scientists are now beginning to suggest more radical inventions that might save us from disaster by actually putting the greenhouse effect into reverse.

One scientist is proposing to put a huge glass sunshade in space which would orbit the Earth so that it would always face the sun. This would deflect some of the sun's rays back into space, so the temperature of the atmosphere would be reduced.

Another proposal is to fire rockets loaded with sulphur into the stratosphere. The sulphur would be released and it would form a thin cloud-like layer around the Earth, which would block some of the sun's rays.

Another interesting idea is to pump fine particles of sea water into the clouds. This would increase the thickness of the clouds, so the sun's rays would be reflected. This could be done using remote-controlled yachts, so the energy cost would be zero.

Another possibility would be to create enclosed 'plankton farms' in the sea, where plankton could be fed huge quantities of fertiliser. This would make the plankton grow and absorb CO_2 from the air.

Proposals like these may seem like science fiction, but some experts believe we may soon be forced to take them seriously, for the sake of our planet.

Artificial trees

1 **Look at the image that was not mentioned in the article. What do you think it shows and how might it work? Read more about it on p133.**

LANGUAGE FOCUS

Active and passive infinitives

2 **a** **After could and would, we can use an active or a passive infinitive. Complete the gap.**

Active: The apparatus would extract carbon dioxide.

Passive: Carbon dioxide would ______.

b **Find more examples of each type in the article on p133.**

3 **a** **Cover the article above and complete the sentences. Choose an active or passive infinitive, using the verbs in the box.**

release reduce form feed increase reflect block absorb ~~deflect~~

1 **Giant sunshade:** the sunshades would deflect a small percentage of the sun's rays back into space, so the temperature of the atmosphere would ...
2 **Sulphur rockets:** the sulphur would ... and it would ...
3 **Pumping sea water:** this would ... The sun's rays would ...
4 **Plankton farms:** plankton would ... The plankton could ...

b **Read the article again. Did it use the verbs you chose?**

SPEAKING

4 **Consider each of the five proposals in turn.**

1 Do you think it is likely to work?
2 Do you think it would help combat global warming?
3 In which proposals would cost or energy consumption be a problem?

Glaciers

11.2 goals

- describe an ongoing process
- understand imagery in a poem

1 

2 

READING

1 What is the difference between the two photos? How many years, do you think, have elapsed between them? What could have caused the changes to take place?

2 a Read the beginning of an article about Greenland. What does the writer mean by:

1 "calving season"? 2 "a flotilla of icebergs"? 3 "eerily beautiful"?

The Sermilik fjord in Greenland: a chilling view of a warming world

It is calving season in the Arctic. A flotilla of icebergs, some as jagged as fairytale castles and others as smooth as dinosaur eggs, calve from the ice sheet that smothers Greenland and sail down the fjords. The journey of these sculptures of ice from glaciers to ocean is eerily beautiful and utterly terrifying.

The wall of ice that rises behind Sermilik fjord stretches for 2,400 km from north to south and smothers 80% of this country. It has been frozen for three million years.

b Why do you think the writer says this is "a chilling view" and that the icebergs are "utterly terrifying"?

3 a Read the rest of the article quickly. What seems to be happening in Greenland? Do scientists fully understand it?

Now it is melting, far faster than the climate models predicted and far more decisively than any political action to combat our changing climate. If the Greenland ice sheet disappeared, sea levels around the world would rise by seven metres, as 10% of the world's fresh water is currently frozen here.

Experts from around the world are landing on the ice sheet in a race against time to discover why the ice in Greenland is vanishing so much faster than expected. Gordon Hamilton, a Scottish-born glaciologist, hit upon the daring idea of landing on a moving glacier in a helicopter to measure its speed. When Hamilton processed his first measurements of the glacier's speed, he found it was marching forwards at a greater pace than a glacier had ever been observed to flow before. "We were blown away because we realised that the glaciers had accelerated not just by a little bit but by a lot," he says. The three glaciers they studied had abruptly increased the speed by which they were transmitting ice from the ice sheet into the ocean.

Driven by the loss of ice, Arctic temperatures are warming more quickly than other parts of the world: last autumn air temperatures in the Arctic stood at a record 5°C above normal. For centuries, the ice sheets maintained an equilibrium: glaciers calved off icebergs and sent melt water into the oceans every summer; in winter, the ice sheet was then replenished with more frozen snow. Scientists believe the world's great ice sheets will not completely disappear for many more centuries, but the Greenland ice sheet is now shedding more ice than it is accumulating.

Research is focusing on what scientists call the 'dynamic effects' of the Greenland ice sheet. It is not simply that the ice sheet is melting steadily as global temperatures rise. Rather, the melting triggers dynamic new effects, which in turn accelerate the melt. "It's quite likely that these dynamic effects are more important in generating a rapid rise in sea level than the traditional melt," says Hamilton. Some scientists are astounded by the changes. "We can't as a scientific community keep up with the pace of changes, let alone explain why they are happening," says the glaciologist.

b Read the article more carefully and make notes about:

1 the Greenland ice sheet.
2 Gordon Hamilton.
3 air temperatures.
4 'dynamic effects'.

LANGUAGE FOCUS
Processes

4 a The verbs in the box all describe processes. How could you use them to answer these questions?

1 What is happening to: the ice? the glacier? the ocean?
2 What used to happen before?

melt shed disappear replenish flow rise transmit trigger accelerate march maintain vanish

b Check in the article.

c Talk about the notes you made in 3b, using the verbs in the box to talk about them. Did you make the same points?

d Do you know of any other 'dynamic effects' connected to climate change?

2084

READING

1 a You are going to read a poem called *2084* by Carol Rumens about a future vision of the world. Before that, read about Phaethon on p133. What could Phaethon be a metaphor for in the poem?

b *2084* echoes the year 1984. What significance does 1984 have for you, if any?

2 a 3.17 Read and listen to the first part of the poem. What expressions talk about climate change?

that flood, in motion inches from the cross-roads

b Find expressions which refer to:

- bicycles.
- solar heating.
- computers.
- a group of houses / flats.

2084

Paired wheels and PV panels, ponds and hives
and garden-fields (citron and silvery-green
samplers, stitched by hand) declare our ground.
We're scripture-safe in our examined lives;
for each estate, one bin, one fridge, one screen
only, daily rationing of down-loads.
That ice-bar, frilling in the distant sound,
that flood, in motion inches from the cross-roads
where we abolished run-ways and re-wound
the windmills, will be measured and contained –
the government says so. And the world will sail
over the carbon peak: we'll be in free-fall
the whole sweet way to paradise regained.

3 3.18 Read and listen to the second part of the poem.

1 How many references to Phaethon can you find?
2 Find expressions that refer to 'fire'.
3 Who are the 'unfortunate' ones in this case?

It's slow, of course. The children want to burn
anything that burns. They say we stole
the magic brand, and scraped the sun's wheel
to spark it, so shut up: it's their turn
to hit the gas, light out, ignore the brakes,
as children should. Just let us be children
they wail from blazing consoles. And we tell them,
or try to, what it was to drive that borrowed
chariot, rocketing, spiralling with its florid
machinery in a thunder of gold tyres
down, down the yellowing sky-waste. Oh infelix
Phaethon, earth grew nothing, then, but fires.
We drove death into childhood, just being children.

LISTENING and SPEAKING

4 a 3.19 Listen to someone commenting on the poem. What does he say is its main message? Do you agree?

b Which parts of the poem talk about:

- people's lifestyle in 2084.
- the kind of society it will be.
- what the children want.
- what their parents did to the Earth.

5 a 3.20 Read and listen to the whole poem. What connections are there with the article on page 108?

b What other visions of life in the future can you think of (films, books, etc.)?

11.3 Target activity

11.3 goals

- talk about climate change
- describe an ongoing process
- say if actions are justified
- conduct a debate

The Doomsday debate

TASK LISTENING

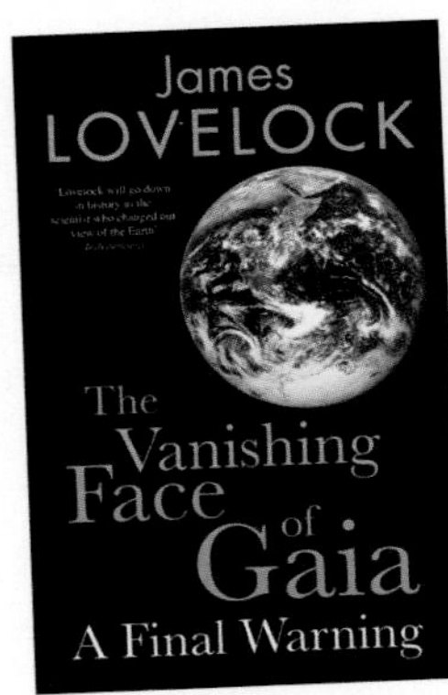

1 a You are going to listen to part of a radio discussion about the book *The Vanishing Face of Gaia* by scientist James Lovelock.

1 What do you think this title means?
2 What do you think it says about James Lovelock's view of climate change?

b 3.21 Listen to the discussion.

1 Which of these opinions does the book express?
- Global warming is irreversible.
- Humans are not responsible for causing climate change.
- Humans caused climate change without realising what they were doing.
- It's now impossible to slow down climate change.

2 Why do you think Moira laughs?

TASK LANGUAGE

Saying if actions are justified

2 a Which sentences best match James Lovelock's point of view?

1 Global warming is now **inevitable**.
2 It's absolutely **crucial** that we reduce CO_2 emissions over the next 50 years.
3 Using low-energy light bulbs is **pointless**.
4 It would be quite **feasible** to reverse global warming if we act soon.
5 The amount of money which we invest in wind power **isn't really justified**.
6 It's certainly **worthwhile** holding conferences on climate change.

b Which highlighted adjectives in 2a mean:

a it has no purpose?
b it's possible to do it?
c there's no good reason to do it?
d we really must do it?
e it's certain to happen?
f it's a good idea?

c How could you use these words in sentences 1–6 to express the same meanings?

justification difference sense worth point nothing achieve

1 There's nothing we can do to prevent global warming.

TASK PREPARATION

3 a Which view is closer to your own?

A Today's society is ever more irresponsible and selfish, so the world as we know it is unlikely to survive.

B We are better informed than ever about the harm we do to the planet, so there is real hope for humanity.

b Divide into group A or group B according to your point of view.

- Group A, read about James Lovelock on p134 and answer the questions.
- Group B, read about the 'Doomsday Clock' on p139 and answer the questions.

TASK

4 a Prepare to debate the issue. Draw on arguments used in the information you read, and any others you can think of to support your view.

b Conduct a debate with the other group.

Across cultures Living 'off-grid'

1 What do you think 'off-grid' refers to? What clues can you find in the photo?

2 a Read the first paragraph of the article to check.

b Which verbs collocate with these nouns to describe what an 'off-gridder' does?

electricity own water own waste disposal

3 Now read *all* of the article.

1 Find nouns and adjectives which describe 'off-gridders' and their lifestyle.
noticeable glee, smug …

2 Which ones show the 'off-gridders' in a positive light? Which in a negative light?

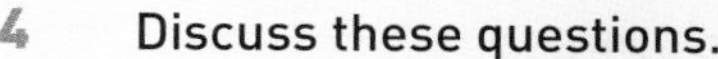

4 Discuss these questions.

1 How do you think 'off-gridders' would be viewed in your country: as pioneers or dreamers?

2 How would you describe Perez's tone at the start and the end of the article? Do you see a contradiction in living 'off-grid', but having a 21st-century lifestyle?

3 Why do you think it is becoming more popular? Do you think 'off-grid' living could become popular where you live? Why / Why not?

4 Think about three different regions of the world. How easy would 'off-grid' living be in each of them? Give reasons.

home | about | blog — **Feeds:** posts comments

Unplugging from the grid

"I haven't paid an electricity bill since 1970," says Richard Perez with noticeable glee. He can afford to be smug. He lives "off-grid" – unconnected to the power grid and the water, gas and sewerage supplies that most of us rely on. He generates his own electricity, sources his own water and manages his own waste disposal – and prefers it that way. "There are times when the grid blacks out," he says. "I like the security of having my own electricity company."

Perez is not alone. Once the preserve of mavericks, hippies and survivalists, there are now approximately 200,000 off-grid households in the US, a figure that Perez says has been increasing by a third every year for the past decade. For people who live off-grid, self-sufficiency means guilt-free energy consumption and peace of mind. "It feels brilliant to use clean, free energy that's not from fossil fuels," says Suzanne Galant, a writer who lives off-grid in rural Wales. "And if something goes wrong, we can fix it ourselves." Now even urbanites are seeing the appeal of generating some if not all of their own power needs. So is energy freedom an eco pipe-dream or the ultimate good life?

Well, there's only one way to find out: begin to explore the possibilities of solar, wind or hydro-power. But unless you live on a sunny, south-facing hillside with access to a nearby river or stream, that might prove prohibitively expensive!

There is no doubt that being off-grid has its problems, and it is not always the cheapest way to get your energy. Even so, pioneers like Perez have proved that it can be done, and without giving up a 21st-century lifestyle: "I've got five computers, two laser scanners, two fridge-freezers, a microwave, a convection oven, vacuum cleaners – you name it," says Perez. "There's an external beam antenna on the roof for the phone and a satellite dish for an Internet connection. I've got 70 kWh in batteries that could last me five days. I have too much electricity." Too much electricity and no more bills. That's got to be worth aiming for. ●

Keywords describing similarities and differences

1 **Look at these examples from the unit.**

> 1 Just like a real tree, an artificial tree would have a structure to hold it up - the equivalent of a trunk, probably a pillar.
> 2 Unlike in a real tree, he explains, where the leaves are spread out because they have to see sunshine for the purpose of photosynthesis, the leaves on an artificial tree could be packed much more tightly.

How could you express the same meaning using these expressions?

as	with	similar to	whereas	rather than

2 **a** **Here are some more examples. Complete the gaps with like or unlike. What words in the sentence helped you to choose the answer?**

1 ______ the rugged west coast, the east coast of the island has wide sandy beaches.
2 The final was played mainly without disciplinary problems, ______ last Friday's stormy quarter-final.
3 ______ all forms of art, popular music deserves to be discussed and analysed.
4 Desktop PCs, ______ notebook computers, are prohibitively expensive to ship overseas.
5 Tamarind pulp has a sour taste, rather ______ lime juice.
6 He sold fruit from a small box on wheels which looked a bit ______ a child's pram.

b **Add information with like or unlike to these sentences to expand the meaning.**

1 The president is committed to finding a diplomatic solution to the crisis.
The president, like many other world leaders, is committed ...
2 Eco-cola is made only from natural ingredients.
3 I live in constant fear of being made redundant.
4 Coyotes do not normally attack humans.
5 Basketball players usually reach their peak at about 25.

3 **a** **These examples show other ways of saying things are similar or dissimilar. How do you think they might continue? What will the next word probably be?**

1 Synthetic trees resemble real trees in many ways. For example, they have the equivalent ...
2 The DNA analysis found that the bloodstains were identical ...
3 One euro is now equivalent ....
4 Traditions run deep here. On special occasions, people still sing traditional folk songs, just ...
5 We believe that banks should be regulated in the same way ...
6 Her refusal to answer the question in court was tantamount ...
7 I'd prefer to cycle to work, as opposed ...
8 Many antibiotics are not available over the counter in pharmacies in the US, in contrast ...

b 3.22 **Listen to check.**

4 **a** **Look at these pairs of images. How many sentences can you make about their differences and similarities?**

A

B

C
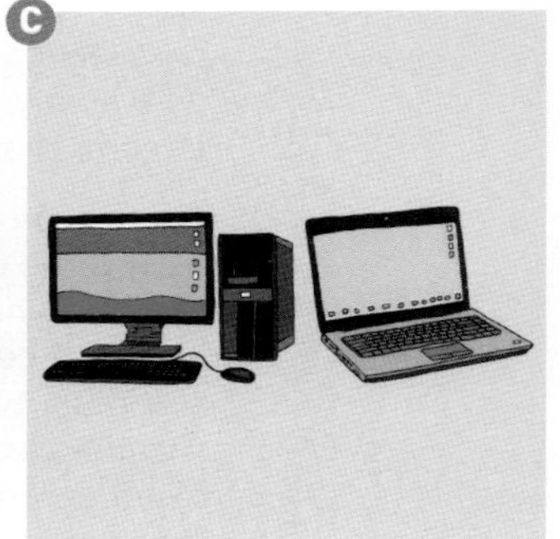
D

b **Think about different aspects of where you live (society, people, neighbourhoods, etc.). Write about them expressing similarities and differences. Give reasons.**

EXPLORESpeaking

Goals
- report a point of view
- react to a point of view

1 a 3.23 You will hear Pilar, Uri, Patrick and Jane reacting to James Lovelock's ideas about global warming. Cover the scripts and listen to each speaker in turn.

1. Does the person agree, partly agree or disagree with James Lovelock?
2. What is each speaker's view?

Pilar

What he's really saying is that global warming is already happening. We can't stop it, so there's no point in doing anything. I [1]_______ (**agree**), I think things aren't nearly as bad as he says they are. I [2]_______ (**exaggerating**) a bit.

Uri

[3]_______ (**agree**) when he says that there's no point in using low-energy light bulbs, I think he may be, maybe he's right about that, it, it's not going to make any difference. But I [4]_______ (**see**). I think, I think it's worth trying anything – but it would probably have to be something quite radical, like taking CO_2 out of the atmosphere again.

Patrick

His point really is that politicians are never going to say how bad things really are, right? I [5]_______ (**a point**). Politicians, yeah, OK, they're talking a lot, but what are they actually doing? That's exactly what he's saying. Lovelock makes the point that people don't react to things until it's too late. I [6]_______ (**a valid point**).

Jane

When he says it's too late, I think what he really means is that we'd have to do something quite drastic, like – oh, I don't know – invent new technology to deal with it. Something like that. I think [7]_______ (**spot on**), [8]_______ (**right**).

b Read what the people said. What expressions do you think go in the gaps?

c 3.23 Listen again to check.

2 a Compare these two ways to give the same information. How do the expressions in B change the meaning?

A	B
1 He says that global warming is already happening.	1 What he's really saying is that global warming is already happening.
2 He says that politicians are never going to say how bad things really are.	2 His point really is that politicians are never going to say how bad things really are.

b 3.24 Listen to the two sentences in B again. Where is the emphasis placed each time?

c Look again at what the speakers say. Find three more expressions like those in B. Practise saying them.

3 a 3.25 Listen to four people expressing opinions.

1. What is each person talking about? Match them with the photos.
2. What seems to be their point of view?

A

B

C

D

b 3.26 Listen to check. Do you agree, partly agree or disagree?

c Choose one of the opinions you heard and prepare to comment on it. Note down expressions you could use.

1. Think of ways to report the opinion.
   - What he's saying is ...
   - The point she's making is ...
   - One example she gives is ...
2. Think of ways to agree, partly agree or disagree.
   - I partly agree with ...
   - I think he makes a valid point ...
   - I think she's spot on ...
3. Think of ways to express your own opinion on the topic.
   - It seems to me ...
   - I think it's terrible the way ...
   - I don't approve of ...

d Talk about the opinion you chose. Do other people agree with you?

Grammar

Present progressive active and passive

1 a We can use the present progressive to describe:

a gradual ongoing processes (= it's happening all the time).
b temporary situations and activities (= it's happening around now).

Look at these examples. Which use do they show? Which uses the passive?

1 Climate change is being experienced everywhere in the world.
2 One scientist is proposing to put a huge glass sunshade into space.
3 Richard Branson is offering $25 million.
4 Experts from around the world are landing on the ice sheet.
5 Arctic temperatures are warming more quickly than in other parts of the world.

b Look back at *The Sermilik Fjord in Greenland* on p108. Which examples of the present progressive can you find?

2 a These sentences are from environmental news items. Continue each with a verb from the box, using the present progressive active or passive. More than one answer may be possible.

erode introduce increase decline disappear

1 The government are refusing to allow continued industrial development at Cherry Point, a major fish-spawning ground where the fish ...
2 The low-lying farmland near the coast is susceptible to flooding, and the coast itself ...
3 In many areas, new drought-resistant crops ...
4 The number of sea turtles coming to the island to breed ...
5 The population of foxes in the region, who benefit from the presence of humans, ...

b Which of these adverbs could you add to each sentence in 2a?

gradually rapidly noticeably experimentally imperceptibly steadily alarmingly dramatically

Which adverbs go most naturally before the main verb? Which go after it?

3 Write sentences about three things happening where you live. Include adverbs if appropriate.

Unemployment is rising rapidly ...
Many people are being laid off ...

Cleft sentences

4 a Here are examples of speakers giving emphasis and focus to an idea. Are they similar to the ones on p113? How are they different?

The place I'd really like to live is Vancouver, Canada.

What I'd like more than anything is a good, strong cup of coffee.

b How could you emphasise and focus on the underlined parts of these sentences?

1 Light green really works well for a bedroom.
2 I think she's trying to get attention.
3 I hate rude shop assistants.
4 I remember our first holiday together clearly.
5 I like living here because it's close to the sea.

c 3.27 Listen and compare your answers. Did the speakers add other words or expressions? Which words did they emphasise?

5 a Look at these examples. The speakers divide their message into two parts to add emphasis.

1 What is the person talking about in each case?
2 How would you say the sentences in a non-emphatic way?

a It's people who have no civic responsibility that annoy me – they just leave this here, they don't put it in the bins provided.
b What Erika did have was a rare gift – she'd always have time for you, always be ready to listen.
c The company they give you is special – it's something no other animal can give, they depend on you but they give you a lot back.
d The reason why I left is that I just couldn't stand the noise any more – the walls were wafer-thin, you know, I could hear everything.

b Think of something that irritates or pleases you. Talk about it in an expressive way.

What really irritates me at the moment are the road works going on outside my front door – it's practically all day long.

Grammar reference, p145

Vocabulary

Adverb / adjective collocations

6 a Look at this sentence from the unit.

> The journey of these sculptures of ice from glaciers to ocean is eerily beautiful and utterly terrifying.

We could also describe the icebergs using these adverbs. How would they change the meaning?

- strangely beautiful
- breathtakingly beautiful
- exquisitely beautiful
- astonishingly beautiful
- stunningly beautiful
- heart-rendingly beautiful

b Which expressions from 6a could describe:

1 a dream?
2 a fashion model?
3 a romantic song?
4 a mountain landscape?
5 a piece of jewellery?

7 Add adverbs from the box to 1–7. How do they add to the meaning?

bitterly highly notoriously blissfully hideously stiflingly wildly

1 hot weather
2 a cold wind
3 ugly apartment blocks
4 an intelligent person
5 a dangerous road
6 a happy couple
7 a successful book

8 Match each pair of adverbs with a sentence. How do the two adverbs in each pair differ in meaning?

~~critically / terminally~~	dangerously / terrifyingly
reassuringly / strangely	eerily / pleasantly
deceptively / relatively	obstinately / tactfully
impossibly / frustratingly	
resolutely / irrepressibly	

1 Unfortunately he is *critically / terminally* ill in hospital.
2 In spite of all her problems, she remained ______ cheerful.
3 He remained ______ silent throughout the meeting.
4 We were driving ______ close to the edge of the road.
5 I heard ______ familiar voices in the next room.
6 The river looks ______ easy to cross.
7 The crossword was ______ difficult to solve.
8 The streets were ______ quiet.

9 a Think of adverbs and adjectives to describe these images from the 1960s. Compare with a partner and give reasons.

A

B

C

b 3.28 Listen to these descriptions. How similar were they to yours?

10 a Work alone. Choose three expressions from 7 or 8 which describe experiences you have had.

b Work with a partner. Listen to each other's experiences and ask questions to find out more.

Self-assessment

Can you do these things in English? Circle a number on each line. 1 = I can't do this, 5 = I can do this well.

talk about climate change	1	2	3	4	5
describe inventions and how they work	1	2	3	4	5
discuss proposals	1	2	3	4	5
describe an ongoing process	1	2	3	4	5
understand imagery in a poem	1	2	3	4	5
say if actions are justified	1	2	3	4	5
conduct a debate	1	2	3	4	5
report a point of view	1	2	3	4	5
react to a point of view	1	2	3	4	5

- For Wordcards, reference and saving your work → e-Portfolio
- For more practice → Self-study Pack, Unit 11

12

12.1 goals

- talk about knowledge and technology
- discuss how to access information

Knowledge and technology

The end of general knowledge?

SPEAKING

1 In what ways could you find out:

- how to kayak?
- biographical data about a person for a research project?
- the capital of Burkina Faso?
- about disabled facilities at a particular hotel?
- your current destination when travelling by car?

READING

2 a Read the start of an article about technology and general knowledge.

1 Why do you think the mistake happened?
2 Whose fault do you think it was?

One day last year a middle-aged man asked a taxi to take him to see Chelsea play Arsenal at football. He told the driver "Stamford Bridge", the name of Chelsea's stadium, but he delivered him instead to the village of Stamford Bridge in Yorkshire, nearly 150 miles in the opposite direction. Of course, he missed the match.

b What point is the journalist making? What do you think he will go on to say? Read the next part to check.

What had happened? The man in this story had handed over responsibility for knowing geography to a machine. With the Sat-Nav system in place, he felt that he did not need to know where he was going. That was the machine's job. He confidently outsourced the job of knowing this information, or of finding it out, to that little computer on the dashboard ... Is that what the future holds for us? Using an Internet search engine (once you have keyed the words in) takes a broadband user less than a second, and the process will only get quicker. And soon with our smartphones at hand, almost all of us will be online almost all of the time.

The same could be true of university education. Today, the average student seems not to value general knowledge. If asked a factual question, they will usually click on a search engine without a second thought. Actually knowing the fact and committing it to memory does not seem to be an issue, it's the ease with which we can look it up.

However, general knowledge has never been something that you acquire formally. Instead, we pick it up from all sorts of sources as we go along, often absorbing facts without realising. The question remains, then: is the Internet threatening general knowledge? When I put that to Moira Jones, expert in designing IQ tests, she referred me to the story of the Egyptian god Thoth. I looked it up. It was told by Plato 2,400 years ago. It goes like this: Thoth invents writing and proudly offers it as a gift to the king of Egypt, declaring it an 'elixir of memory and wisdom'. But the king is horrified, and tells him: "This invention will induce forgetfulness in the souls of those who have learned it, because they will not need to exercise their memories, being able to rely on what is written. Writing is not a remedy for memory, but for reminding them of what they have discovered."

Who wants to be a millionaire finalist David Swift, responding to the same question, recognises that there was a problem of young people saying: "I don't need to know that", but he is far more excited about the educational potential of the Internet. "There is so much more info out there, giving people far more opportunities to boost their general knowledge."

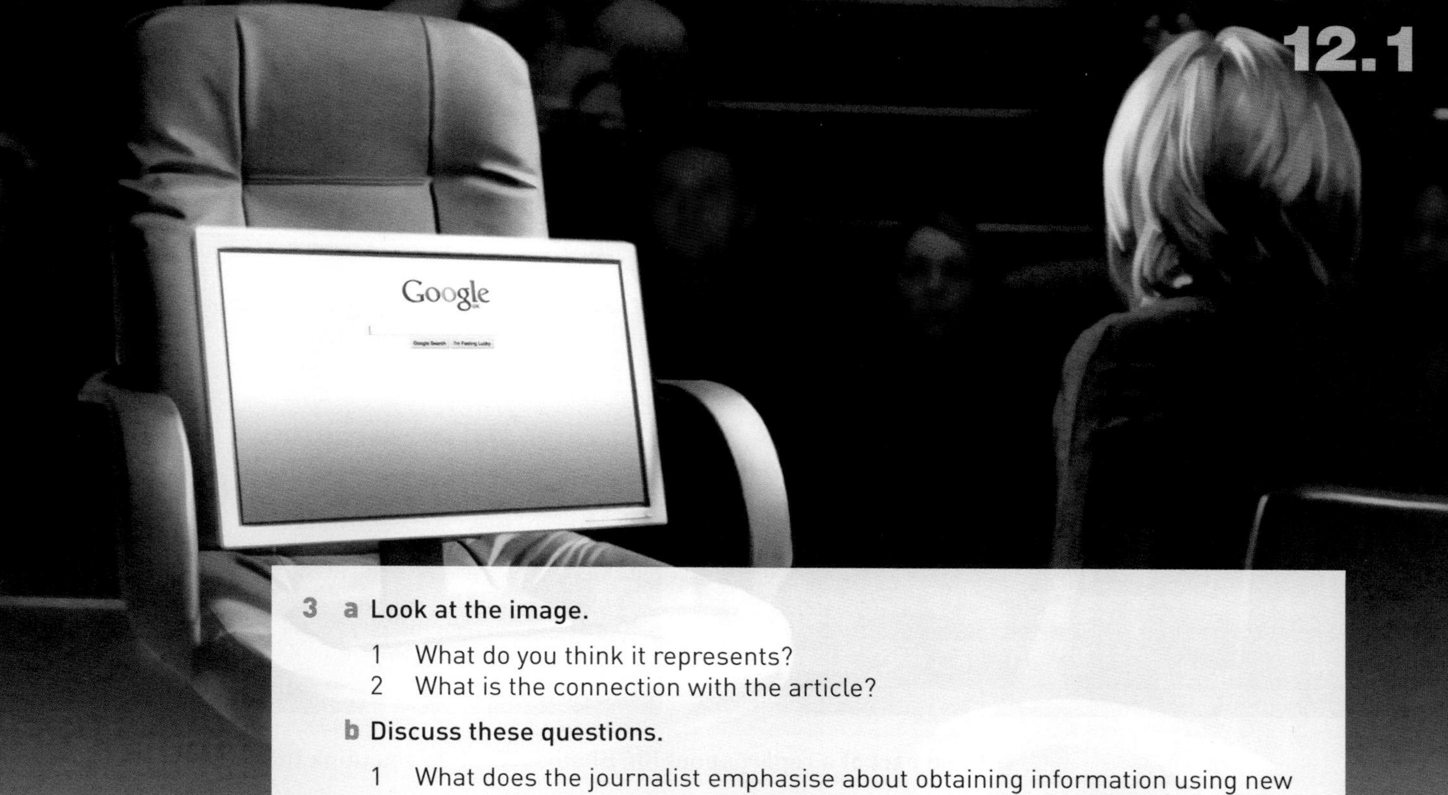

3 a Look at the image.

1 What do you think it represents?
2 What is the connection with the article?

b Discuss these questions.

1 What does the journalist emphasise about obtaining information using new technology?
2 What do you understand 'general knowledge' to mean here?
3 What are the parallels between technology and writing in the story of Thoth?
4 What is the difference between Jones's opinions and Swift's?

c How do you think the writer will conclude the article? Do you think he will agree that general knowledge is now dead?

d Read the final paragraph on page 134. Are you surprised by the ending? Why?

LANGUAGE FOCUS
Talking about information and knowledge

4 a Cover the article.

1 Which of these verbs collocated: with information or facts? with knowledge?

value	look up	find out	commit (to memory)
know	acquire	pick up	absorb

2 Which verbs have a similar meaning?
3 Which could collocate with both information and knowledge?
4 Can you remember how these other verbs were used?

hand over	key in	click on	outsource	boost

b Read the article again to check.

LISTENING and SPEAKING

5 a 3.29 Listen to three people discussing the ideas in the article. Which of those topics do they talk about?

- going out
- going on a long journey
- travelling to work
- knowing historical facts

Are they generally in favour of, or against technology?

b Match these opinions with the speakers.

1 Technology makes going out more interesting.
2 It saves you time when travelling.
3 It saves you having to memorise useless information.
4 It helps you to understand things in greater depth.

c Which opinions do you agree with? Why?

6 Discuss these questions.

1 Think of some information you looked up online. Was it easy or difficult to find? Were you satisfied with the result?
2 Have you ever received unreliable information?

The Hole in the Wall

12.2 goals

- describe technological advances
- talk about how things develop

LISTENING

1 a **What do you think these photos show?**

A

B

b **Read part of a report about the photos. What do you think the project consists of?**

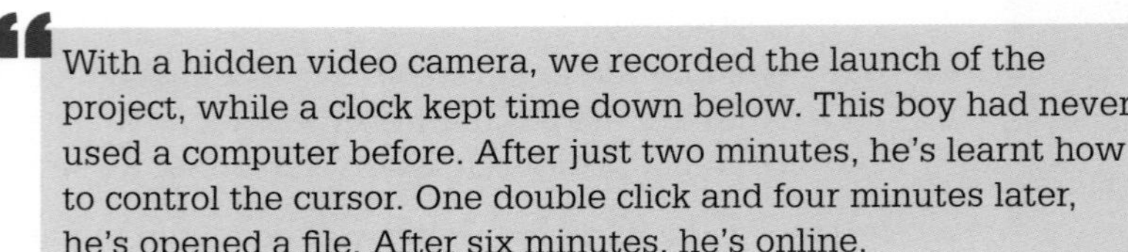

"With a hidden video camera, we recorded the launch of the project, while a clock kept time down below. This boy had never used a computer before. After just two minutes, he's learnt how to control the cursor. One double click and four minutes later, he's opened a file. After six minutes, he's online."

c **Look at the photo on page 139. What do you understand about the project now that you didn't before?**

2 a 3.30 **Listen to a TV news report about the *Hole in the Wall* project.**

1 What was the main conclusion that the researchers reached about the children's behaviour?
2 How do the children learn to use the computers?
3 What is installed on the computers?
4 What is the reporter's final point and message for the future?

b **What images do you think were shown on screen at these points?**

"The children are falling over themselves to look at something new."

"He's been coming here from the start, learning by watching others."

"... which would go on to inspire the hit movie *Slumdog Millionaire*"

"giving the children access to a whole new world and valuable life skills"

READING

3 a **Talk together.**

1 What kind of online sites do you think the children will access?
2 What do you think they like best about computers?
3 How do you think they benefit from the project?

b **Read the interview. Were your ideas the same?**

The project has now expanded throughout India to many different provinces. Psychologist Ritu Dangwal has observed kids using the kiosks since its inception. Who's looking through the *Hole in the Wall* and what are they really getting out of it?

1 ______________________________?

Definitely – there has been a marked difference in how the children and community react to a computer, depending on the geographic location and on cultural, ethnic and racial backgrounds. In some places there is no gender difference. At the other extreme, girls, though eager, do not come to the kiosk. They just stop near the kiosk site and watch.

2 ______________________________?

I don't see the *Hole in the Wall* as a purely Indian phenomenon. Children are the same all across the world. If it can hold true in India, it can work as well anywhere in the world. Cambodia, Ethiopia and the Philippines have all shown interest in this project.

3 ______________________________?

There was a study done by a professor teaching in Delhi University entitled *Computer Environment and Cognitive Development*. She found that children using the kiosk were more persistent, more tolerant toward ambiguity – their aspirations were more realistic than children who were going to school but not using the kiosk.

4 ______________________________?

Clicking around the Internet may not directly lead to any kind of improvement. But yes, browsing the Internet is like a child sitting with a book in their hands. Without knowing it, children are going to sites like tours and travels, reading news, or making attempts to do so. At the end of the day, they are doing far more constructive work than they would have done in a classroom.

5 ______________________________?

Just about everything. How intuitively these slum children have taken to computers. How well they seem to have organised themselves to pick up skills. Their quest for information is the greatest wonder.

c **Write a question for each of the answers. Then check on page 135.**

d **Do you think the project could be criticised? Think of arguments for and against.**

LANGUAGE FOCUS
Developments and advances

4 a **Do the highlighted verbs mean: become popular or successful? improve? increase?**

1. It gives people far more opportunities to boost their general knowledge. *increase*
2. The idea has caught on across the world.
3. This educational project has spread like wildfire over the past six years.
4. We ask why DJ schools are thriving in a recession.
5. We enhanced the help section for the software, added pictures, etc.
6. Telecity is looking at raising capacity in its data centres across Europe.
7. The title of the talk is 'Computers and how they have advanced'.
8. Apple are still gaining ground in computer sales.
9. Rajinder's self-confidence soared after he taught himself how to use a computer.
10. The project has now expanded throughout India.

b **Write about something that has become popular or increased.**

Unemployment is soaring right now. It's nearly 10%.

c **Read out your sentence, but don't mention the topic. Can other people guess what it is about?**

It's soaring right now. It's nearly 10%.

SPEAKING

5 **Talk together.**

1. How did you learn your own computer skills? How much were you taught? How much have you picked up by yourself?
2. What do you think this tells us about the way we acquire new skills?
3. What impact do you think computer technology has had on your life? Think about
   - ways it has improved.
   - ways it has got worse.

Deliver a confident message

12.3 goals
- explain an idea
- deliver a positive message

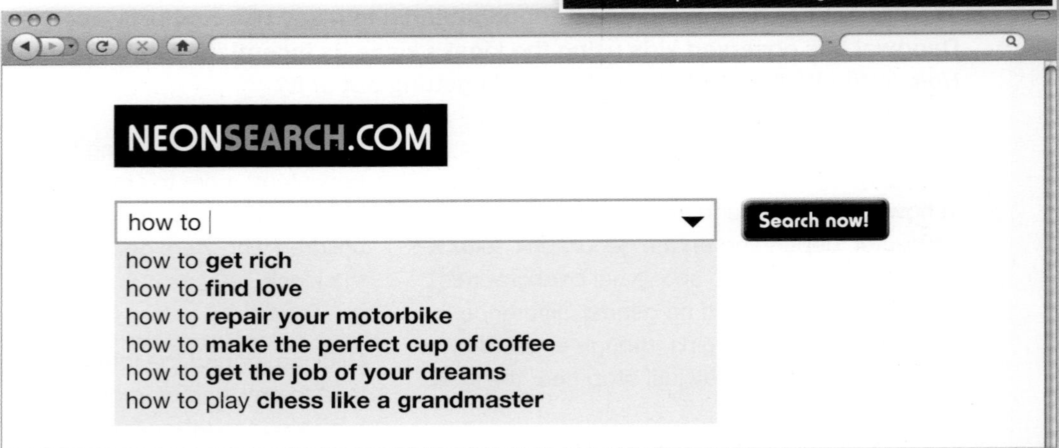
NEONSEARCH.COM
how to
Search now!
how to get rich
how to find love
how to repair your motorbike
how to make the perfect cup of coffee
how to get the job of your dreams
how to play chess like a grandmaster

TASK PREPARATION

1 a Demand Media is an online company which aims to answer the general public's most burning questions on their websites. What kind of questions do you think people might ask?

b Read the article on p137 and answer the questions.

c Compare what you found surprising in the article.

2 3.31 Listen to an interview with the CEO of Demand Media, Richard Rosenblatt.

1 What information does he add about his company and how it works?
2 How is it different from the way traditional content media worked?
3 What does he mean by "We added a science to the art of creating content"?
4 How would you describe his attitude?

3 a Look at these statements from the interview. Which words contribute to the strength of Rosenblatt's message and make him sound confident?

b Where you would place the emphasis in each statement? Try saying them out loud.

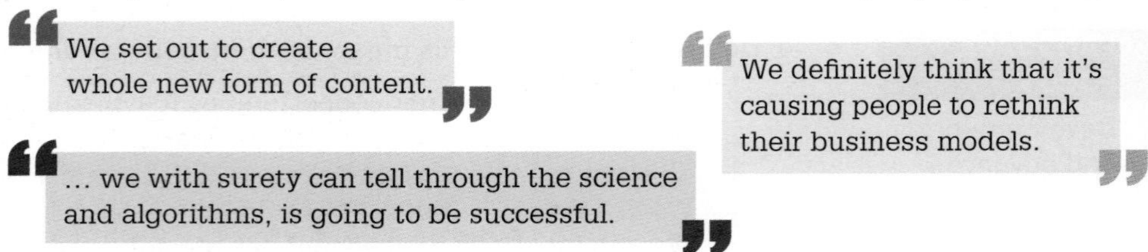
We set out to create a whole new form of content.
We definitely think that it's causing people to rethink their business models.
... we with surety can tell through the science and algorithms, is going to be successful.

c 3.32 Listen to check.

d Which sentences in 3a could these expressions be used in? How would the sentences need to change?

cutting-edge	there's no question	totally unique	innovative	to flourish
without any doubt	absolutely certain	ground-breaking	catch on	

TASK

4 a Work alone.

1 Think of an idea that you think is unique. Use these ideas or your own:
   - an idea for improving your town.
   - a way of solving a social or an environmental problem.
   - a business idea that would fill a gap in the market.
2 Prepare to explain your message in a clear, detailed way. Plan to deliver it in a positive light, so that you sound confident and have complete belief in it.
3 Anticipate any questions that you might be asked, and how to deal with them.

b Work in pairs.

1 Take turns to explain your message.
2 As your partner is speaking, think of difficult questions to 'test' or criticise that message. Find as many 'holes' in their argument as you can.

Across cultures Technology

1 a Look at the images. Discuss these questions.

1 What do you think they show?
2 Where were the photos taken?
3 Why have they been placed together?
4 What do they say about technology in the world today? Do you think it is a fair representation?

b Read the captions which accompany the images. Do they make you change your mind about your answers to 1a?

2 a 3.33 Listen to the introduction of a programme about technology in different parts of the world.

1 Do you agree with the presenter's interpretation of the two images?
2 What do you think the report will go on to say about mobile phone usage in the West and in the developing world?

b 3.34 Listen to the full report. Discuss these questions.

1 What perspective is the reporter speaking from? How do you know?
2 What does she see as the key difference between the USA's attitude towards technology and that found in many developing countries?
3 According to the reporter, why has the mobile phone opened "a new frontier of innovation"?
4 What uses can mobile phones have in:
- India?
- Kenya?
- Moldova?

5 What lesson does the reporter think developed countries can learn from the developing world?
6 What conclusion does the reporter leave us with?

3 Think about where you live. Discuss these questions.

1 What percentage of people do you think have:
- an Internet connection at home?
- a mobile phone or another, similar device?

2 What do people use their mobile phones for?
3 Do most people feel any pressure to own the most innovative new gadget on the market? Why / Why not?
4 Is it common to replace or upgrade technological devices? Why / Why not?

A

Hamar, Norway
Computer nerds of the world unite!
The world's largest convention of computer enthusiasts is called, simply, 'The Gathering'. Over 5,000 young people come together each spring, some travelling long distances, each carrying their own computer equipment to the massive Vikingship sports hall in the city of Hamar. Many hardly see daylight or taste fresh air for the entire five days as they compete with their fellow geeks for cash prizes and the honour of being the best computer programmer.

B

Accra, Ghana
Rubbish dump 2.0
Move to the recycle bin. It's an operation we perform every day on our computer desktops. But what happens when the virtual becomes real? Where do our computers go when they die? Increasingly this i-waste is finding its way to West African countries like Ghana. Their final resting place is the Agbogbloshie dump where they are broken apart, mostly by children, to salvage the copper, hard drives and other components that can be sold later on.

Keywords *sure, certain*

1 a Look at these sentences. Try replacing the highlighted words with certain or certainly. Does it change the meaning?

```
1  Be sure to write about something you enjoy.
2  Schools are surely right to encourage them.
```

b How could you replace the highlighted words with the words in the box? What other changes would you need to make to the sentence?

ensure doubt hesitation fundamental of course unquestionably make

2 a Sure can modify nouns. How do you think these sentences continue?

1 It was a sure sign that we hit the 'terrible twos' when my daughter ...
2 It is a sure bet that no classical music release this season offers ...
3 What was once a sure thing suddenly became much more competitive. Hong Kong now faces ...
4 Being English, she thought that a sure way of greeting her new friends ...
5 Ahead 7–6, 2–1, Mauresmo looked like a sure winner, but ...

b 3.35 Listen to check.

3 a Where could you add surely in these examples? How would it affect the meaning of each sentence?

1 They're just late. They wouldn't have forgotten, would they?
2 Their achievement in reaching the final must be viewed as a success, regardless of the outcome.
3 You're joking with me!
4 It's never happened before, though.
5 But that's not the point.

b Which sentences could be replies? What are they replies to?

c Do the sentences in 2a and 3a sound written or spoken? What does that say about how sure and surely are often used?

4 a How could you express these sentences in different ways? Use the words in the box to help you.

1 It's certainly going to be successful.
2 The Democrats will certainly win again.

bound certain chance chances undoubtedly shadow of a doubt foregone conclusion inevitable sure

The Democrats <u>are sure to</u> win again.
<u>Chances are</u>, the Democrats will win again.

b What do you think is happening or going to happen in each photo? Write sentences using expressions in 4a.

c Read out your sentences. Do other people agree with you?

A

B

C

D

EXPLOREWriting

Goals
- give written advice
- write steps in a process
- describe how to do something

1 a Read these two examples giving advice on writing an online article. Add imperatives to the gaps.

bear	get	write	be	try	choose	bore	use	learn	add

A

- [1]_______ your topic wisely. Be sure to write about something you enjoy as your enthusiasm will be evident in your writing. The topics that seem to be most profitable for me are related to finance, making money online, health, credit cards, and business.
- [2]_______ your audience in mind. If your article is intended for beginners, then you need to cater for them. Spelling things out might be annoying for those who already know the subject, but could prove invaluable for newcomers to the subject. If your article is for experts, then similarly, don't [3]_______ them with needless descriptions.
- [4]_______ the word out! Share your article with friends and family by emailing it to them, or simply ask them to go online and check it out where they can leave comments on what they think. Listen to their critiques and [5]_______ from them. They are only trying to help you.

B

- [1]_______ familiar with the topic, because you'll want to share what you know. People want to learn from the best, so you should be the best – or at least have enough experience to teach others. When coming up with the topic, think about your hobbies and interests – your best articles will come from there.
- [2]_______ content. Starting with the title, [3]_______ to use words that people will search for on the Internet. Those words will make it easier for people to find your article. Steps should be written in laymen's terms so that anyone can follow their direction to get to the result.
- Always [4]_______ the spell check! You are the expert and experts don't make mistakes, right? Articles should be well written and free of spelling, grammar and punctuation errors. Once you have checked it all, check it again!
- Most of all, [5]_______ something appealing! People can tell if you're writing about a subject that bores you. You don't have to be a comedian, but try to give your article a bit of flair. Remember, people enjoy reading something with a bit of personality to it.

b What is the difference between A and B? What do they have in common? Consider style, content and tone.

c Can you think of any other advice that would be useful on this subject?

2 What kinds of expressions are typically used for giving advice in the texts?

1	**imperatives and modals:**	*Try to ...; You should ...*
2	**linking words:**	*if ...; so that ...*

3 a Look at these examples from different articles. Complete the gaps with possible words or expressions.

1. Organise your desk. _______ working, throw away any unused papers, receipts, etc.
2. When _______ for clothes, always make sure you look at the label for natural fibres.
3. It _______ more than just writing down words on a piece of paper to create a song.
4. The _______ here is to use a strong deodorant, not a cheap supermarket kind.
5. Creating a cosy home will help you feel comfortable and warm, _______ can stay depressed for long when cuddling up..
6. _______ you find out what you're good at, stick with it!

b What 'how to' articles do you think the extracts are from?

4 Write your own 'How to ...' article.

1. Work in groups. Choose one of these topics or your own.

   How to ...
   - keep your car clean.
   - get rid of a ghost.
   - enjoy a party.
   - meet people like you.
   - keep your desk tidy.
   - read someone's palm.
   - appreciate abstract art.
   - behave well on the road.
   - visit a patient in hospital.
   - remember your dreams.
   - overcome a fear of spiders.
   - improve your handwriting.

2. Brainstorm ideas, then write the article together. Include between three and six steps.

5 Read out your advice to other class members. Decide on the best piece of advice.

Grammar

Participle clauses

1 a Look at these examples from the unit, and underline the participles. Which are present and which is a past participle?

```
1  When coming up with the topic, think about
   your hobbies and interests.
2  Starting with the title, try to use
   words that people will search for on the
   Internet.
3  If asked a factual question, they will
   usually click on a search engine without a
   second thought.
```

b Express the sentences without using a participle clause. What words do you have to add in each case? Which of these examples are more common in spoken or written English?

2 Look at this example. The underlined expression can be replaced by a participle clause.

```
Once you have checked it all, check it again!
```

Having checked it all, check it again!

If possible, change the underlined expressions in these sentences, using a present or past participle. Why is it not always possible?

1. When I put that to Moira Jones, she referred me to the story of the Egyptian god Thoth.
2. Using an Internet search engine, (once you have keyed the words in) takes a broadband user less than a second, and the process will only get quicker.
3. "I come here every day, that's why I am happy," says 9-year-old Shabanam as she plays with the educational games.
4. He told the driver "Stamford Bridge", the name of Chelsea's stadium, but he delivered him instead to the village of Stamford Bridge in Yorkshire.
5. When you shop for clothes, always make sure you look at the label for natural fibres.

3 a We often use participles after prepositions. Think of a context for the expressions below. What might come before and after them?

despite being injured	far from apologising
after resigning from the job	without being searched
without saying goodbye	on arriving at the airport
before opening the door	on hearing the news

b Work in pairs. Writing game.

1. Choose one of the expressions in 3a and expand it into one or two sentences, as if part of a story. Pass it to another pair.
2. Add one or two more sentences to continue the story, including another expression from 3a. Pass it to another pair.
3. Continue the story, adding another expression from 3a.
4. Read out your stories.

He left without saying goodbye ...

4 a Join these sentences using participle clauses. Then write a single paragraph from all four sentences.

1. I decided to take the experiment out to a village called Madantusi. I built another hole-in-the-wall there.
2. I left the computer there with lots of CDs. I returned three months later and found these two kids who were playing a game on the computer.
3. As soon as they saw me they said "we need a faster processor and a better mouse" in English!
4. So then I measured their performance, and I realised they were using 200 English words with each other. Words like *exit, stop, find, save*, that kind of thing, not to do with the computers but in their day-to-day conversations.

b Check on p138. What are the differences? Which version sounds more formal?

5 a We often use participle clauses in formal speeches, to sum up experiences, thoughts or feelings. Complete each sentence in a way that is true for you.

1. Having lived here for ______ years, I ...
2. When asked why ______, I usually ...
3. Having been ______ for ______, I ...
4. Thinking back over my life, I ...
5. Looking to the future, I think ...

b Compare sentences. Ask each other questions to find out more.

Grammar reference, p145

Vocabulary

Computer icons and collocations

6 **a Look at these icons, commonly used in computers and mobile phones.**

1 How many are familiar to you?
2 Can you guess what the others mean?
3 Which ones now look out of date? Why?

b Make collocations about computing.

a file a system the net the cursor an image a program

1 browse ______
2 open ______
3 control ______
4 run ______
5 download / upload ______
6 crash ______

c Discuss these questions.

1 In what other contexts can browse, surf and crash be used?
2 What do these words mean in relation to computers? What is their 'normal' meaning?
- mouse
- bug
- virus
- cookie
- bookmark
- spam
- desktop
- home

3 Do you know any technology-related brand names that have become everyday words? *google, photoshop ...*

knowledge and *information*

7 **a Which of these words can collocate with knowledge or information?**

new prior further / additional background relevant / useful common confidential general accurate

b Complete the gaps with a collocation from 7a.

1 Every child comes to school with different ______ because of what they've been exposed to in their lives.
2 It's ______ that late-onset diabetes is more common in overweight people.
3 This is not the time to subject me to some ______ quiz.
4 For ______ about Dr Takada and her book, go to her website at ...
5 In our world we learn by way of ______ rushing through our brain every day.
6 It's not clear if Mr Yu had any role in the leak of ______ to a Hong Kong couple accused of insider trading.
7 Labels should have ______ which will not scare consumers.
8 Authorities revealed that they had no ______ about the suspect's whereabouts.

c Discuss these questions.

1 How much information do you take in on a daily basis?
2 How would you describe it?
3 Where do you access it?
4 How much of it do you remember the next day?

Self-assessment

Can you do these things in English? Circle a number on each line. 1 = I can't do this, 5 = I can do this well.

talk about knowledge and technology	1	2	3	4	5
discuss how to access information	1	2	3	4	5
describe technological advances	1	2	3	4	5
talk about how things develop	1	2	3	4	5
explain an idea	1	2	3	4	5
deliver a positive message	1	2	3	4	5
give written advice	1	2	3	4	5
write steps in a process	1	2	3	4	5
describe how to do something	1	2	3	4	5

• For Wordcards, reference and saving your work → e-Portfolio
• For more practice → Self-study Pack, Unit 12

Activities

Unit 1, p8, Memory 1a

1 Work with a partner. Discuss questions 1–3. Who remembers most clearly?

2 Now discuss questions 4–10 about the pictures you looked at.

1 Think about your first school.
- What was it called?
- What street was it in?
- What was your first teacher's name?

2 Think about last Saturday.
- What time did you get up?
- What colour clothes did you wear?
- Did you go to a shop? If so, what did you buy? How much was it?

3 Think about the children on page 6. Which seven countries did they come from?

4 Think about the student.
- What is her name?
- When was the card valid?
- What is her card number?

5 What kind of hair has the student got?
6 What kind of university is Athabasca?
7 What images can you remember from the sign on the road?
8 What kind of trousers is the woman wearing?
9 What time of year is it? How do you know?
10 What colour is the pram? What about the wheels?

Unit 2, p20, Target activity 3 (Student A)

You are an employer.

1 Decide on the qualities and abilities you are looking for and how formal the interview should be. Prepare what to say and what questions to ask. Think about tone and register. Remember that you want to create a relaxed atmosphere, but have not met the candidates before.
2 Welcome the first candidate. Make him / her feel at ease and ask questions. Then repeat the interview with another candidate.
3 Decide who is the best candidate and why. Report back to the class.

Unit 3, p33, Explore speaking 1b

alien *adj* foreign; repugnant (to); from another world *n* foreigner; being from another world

Is unbelievable, I arriving London, 'Heathlow Airport'. Every single name very difficult remembering, because just not 'London Airport' simple way like we simple way call 'Beijing Airport'. Everything very confuse way here, passengers is separating in two queues.

Sign in front of queue say: ALIEN and NON ALIEN. I am alien, like Hollywood film *Alien*, I live in another planet, with funny looking and strange language.

I standing in most longly and slowly queue with all aliens waiting for visa checking. I feel little criminal but I doing nothing wrong so far. My English so bad. How to do?

In my text book I study back China, it says English peoples talk like this:
'How are you?'
'I am very well. How are you?'
'I am very well.'

Unit 4, p37, Maps of the world 3b (Student A)

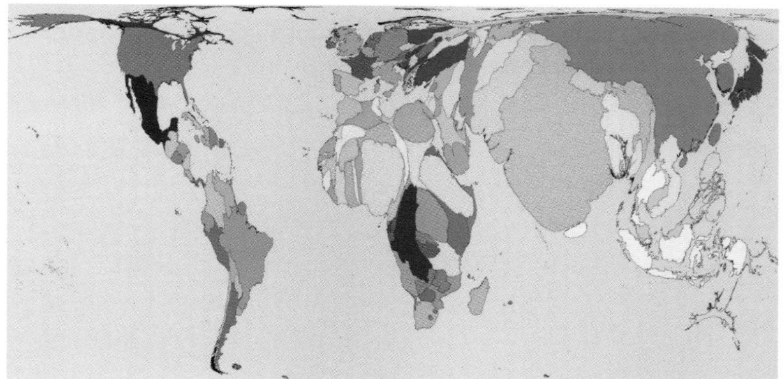

The world's population in the year 2050

"The choices that today's generation of young people aged 15–24 make about the size and spacing of their families are likely to determine whether Planet Earth will have 8, 9 or 11 billion people in the year 2050." (United Nations Population Fund, 2005)

By 2050, the Earth's population is due to reach 9.07 billion. 62% of people will be living in Africa, Southern Asia and Eastern Asia – numerically this is the same as if all the world's current population lived just in these regions. In addition, another 3,000,000,000 are set to spread across the rest of the world.

Unit 3, p30, Target activity 4a

Complete these sentences about your general situation.

1 I started learning English ...
2 I use English (when? where?) ...
3 I need English for ...
4 English is helpful when ...

Choose the best option about your current abilities in English.

1 I have no / little / some / plenty of opportunity to use English outside class.
2 I feel not at all / reasonably / very confident when speaking in public.
3 Improving my grammar is often / always / no longer an issue for me.
4 I feel I have a limited / extensive active vocabulary.
5 Of the four skills, writing / listening / reading / speaking remains my weak point.
6 I am only slightly / quite / highly motivated to improve my English level.
7 I've sensed a slight / some / a great deal of improvement recently.

Are these statements true for you? Rank them 1–10 (10 = very true / important).

- ☐ I need to socialise more with English speakers.
- ☐ I want to become familiar with different world 'Englishes'.
- ☐ English remains just another 'subject' that I study.
- ☐ I'd like to immerse myself in an English-speaking environment.
- ☐ Reading more in English is how I can best pick up new vocabulary.
- ☐ A knowledge of colloquial / informal expressions is what I need right now.
- ☐ I get a lot of benefit from classroom work.
- ☐ I still tend to translate from my mother tongue – I need to learn how to think in English.
- ☐ Learning another language may help me with my English.
- ☐ I have a set way of saying things – I need to vary that and move on.

Unit 6, p57, Fake photos 2 (Student A)

This nearly iconic portrait of US President Abraham Lincoln, taken around 1860, is a composite of Lincoln's head and the Southern politician John Calhoun's body, carried out with the aim of enhancing the President's stature. No 'heroic'-style photos of Lincoln had been taken by that point. This composite may have been created so as to address that. Putting the date of this image into context, note that the first permanent photographic image was created in 1826 and the Eastman Dry Plate Company (later to become Eastman Kodak) was created in 1881.

Unit 4, p39, Nutrition transition 4 (Student A)

You are the successful owner of a large farm and use modern methods of intensive farming. You think developments to food production are beneficial to everyone. Prepare some ideas to support your point of view. Think about:

- the transport of food.
- multinationals.
- GM foods.
- pesticides and artificial fertilisers.
- intensive farming.
- developing new crops and types of food.
- hygiene.
- processed and packaged food.

Talk about your ideas with Student B.

Unit 4, p43, Explore writing 4

Choose a photo. Write a caption of two or three sentences.

1. Imagine the place, its atmosphere and what would be worth saying about it.
2. Look at what you have written. Can you:
   - make your caption more economical and more vivid?
   - think of other adjectives, verbs or expressions which would better capture the atmosphere you want to describe?
3. Read out your finished captions to other students.

A

Cattle ranching, Montana, USA

B

Nanzen-ji Temple, Kyoto, Japan

C

Sunday in Käthe-Kollwitz Park, Berlin

D

Going to work, Hanoi, Vietnam

Unit 6, p58, Genuine fakes 2b

Maisons sur la Colline is a genuine Picasso, painted during his Cubist period in 1909.
It can be seen at the Museum of Modern Art, New York. *Cadaqués* is the fake, painted by John Myatt.

Unit 5, p48, Surveillance 3

But that, say the critics of CCTV, is the problem: the House of Lords constitutional committee recently noted that there was no regulatory framework for adequate protections against invasion of privacy by CCTV. No-one even knows how many cameras there are in Britain. The best guess is over four million. CCTV is reckoned to operate in around 500 British towns and cities, as against 50 in Italy, 11 in Austria, and one in Norway. Professor Clive Norris, head of the department of sociological studies at Sheffield University, thinks public funding explains much of the difference. During the 1990s, roughly 75% of the Home Office crime-prevention budget is said to have been spent on installing CCTV, even though no-one can be sure that it works: "The primary justification for CCTV is the reduction of crime. There has been a singular failure to produce evidence that it has achieved that."
Norris quotes case studies in Australia and the United States showing CCTV's paltry success in leading to prosecutions. Police hours spent going through the tapes must also be considered. It has also been shown that improving street lighting "is a rather more effective form of prevention". Meanwhile, the hunt for all the identified Manchester hooligans is still continuing, a year later.

1 Does the writer of the article think surveillance cameras have helped to reduce crime?
2 What do you think might be the reasons for this?

Unit 5, p50, Target activity 4a

Role play. Work in groups of four to find a solution for the square at Harras.

Student A
You work in the town council.
Your priority is that the traffic flow should not be blocked on the three access roads leading to the square. The square should be attractive to pedestrians, but also consider the needs of drivers, buses and cyclists. There is money available, but you should not agree to any solution which would involve unnecessary expense.

Student B
You are a landscape architect.
Your main contribution is to suggest creative ideas for using the space. You would like to create an attractive area that will be used by people, including children and old people.

Student C
You own a shop on the square.
Your main interest is in making it easier and safer for people to use the shops around the square, but you will agree to any solution that makes the square an attractive place for people to come to.

Student D
You live on the square.
You want the square to be a quieter, more pleasant place to live, and a place where it is safe for children to play. You will agree to any solution that gives priority to pedestrians and cyclists rather than cars.

Think about:
- the layout of the roads.
- traffic lights and pedestrian crossings.
- pavements and pedestrian areas.
- car parks, cycle paths and bus stops.
- making the square accessible to people.
- the appearance of the square (trees, flowers, paving stones, grass ...).
- other features (seats, water features, play areas, sculptures ...).

When you reach agreement, draw your solution on the plan and make notes for a presentation. Include:
- an analysis of the main problems.
- how you propose to solve them.
- the advantages of your solution.

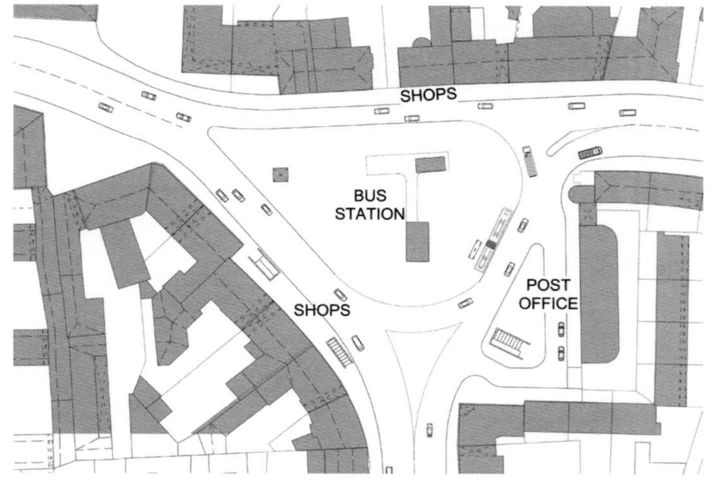

Unit 4, p38, What the world eats 3a (Group A)

1 What are the main things the Casales family seem to eat and drink?
2 How much of their food is:
- fresh?
- processed?
- packaged?

3 Do you think they have a healthy diet?
4 What seems to be their main source of:
- vitamins?
- carbohydrates?
- protein?

Mexico: the Casales family of Cuernavaca
Food expenditure for one week: $189.09

Unit 6, p59, Genuine fakes 5 (Student A)

You are an art dealer.
You want to sell B this painting. Although you know it's a fake (painted by John Myatt), try to convince B that it's genuine, and be prepared to bluff. Tell B that:
- it's typical of Anton Mauve's early style. He often painted people on horseback by the sea during this period.
- you have documents stating that it was painted in 1851 when Anton Mauve was living on the Dutch coast.

Morning ride on the beach (Anton Mauve 1838–1888)

Unit 6, p64, Look again 4b

1 He lay on the beach, gazing up at the Milky Way and listening to the distant sounds of music floating across the water.
2 She cantered along the path, the wind streaming through her hair and the mud flying up from under the horse's hooves.
3 He was sitting on a park bench, looking nervously up and down the path. From time to time, he would glance anxiously at his watch.
4 He paused, his fingers drumming on the desk as he considered how best to break the news.
5 She stood by the window, watching as two men in their late 20s got out of the car and walked towards the house.

Unit 7, p70, Target activity 2

Malaria is a serious disease which can affect anyone. It is an infection spread by mosquito bites. Symptoms include fever, headache, muscle ache and fatigue. These problems can appear at any time between one and fourteen days after being bitten. If not treated, malaria can become fatal.

An estimated 300–500 million cases of malaria occur every year, with more than one million fatalities. It is a risk for nearly half the world's population, and provides a constant challenge for almost 100 governments.

Malaria is one of the most severe health problems worldwide, especially in developing countries. Most victims are young African children. Every minute, two African children die of the disease.

Treatment is available. So are methods of prevention. Mosquito repellent and mosquito nets are often enough to prevent the one, small bite which would transmit the disease. It is necessary to spread knowledge and resources to those regions most in need.

But those regions are increasing. Malaria causes a negative cycle. People without access to preventative resources or health care are among those most at risk. The spread of malaria to countries with fragile governments and social services reduces those countries' economic growth. This leads to more widespread poverty, and thus increases the number of vulnerable people.

Unit 9, p86, Apples 5

Explain the relationship with apples in each image.

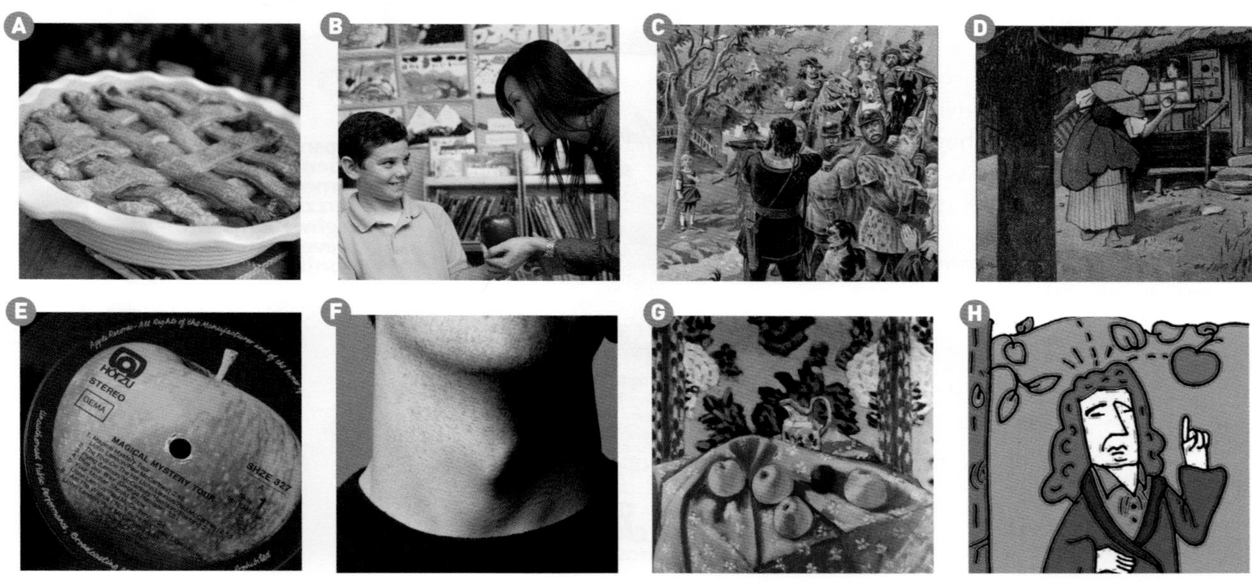

Unit 9, p90, Target activity 5 (Group A)

1 Choose the images you think are most suitable as icons for our time. Then agree on an icon to add in the empty space.
2 Think of arguments to defend your choice.
3 Look at Group B's images on p137. Think of arguments *against* them being chosen as icons for our time.

A

GM food

B

David Beckham

C

the iPhone

D

Deepwater Horizon oil spill

E

Unit 8, p77, Brand images 3b

1 **Work in A/B/C groups. Group A, look at adverts 1 and 2. Group B, look at adverts 3 and 4. Group C, look at adverts 5 and 6.**

1. What effect do the adverts suggest the drink has on people?
2. What qualities do you think they promote? What do the people represent?
3. How old do you think the adverts are? How do you know?

2 **Work with students from the other groups. Look at all the adverts together.**

1. Put the adverts in chronological order. What helped you decide? Which advert is clearly linked to a particular time?
2. Match these qualities to the adverts.

energy victory friendship popularity taste health youth refreshment attractiveness modernity

3. Which advert is associated with a particular:
   moment or feeling?
   pleasure or leisure activity?
   country?
   form of wordplay?
4. How are women presented in adverts 4 and 5? What does this say about how the presentation of women in advertising has changed?
5. Which advert do you think is most effective? Why?
6. One of these adverts became very well-known. Can you guess which one and why?

1

2

3

4

5

6

Unit 8, p80, Target activity 4a (Student A)

The AIRpod is powered by compressed air, which is stored at high pressure in shatter-proof thermoplastic tanks surrounded by a carbon-fibre shell (the same tanks used to contain the fuel in gas-powered buses). The air is released through pistons in the engine, which drive the wheels.

Unlike conventional internal combustion engines, air-powered engines run very cold and thick ice quickly forms on the engine. This means that the engine can be used to cool the inside of the car, but not to heat it.

Each car has an onboard pump that can refill the tank overnight. But Negré has also developed a high-pressure air pump – like a version of the tyre pumps found on a garage forecourt – that can fill the tanks in less than a minute. These could be powered by clean electricity – hydro, wind or solar – making the air car completely pollution-free. Even if carbon-generated electricity is used, CO_2 emissions are still only 10% of a petrol engine's.

The car has a range of more than 112 miles, and it takes less than two minutes to refill the 210-litre air tank. It can reach speeds of just less than 45mph, although the air-powered engine produces only 8 horsepower, so acceleration is slow.

Unit 10, p100, Target activity 1b

1

This annual, international event brings together homeless people for a once-in-a-lifetime chance to represent their country in the name of football! Grass-roots football projects have been kicked off in more than 60 countries, working with 25,000 homeless and excluded people around the year.

2

In cities around France, homeless people and middle-class home owners come together in this open-air event, raising public awareness of the fragility of the housing market, and growing homelessness.

Unit 11, p107, Artificial trees 1

Read the proposal and answer the questions.

Professor Klaus Lackner has invented an ingenious way of counteracting CO_2 emissions, which he believes could solve global warming. His invention is an artificial tree. It's made of metal but works in the same way as a real tree by extracting CO_2 from the air as it flows over its 'leaves'. Large quantities of CO_2 could be removed from the atmosphere, and could be stored deep beneath the earth's surface in a solid form which would be stable and safe.

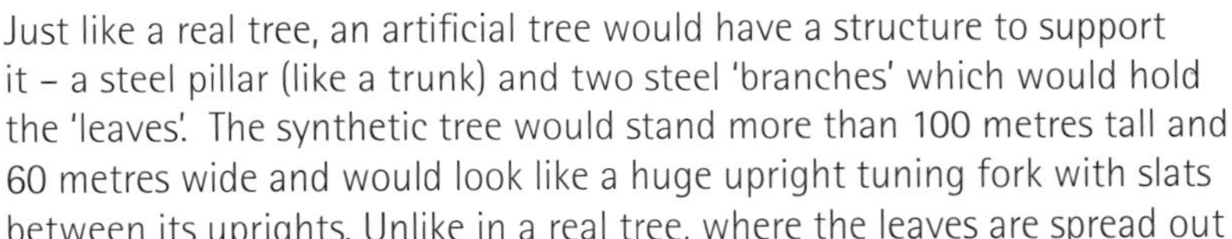

Just like a real tree, an artificial tree would have a structure to support it – a steel pillar (like a trunk) and two steel 'branches' which would hold the 'leaves'. The synthetic tree would stand more than 100 metres tall and 60 metres wide and would look like a huge upright tuning fork with slats between its uprights. Unlike in a real tree, where the leaves are spread out as much as possible because they need to catch sunlight, the leaves on an artificial tree could be packed much more closely together and be parallel with each other, like a Venetian blind. So an artificial tree could extract far more CO_2 than a natural tree; and of course, unlike a real tree, they could be 'planted' anywhere, even at the North Pole or in the Sahara Desert.

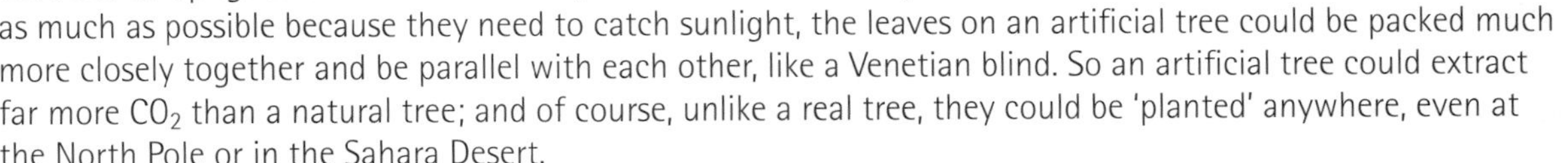

The apparatus would work by using a series of simple chemical reactions. The slats would be coated in liquid sodium hydroxide, so as the air passed over them the CO_2 would be extracted and converted into sodium carbonate. A series of further chemical reactions would extract the carbon from the sodium carbonate and turn it into a concentrated, solid form of CO_2 that could be buried deep underground.

It would be quite feasible to produce thousands of artificial trees and put them in any available space. Each tree would collect 90,000 tonnes of CO_2 a year from the atmosphere – as much as is produced by 20,000 cars.

1 In what ways are the 'trees' like real trees? In what ways are they different?
2 How do they absorb CO_2?
3 What happens to the CO_2 after it has been extracted?

Unit 11, p109, 2084 1a

Article | Discussion | Log in/create account

In Ancient Greek mythology, Phaethon was the son of Helios, the sun god. His father allowed him to drive the sun chariot for a day, but Phaethon couldn't control it and the chariot fell out of the sky and threatened to burn up the Earth. To prevent disaster, Zeus killed Phaethon with a thunderbolt.

The story was retold by the Roman poet Ovid, who referred to Phaethon in Latin as 'infelix Phaethon' (= unfortunate Phaethon).

Unit 11, p110, Target activity 3b (Group A)

Lovelock's prophecy

At nearly 90 years old, James Lovelock has arrived at a worrying conclusion: we are doomed. Like tourists enjoying a boat ride at the top of Niagara Falls, we have no idea that the engines are about to break down. Lovelock believes drought and other extreme weather will become normal by 2020. By 2040, Europe will be a desert, and Paris will be as hot as Cairo. Beijing, Miami and London will suffer drought, rising seas, or floods. Millions will go north looking for food and water. By 2100, he believes, more than 6 billion people will have died. The survivors will mostly be in Canada, Scandinavia and the Arctic.

Here, simplified, is how Lovelock views this doomsday scenario. Increasing temperatures melt the ice at the poles. This means more water. This increases the temperature (ice reflects sunlight but open land and water absorb it), and more ice melts. Methane (a more powerful greenhouse gas than CO_2) is released from the previously frozen areas of the north. The seas rise. There will be intense rainfall in some places, drought in others. The rainforests will collapse. And so on …

This nightmare vision of a 'tipping point' has been rejected by many climate researchers. However, Lovelock stands by his opinions. Let's assume he's right. What can we do?

Well, not much. We've already passed the moment, he believes, where cutting greenhouse gas emissions would help us. What about using biofuels, renewable energies? It won't make a difference. Sustainable development, he says, is entirely the wrong approach. At this point, we should be concentrating on a sustainable retreat.

1 What does Lovelock think will happen to: most major cities? people in tropical countries? people in northern countries?
2 Why does he think this will happen?
3 What does he think we should and should not do?
4 Mark any points you agree and disagree with.

Unit 12, p117, The end of general knowledge? 3d

Fools will always be here. And their foolishness will always make the news headlines. But on the other hand, there will always be teachers and parents who see the real value in possessing and sharing knowledge. The Internet, however, changes everything. We can't help but use it to check what's happening (or has happened) in the world.

Schools are probably right to encourage young people to use the Internet to find out about the world. It may be right that such a tool will just help us to forget more and more. But at the same time, the continuing popularity of quizzes and game-shows shows us that general knowledge – shared knowledge among a mass of people all part of the same culture and time – is strong enough to remain.

Unit 2, p20, Target activity 3 (Student B)

You are a candidate.

1 Think of skills and abilities which might be suitable for the job. Remember to present yourself in a positive light: how can you appear confident, but not arrogant? How will you sell yourself? What will you ask the employer? Use strategies from p20.
2 Introduce yourself appropriately. Describe your skills and abilities in line with what the interviewer asks. Then move to another interview.
3 Listen to the evaluation. Do you think it is fair? What comments do you have about the employers and the interviews?

Unit 4, p39, Nutrition transition 4 (Student B)

You work for an environmental organisation.
You think developments to food production have mainly had a negative effect on the environment and on people's diet. Prepare some ideas to support your point of view.
Think about:
- the transport of food.
- multinationals.
- GM foods.
- pesticides and artificial fertilisers.
- intensive farming.
- developing new crops and types of food.
- hygiene.
- processed and packaged food.

Talk about your ideas with Student A.

Unit 12, p119, The Hole in the Wall 3c

1 Have you observed any differences between urban and rural areas in how children interact with the Hole in the Wall kiosks?
2 Are there elements of the Hole in the Wall project that make it uniquely Indian? Do you see a Hole in the Wall program catching on in other countries?
3 Have you seen any differences in problem-solving behaviors and academic achievement between the kids who regularly use the Hole in the Wall computer kiosks and the kids who don't?
4 Some argue that just letting kids click around the Internet will not improve their performance in educational domains like reading and science. What do you say to that?
5 What has surprised you the most over these past few years as you've observed how children use the Hole in the Wall computer kiosks?

Unit 8, p80, Target activity 4a (Student B)

The AIRpod is small, holding just three passengers, with a single seat facing forwards for the driver and a bench facing backward for two more people. The car is designed to be exceptionally light, weighing in at 220kg.

Because the air tank and engine don't take up much room, most of the car is devoted to passenger space. The car is a three-wheeler, and the driver uses a joystick to turn, rather than a conventional steering wheel.

In spite of its flimsy appearance, the car is actually very safe, as it has airbags outside the car which inflate when a crash is imminent. The Pod itself is made of strong composite materials that make a safe cell protecting the passengers.

The technology of air-powered engines is relatively cheap and simple, so the car would probably cost about £3,500.

Although air power means the car drives emission-free, some energy is required to compress air into its tank. But the cost of a tank refill would probably only be about £1!

Unit 6, p57, Fake photos 2 (Student B)

Great white shark attack!

Two completely different photos have been joined together to give the impression of a shark attack in front of San Francisco's famous landmark, the Golden Gate Bridge.

This fake photo was circulated by email in 2001, accompanied by a message saying that it had won "*National Geographic* Photo of the Year". It was not clear whether the email was hoping to convince people that the photo was real, or whether it was intended as a joke.

The original image of the shark was actually taken by a contributor to National Geographic – it was presumably chosen so that the claim would seem more genuine.

Unit 4, p37, Maps of the world 3b (Student B)

Prepare to tell Student A about your map.

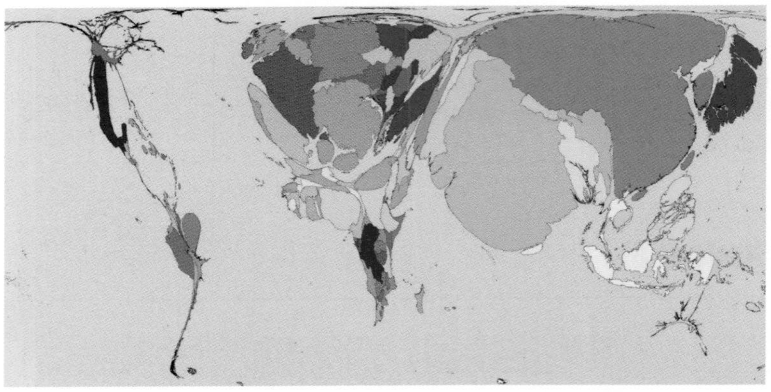

The world's wealth in the year 1500

"Slaves captured in raids and war grew in importance as a commodity. Kola nuts were also important, as were the dyestuffs of northern Nigeria. All these goods were highly prized in and around the Mediterranean basin." (Richard Effland, 2003)

In the year 1500, European territories were some of the wealthiest on earth, when measured by GDP per person. The regions with the largest total GDPs were Eastern Asia and Southern Asia. These were also the most populous regions at that time. The regions with the lowest GDP in 1500 were central and south-east Africa. These regions also had the lowest GDP per person.

Unit 4, p38, What the world eats 3a (Group B)

1 What are the main things the Batsuuri family seem to eat and drink?
2 How much of their food is:
   - processed?
   - packaged?
   - fresh?
3 Do you think they have a healthy diet?
4 What seems to be their main source of:
   - vitamins?
   - carbohydrates?
   - protein?

Mongolia: the Batsuuri family of Ulaanbaatar
Food expenditure for one week: $40.02

Unit 12, p120, Target activity 1b

If **Christian Muñoz-Donoso is going** to make this job pay, he's got to move quickly. He has a list of 10 videos to shoot on this warm June morning, for which he'll earn just $200. To get anything close to his usual rate, he'll have to do it all in two hours. Today's topic is kayaking. Muñoz-Donoso has enlisted a local instructor to meet him and to bring along four of his boats. Muñoz-Donoso gets most of his shots in one take. But conditions are working against him. Shifting winds and changing light require him to adjust his setup. Even so, within a few hours, he has uploaded his work to Demand Media, his employer for the day. It isn't Scorsese, but it's fast, cheap, and good enough.

Thousands of other filmmakers and writers around the country are operating with the same loose standards, racing to produce the 4,000 videos and articles that Demand Media publishes every day. The company's ambitions are so enormous as to be almost surreal: to predict any question anyone might ask and generate an answer that will show up at the top of Google's search results. To get there, Demand is using an army of Muñoz-Donosos to crank out articles and videos. They shoot slapdash instructional videos with titles like 'How to draw a Greek helmet' and 'How to stop snoring'. They pump out an endless stream of bulleted lists and tutorials about the most esoteric of subjects.

Plenty of other companies have tried to corner the market in online advice. But none has gone about it as aggressively, scientifically, and single-mindedly as Demand. Pieces are not dreamed up by trained editors nor commissioned based on submitted questions. Instead they are assigned by an algorithm, which mines nearly a terabyte of search data, Internet traffic patterns, and keyword rates to determine what users want to know and how much advertisers will pay to appear next to the answers.

The process is automatic, random, and endless. It is a database of human needs, and if you haven't stumbled on a Demand video or article yet on sites like ehow or livestrong, you soon will. By next summer, according to founder and CEO Richard Rosenblatt, Demand will be publishing a million items a month, the equivalent of four English-language Wikipedias a year.

In an era overwhelmed by FlickrYouTubeWikipediaBloggerFacebookTwitter-borne logorrhea, it's hard to argue that the world needs another massive online content company. But what Demand has realized is that the Internet gets only half of the simplest economic formula right: It has the supply part down but ignores demand. Give a million monkeys a million WordPress accounts and you still might never get a seven-point tutorial on how to keep wasps away from a swimming pool. Yet, that's what people want to know.

1 Are these sentences true or false?
   a Christian Muñoz-Donoso works for Demand Media.
   b There are thousands of people doing similar work.
   c They all work to a high professional standard.
   d Demand Media finds out what people want to know by tracking Internet search data.
   e Demand Media employs highly trained staff to interpret the data.
   f Demand Media are successful because they can find out what people really want to know.
2 What does the writer think of Demand Media's approach? What adjectives reveal his attitude?
3 How does the writer provide human interest and humour in this story? What do you think is his opinion of the general public and their interests?

Unit 9, p90, Target activity 5 (Group B)

1 Choose the images you think are most suitable as icons for our time. Then agree on an icon to add in the empty box.
2 Think of arguments to defend your choice.
3 Look at Group A's images on p131. Think of arguments *against* them being chosen as icons for our time.

A

graffiti

B

stock market crashes

C

Nelson Mandela

D

Burj Al Arab hotel, Dubai

E

Unit 5, p50, Target activity 4c

Unit 6, p59, Genuine fakes 5 (Student B)

You are an art collector.
You have seen this painting and you want to buy it, but you're not convinced it's genuine. Other Anton Mauve paintings you know have similar themes, but they are darker and the figures aren't so sharply defined. You have seen no information about where or when it was painted.
Decide:

- how much you are prepared to pay for it.
- what questions you will ask A.

Morning ride on the beach (Anton Mauve 1838–1888)

Unit 12, p124, Look again 4b

Having decided to take the experiment out to a village called Madantusi, I built another hole-in-the-wall. I left the computer there with lots of CDs, returning three months later to find two kids playing a game on the computer. On seeing me they said "we need a faster processor and a better mouse" in English! So then I measured their performance, realising that they were using 200 English words with each other like *exit*, *stop*, *find*, *save*, not to do with the computers but in their day-to-day conversations.

Unit 11, p110, Target activity 3b (Student B)

It's six minutes to midnight …

The *Bulletin of the Atomic Scientists* has been updating its 'Doomsday Clock' since 1947. The clock conveys how close we are to destruction (or midnight) and identifies the ways that humans could obliterate themselves. One of the main reasons since the late 1940s has been a possible nuclear war. However, climate change and new life-science technologies have become important new factors.

The clock was re-adjusted on 14 January 2010, moving from five minutes to midnight to six minutes to midnight. The reasons for this? World leaders are showing a stronger commitment to reducing their arsenals of nuclear weapons and other nations' means to make them. Also, developed and developing countries alike are making promises to limit the climate-changing gas emissions that would make our planet uninhabitable. According to the *Bulletin*, there are positive signs that tackling the two greatest threats to civilisation – nuclear war and climate change – are at last receiving worldwide political attention.

1 Where is the clock and what is its purpose?
2 What areas of risk affect the time shown on the clock?
3 According to the *Bulletin of the Atomic Scientists*, what reasons do people have to be optimistic?
4 Mark any points you agree and disagree with.

Unit 12, p118, The hole in the wall 1c

Grammar reference

1 *will* and *would*

will and *would* for habitual action

We often use *will* and *would* for a habitual (or repeated) action in the present or past:

Present (equivalent to present simple):
People will usually keep to the same brand unless they have a good reason to change.

Past (equivalent to past simple or *used to*):
As a student, I would often work through the night and then sleep in the afternoon.

Other uses of *will*

1 to make predictions:
From tomorrow morning, flights will operate normally.
When acid is added, the impurities in the liquid will gradually dissolve.

2 to make decisions, offers, promises and threats:
Don't worry, I'll talk to him.
I'll carry that.

3 to make requests or give orders:
Will you please stop talking?

4 to make deductions:
That will be the postman now. (= I'm sure it is)

Other uses of *would*

1 past of *will*, in reported speech or thought:
I told you they wouldn't agree.
He knew that only one person would get the job.

2 to mean *wanted to* or *was willing to*:
They would always keep an eye on our flat while we were away.
Sorry I'm late. The car wouldn't start.

3 conditional *would*, for hypothetical ('unreal') situations:
I didn't know you were in town, or I would have called you.
I like the job, but it would be nice to have a bit more free time.

4 to make requests:
Would you help me with these bags?

5 to 'soften' assertions and suggestions:
I'd suggest getting a new printer. (less direct than 'I suggest')
I would think she's probably in her mid 40s. (more cautious than 'I think')

2 Verb tenses in narration

When relating events in the past, we often use these verb tenses:

Past simple

To relate the *main events* of a story:
In 1990 we moved to London and I got a job in an engineering company.

Past progressive: *was + -ing*

To give the *background* to events (what was going on at the time):
At that time I was living in London and working in an engineering company. One day ...

If we use 'state' verbs (e.g. *know, be, have*), they will be in the simple form:
It was the weekend and I had a free afternoon, so I decided to ...
(not *I was having a free afternoon*)

Past perfect simple: *had* + past participle

To go back from the past and relate events that happened earlier:
It was already 8.30 and I was still 10 kilometres from the airport. I'd left the house in good time, but the traffic out of town had been very slow.

Past perfect progressive: *had been + -ing*

To go *back* from the past and describe *earlier activities*:
I felt very relieved when we finally found a flat. We'd been looking for months, but there hadn't been anything suitable.

would / was going to ('future in the past')

To express a future idea which is set in the past:
When she joined Sony, she was 22 and had only a year's experience. It would be (was going to be) an enormous challenge for her.

We often use the above tenses in:

1 reported speech and thought:
They were lucky to find a flat. He told me they'd been looking for months.
She knew that it would be an enormous challenge.

2 relative clauses:
I rented the flat to a young couple who had been looking for somewhere to live for months.

3 Adverbs

We can use adverbs to modify:

1 a verb:
She sang beautifully.
I enjoyed the performance immensely.

2 an adjective:
He seems reasonably happy with his progress.
It's extremely difficult to follow what he's saying.

3 a noun or prepositional phrase:
It's really a form of baseball.
The car was completely out of control.

4 another adverb:
We've read your proposal extremely carefully.

Common adverb / adjective collocations

highly	competitive effective intelligent unlikely significant questionable
perfectly	acceptable clear normal
fully	aware (of) booked informed (of)
deeply	disturbed shocked moved

Common adverb / verb collocations
deeply / profoundly regret
vividly / clearly remember
strongly support
highly / strongly recommend
thoroughly enjoy
entirely / totally agree
fully recognise
strongly / firmly believe

Short responses

We often use adverbs as single-word responses in conversation:
A *I think she did the right thing, don't you?*
B *Absolutely.*

A *Are the classes worth going to?*
B *Oh yes, definitely.*

Adverbs that can be used in this way:

absolutely	*definitely*	*precisely*	*probably*
completely	*certainly*	*exactly*	*possibly*
totally	*not really*	*hardly*	

4 Talking about change

Time comparison structures
Most people eat more meat than they used to.
Problems associated with obesity are more widespread than they were a generation ago.
Fifty years ago, most people in Europe had a much more restricted diet than they do today.

In comparison structures, auxiliaries are usually repeated (*are ... than they were*). Main verbs are omitted or replaced by a form of *do* (*eat ... than they used to*; *had ... than they do*).

***get / become* + adjective**
The differences between rich and poor have got bigger over the last few decades.
Access to information has become more freely available to everyone.

Other verbs

increase	*decrease*	*improve*
evolve	*develop*	*rise*
collapse	*improve*	*decline*
deteriorate	*fall*	*spread*

Other expressions
undergo a (rapid, gradual) transformation
make a (rapid) transition
undergo a (complete) revolution
go into (gradual, rapid, terminal) decline
show a (marked, noticeable) improvement

Cause / effect expressions

A causes B give rise to lead to result in trigger bring about
B is caused by A result from be a (direct) consequence of stem from have its origin(s) in originate from
A influences B have an effect on have an influence on have an impact on affect have consequences for

5 Passive reporting verbs

Passive structures are often used in reporting what people say or believe, especially in news reports or in academic writing. This enables the writer to distance him/herself from the facts or opinions being reported. Compare:

Informal, less 'distanced'
Many people think that the expression 'OK' is of French origin.

More formal and 'distanced'
It is thought that the expression 'OK' is of French origin.

There are two ways of using passive reporting verbs:

1 *It* + passive verb + *that* ...
It is generally believed that pasta originated in China.
It has been shown that better street lighting reduces crime.
It is reported that the number of teachers retiring early has risen dramatically.

2 Passive verb + *to* + infinitive
Pasta is generally believed to have originated in China.
Better street lighting has been shown to reduce crime.
The number of teachers retiring early is reported to have risen dramatically.

Infinitives after passive reporting verbs

Passive reporting verbs can be followed by:

1 the simple infinitive:
Better street lighting has been shown to reduce crime.
(= it reduces crime)

2 the continuous infinitive:
They are supposed to be living in the Bahamas.
(= they are living)

3 the past simple infinitive:
More than 50 people are reported to have been killed in the blaze.
(= they were killed)

4 the past progressive infinitive:
They are believed to have been conducting informal negotiations.
(= they have been conducting)

Common passive reporting verbs

say	calculate	think
consider	suppose	reckon
acknowledge	show	estimate
understand	report	feel
believe	know	presume

6 Present perfect

Present perfect simple

To refer to events in a period 'up to now':
The country has experienced three major earthquakes this year. (= so far)
You may have to help me. This is the first time I've used this software. (= in my life up to now)

The present perfect simple is often used for announcing news, where the focus is on *the fact* that something has happened, not on *when* it happened. The event is connected with the present (we can see the result now).
There has been a serious train crash on the main London to Glasgow line. (The line is still out of action)
I've bought some strawberries. (Here they are)

Present perfect progressive

To refer to activities or feelings that started in the past and are still going on:
I've been trying to contact her for days, but I don't know where she is. (= I'm still trying).
I've been meaning to email you, but I never seem to find the time. (= I still intend to write)

We also use it to refer to activities that have been continuing up to now, but have now stopped.
Where have you been? I've been trying to contact you for days. (= now I've succeeded in contacting you)
Look – it's been raining. (= now it has stopped, but the ground is wet)

'State' verbs

Some verbs are not normally used in the progressive form. These include:

- verbs describing mental states and feelings: *think, believe, know; love, respect, admire; need, want*
- verbs describing permanent qualities and states: *consist, contain, include, involve, be, have (= possess), own.*

With these verbs, we use the present perfect simple instead of the progressive:
Fashion photography has always involved manipulating images.
We've had this sofa for years.

Some verbs can be used in the simple or progressive with no difference in meaning:
They've lived / They've been living in London ever since the war.

7 Referencing and substitution

Substituting nouns

To avoid repeating a countable noun, we can use *one* (singular) or *some / any* (plural):
Notepads are really useful. You should get one. (= a notepad)
We need to buy some more paperclips. We haven't got any.

To avoid repeating an uncountable noun, we can use *some / any*:
A *Do you want coffee?*
B *Yes, I'd love some.*

After an adjective, we can use *one* (singular) or *ones* (plural) to replace the noun:
I don't need a window envelope. An ordinary one will be fine.
They replaced their beautiful old wooden windows with cheap metal ones.

We can also use other pronouns to avoid repeating a noun:
I spend time in London and New York.
I like them both in different ways.
I've heard Shanghai is an exciting city, but I've never been there.

Substituting verbs

To avoid repeating a main verb, we can use a form of the auxiliary *do*:
Malaria doesn't kill as many people as it once did.
He still smokes, but not as much as he did a year ago.
A *Who wants tea?*
B *I do.*

We usually repeat auxiliary verbs, or (if the meaning is clear) we can omit them:
Malaria isn't as dangerous as it once was.
Fortunately, the accident wasn't nearly as serious as it could have been.
She's more fluent in Russian than (she is) in English.

Referring to earlier ideas

To refer back to an earlier idea, we can use *this* or *which*:
They used detergent to try to disperse the oil slick. This caused further damage to the marine ecosystem.
They used detergent to try to disperse the oil slick, which caused further damage to the marine ecosystem.
(*this / which* = the fact that they used detergent)

8 *whatever*

We can add *-ever* to pronouns to make the following words:
whatever
whenever
wherever
whoever
however

They are used in various ways.

1 = it doesn't matter, regardless
Whenever you want to arrive, let us know and we'll meet you at the station.
Whatever people may say about her, I think she's an excellent leader.
We'll get the job done, however long it takes.

2 = I don't mind, you're free to choose
You can sit wherever you like. (= anywhere)
There's no dress code – just wear whatever you want. (= anything)

3 to give emphasis to a question.
Wherever did you get that tie? It's awful!
Whatever did you say that for? (= What on earth ...?)

Whatever can also be followed by a noun phrase:
Whatever the time, feel free to call me. (= Whatever time it is ...)
Whatever the reason, he's not speaking to me.

In conversation, *whatever* can also be used on its own, to mean 'I don't care' or 'It doesn't matter':
A *Shall we take them flowers or chocolates?*
B *Whatever. (= whatever you like)*

Whenever can also be used to mean 'every time':
We go walking in the mountains whenever we get the chance.

However is also used to express contrast (= *but*):
Schumacher started the race well ahead. However, engine failure forced him to drop out in the third lap.

9 Modifying a sentence

We can use adverbs and expressions to modify a complete sentence. They can come at the beginning or the end of the sentence, or as a parenthesis within the sentence (usually with a comma before and after).
She didn't get into Oxford, unfortunately.
Naturally, we're very disappointed with the result.
We are, of course, delighted to hear that the family are safe and well.

Signalling attitude

Sentence adverbs and expressions are often used to comment on the sentence or signal the speaker's attitude.

1 = it's understood:
naturally, of course, obviously

2 positive comment:
fortunately, luckily, I'm glad to say

3 negative comment:
unfortunately, sadly, I'm sorry to say

4 expressing surprise:
surprisingly, astonishingly, incredibly, amazingly, oddly, strangely (enough)

5 expressing time or duration:
suddenly, gradually, eventually, in the end

6 expressing contrast:
however, nevertheless, all the same

Softening

They can be used to 'soften' what we are saying or make it less definite.
maybe
presumably
I think
probably
perhaps
sort of
possibly
in a way
to some extent

Adding emphasis

They can be used to reinforce or add emphasis to what we are saying.
really
definitely
actually
indeed
clearly
in fact
certainly
literally
as a matter of fact

10 Inversion

Adverbial phrases

Certain adverbial phrases can be moved to the beginning of a sentence to give special emphasis. After these phrases, the subject and verb change position ('inversion').

Compare:
He not only evaded tax, but he then lied about it.
Not only did he evade tax, but he then lied about it.
I didn't realise my wallet was missing until I got home.
Not until I got home did I realise that my wallet was missing.

The following adverbial phrases can be used in this way:
not only
only rarely
at no time
very rarely
in no way
only recently
not once
not until (now)

These phrases can be used with different tenses:
Not once did they get in touch to ask how I was.
At no time have I claimed money from the company for personal expenses.
Only very rarely was I consulted about managerial decisions.

The main sentence stress shifts onto the adverb phrase:
Not only did he evade tax, but he then lied about it.
Not once did they get in touch to ask how I was.
Only very rarely was I consulted about managerial decisions.

The expression *no way* is common in conversation, meaning 'in no way' or 'not at all'. It is followed by inversion:
No way would I want to do a job like that. (= *I certainly wouldn't want to do it*)

We also use inversion after time expressions: *no sooner, hardly, scarcely.* These are usually followed by the past perfect.
No sooner had we taken off than the plane started shaking.
Hardly had I started reading when Jane came in and started telling me about her homework.

11 Cleft sentences

To give emphasis to one part of a sentence, we can divide it into two clauses. This is called a 'cleft' sentence.

Cleft sentences with *What ...*

Compare:
We need a new car.
→ *What we need is a new car.*
I'd really like to give up my job.
→ *What I'd really like to do is give up my job.*

Starting with a clause with *What* ... gives added emphasis to the second part of the sentence (*a new car, give up my job*)

We can also begin the sentence with a general expression referring to time, place, reason, etc.:
the thing
the time
the person / people
the place
the way
the reason

What / The thing I need now is some money.
The time I like best is just before sunset.
The first thing I'll do when I get home is have a hot shower.
The reason it didn't work was (that) it wasn't plugged in.
The people I really admire are traffic wardens.

Cleft sentences with *It ...*

We can also begin a cleft sentence with *It* ...., followed by a clause with *who* or *that*. Compare:
My aunt first got me interested in politics.
→ *It was my aunt who first got me interested in politics.*
We only heard he was ill yesterday.
→ *It was only yesterday that we heard he was ill.*

Starting with a clause with *It* ... gives added emphasis to the first part of the sentence (*my aunt, yesterday*).

We often use cleft sentences with *It* ... to correct people:
It was actually London that I flew to, not Manchester.
It wasn't my husband you spoke to, it was my brother.

12 Participle clauses

There are three kinds of participle clause in English.

Present participle clauses

(form: verb + *-ing*)
We lay on the beach, gazing up at the night sky.
When shopping for clothes, always check the label.

Present participle clauses can be used to shorten a sentence with an active verb:
We lay on the beach and gazed up at the night sky.
→ *We lay on the beach, gazing up at the night sky.*

Present participle clauses often start with prepositions:
after closing the door ...
before going to bed ...
without saying anything ...
on hearing the news (= when I heard)
while walking through the park ...

Past participle clauses

(form: verb + *-ed*)
Although badly wounded, I managed to crawl back into the building.
If asked his opinion, he usually remained silent.

Past participle clauses can be used to shorten a sentence with a passive verb:
Although I was badly wounded, ...
→ *Although badly wounded, ...*

Perfect participle clauses

(form: *having* + verb + *-ed*)
Having lived in London all my life, I couldn't imagine moving.
Having finished the shopping, we went to a café for lunch.

Perfect participle clauses can be used to show the sequence of two events:
We finished the shopping. Then we went to a café.
→ *Having finished the shopping, we went to a café.*

Participle clauses must have the same subject as the main clause. So we can say:
After going online, type a word into Google.
But not:
After going online, Google will appear on the screen.

Unit 1

1.1

1 **SARAH** Yeah, I found it really difficult at first because I didn't speak the language very well, but it was pretty easy to fit in after a while because people are very friendly. I also was lucky to meet a lot of expats here. I really miss my friends at home but the people that I've met here are really, really nice. I've also made a real effort to learn the language, but to be honest most of the expats that I've met here speak English, so it's easier just to talk in English to them. And yeah, I feel that I've adapted to the country and I'm enjoying it and I probably will stay here for a long time.

2 **DANIEL** When I first arrived here everyone was really welcoming, even though I didn't speak the language, I didn't speak a word. I found that hard to get used to, not living in an English-speaking country. There were lots of things I missed from back home – food, pubs, my friends. And although I felt accepted and welcomed at the beginning, the more I learn about the culture here, the more I feel like an outsider. I think I'll never be accepted really until I can speak the language fluently. Yeah, I'll always feel like an outsider, really.

1.2

1 **LIAM** I think I do have a good visual memory and a good spatial memory. I, I think I've a memory for places, for things that I've seen, erm, as long as I'm paying attention. If I'm going back to a place that I've been to before, when I get there, I'll see something that'll **jog my memory**. It'll make me recall where something else was in the scene, even if I couldn't have visualised the place before going back there. When I get there, **it all comes back to me**.

2 **JANE** I'm really bad, I, I can't, I just always leave the house and forget at least something whether it's like my phone or, erm, my bank card or my keys. It's usually my keys. **I've got a mental block** about keys. I think I'm going to have to start writing notes and leaving them on the front door **to remind me** to pick them up. But yeah, now I've given, erm, lots of friends who live nearby, they all have sets of keys now so I tend not to get stuck outside in the cold any more.

3 **OLGA** **I don't have a very good memory**, especially for numbers. So, I used to have one password for everything. Quite an easy one as well, and then a friend told me that's not what a password is about. So, I got different passwords for online banking, erm, for Facebook, for work ... all the different ones. And at the time I thought of some associations that would remind me of those words, but then I forgot them all, so I had to use a different strategy. I had to jot them all down in an address book **as reminders**. So, I don't forget them!

4 **URI** As I got older, my ... **my memory started to fade** a bit, but one thing I can, I can always remember are numbers – people's numbers, telephone numbers but from years ago, and birthdays ... I've no problem with remembering pin numbers, bank account numbers, lottery numbers, that kind of thing.

5 **TINA** I can remember all kinds of things, but I'm really hopeless with people's names and faces. I know their faces **look familiar** but I can't remember where I know them from, that sort of thing. I'm OK with names of things and objects and place names, but when I see someone I find it really hard to know where I remember them from. And I get into a real panic, **my mind goes blank** and I know it's really easy to offend people when you do that, so I have to pretend to know their name. And sometimes the name's **on the tip of my tongue** but I just can't remember it. It's very embarrassing.

1.3

ANDREW I remember when I was little, when I was young. I particularly remember when I was about five or six, that kind of period, going to the beach and we'd stay in a cottage in the New Forest and we'd pack all our things up and set off for the beach and the excitement of that journey, of the preparation, with the buckets and the spades and checking everybody was ready and getting in the car, but the most ... the thing I really remember is that as we would drive towards the coast, the trees – we were staying in a kind of forested area – and as we got towards the coast, the trees would thin out and you'd get glimpses of the sea as you arrived and when we first got the little glimpse of the water reflecting in the distance we'd all open the windows and see if we could smell that particular smell of the beach. So, by the time we arrived at the beach, we were at such a high level of excitement, we'd all spin out and start digging sandcastles and stuff. But I just remember loving that, the first glimpse, the first reflection of light on the horizon – that the beach was nearby – and the first smell of the rotting seaweed was just something that's stayed with me forever, really.

JULIA One of my earliest memories is the day that we went to wash my aunt's wool. She was getting married and beforehand, she had to do this preparing of the mattresses for her future wedding. So, all the family got together, we went down to a small river nearby where we live, near the village. And it was all the family together, all the cousins, my grandparents, my mum, my sisters, my brothers and it was such good fun to go down there and have a picnic ... there weren't any cars at the time. We went down with horses. And looking back now on this occasion reminds me of how beautiful the village childhood was.

BEN Yes, I guess if I think about it, I do have a very early memory from my childhood. I was at school, I think I'd just started primary school. I must have been about four years old. And in my class, well there were a lot of other kids as you can imagine, but the thing I remember which made me feel very unhappy at the time was that I didn't have a partner. So there were 28 other kids, 14 partners, whatever, and I didn't have one and so I had to work and play with the teacher. So, it was kind of embarrassing, or I think it was kind of sad for a four-year-old boy. So one day, I remember the teacher said to me: "Your partner has arrived, there's a new boy who's come to school and he's going to be your partner." And I remember the excitement, the expectation of seeing who this was going to be. I was thinking I'm not going to be on my own any more. Anyway, his name was Noah and he became my partner when I was four years old and the incredible thing is that nearly 40 years later, we're still really close friends. Isn't that incredible? So, I guess that's you know, a happy memory of meeting someone at the, kind of, very earliest time you could do.

1.4

1 **A** Am I OK with him on my own?
B Oh yes, he's usually fine with strangers, once he's got used to you. He does have a tendency to get a bit excited if he thinks you're afraid of him, mind. But you should be OK. Just keep calm, don't let him see you're afraid. I'll be back in about 10 minutes anyway, so don't worry.

2 **A** You need to be very careful on this bit. It's liable to get really slippery when it's been raining.
B Oh, seems to be OK.
A Well, especially on the bends. I'd slow down a bit.
B I'm only doing 70, should be all right ... Sorry!
A See what I mean?

3 **A** Anyway look, you need to keep saving the data, because it tends to crash suddenly, just for no reason. I think it's the program, it's got a bug in it.
B OK, well I'll just keep pressing 'save'.
A Good luck. Just shout if you've got a problem.

4 **A** Anyone else?
B Then there's Amy. She's very bright and tends to know all the answers. And she's always putting her hand up and calling out the answers, I think it really annoys the others sometimes.
A I'll watch out for that, then.
B Yeah, I mean, don't discourage her, though. She's a nice kid.

1.5

BEN I'm the youngest of three boys. This is a story about when I was three or four years old. It's one my mother still tells today because I think the whole family were so embarrassed. I'm the youngest by many years so my other brothers treated me as if I wasn't really a brother. They always felt superior to me. But I was the youngest, so everybody loved me and I could do what I liked sometimes. One day I was watching my father talk in public. He did a lot of public speaking. In fact he was on television quite a lot and of course you had to be quiet at this kind of event. My brothers – Gary and Chuck – always made sure that they kept their distance from me because I could be really naughty and they couldn't bear that. So, I was in this very formal setting with my mum and my brothers, watching my father speak. On one occasion, I got lost. Nobody could find me. My mother got quite worried and I think she wanted to interrupt my father speaking, but she couldn't because it was a public event. Then, I appeared. I was up on stage with my father in full view of the cameras, holding on to my dad and waving at everyone, smiling. My brothers were embarrassed. They couldn't look. The press loved it and my father, who at first was really angry, also thought it was funny in the end. I think I couldn't bear not to be the centre of attention. I think I'm still like that today, in fact. Once the youngest, always the youngest.

1.7

1 Would you open the door?
2 I asked him but he wouldn't say a word.
3 Would you prefer to go by bus?
4 She would never forget that favour.
5 I would go there every year in August.
6 He said he would leave early today.
7 She would say that, wouldn't she?

1.8

1 The rains have not stopped for over 48 hours. Villagers say that they're the worst in living memory. Most of their houses are flooded and treasured possessions have been lost beneath the waters.
2 He's suffering from short-term memory loss, but there's nothing to worry about. It's quite understandable after a blow to the head like that. He'll be back to normal soon.
3 **ANA** So, what were you meant to do today?
WILLEM Eh? Sorry, I'm not with you.
ANA Willem, you've got a memory like a sieve, you really have! Really, I …
WILLEM Oh, yes. You're right, the mortgage. I always forget to do anything related to paying money.
4 **SALESMAN** And there's this one.
CUSTOMER Well, this is a lot more expensive.
SALESMAN That's because this model has plenty of memory. 150 GB.
5 **STUDENT 1** OK, I'm going to test you on unit 13. Do you want me to give you a prompt?
STUDENT 2 No, I think I can do it from memory. Right here goes. Unit 13 focuses on family law …
6 **OFFICER** Are you sure that's the man you saw at the scene of the crime?
WITNESS I think so.
OFFICER You have to be sure about this. "Think so" is no good.
WITNESS Sorry, memory's playing tricks again. I think so, yeah.

1.10

1 You missed the show, that's just too bad!
2 Oh, it's just so you – you should buy it!
3 Hello, it's just so nice to be back home!
4 Arriving on time? I guess that's just too much to expect!

Unit 2

1.11

NORMAN Probably what defines me most is the background where I grew up. I grew up in the south-west corner of Germany and I spent most of my childhood there, and the language and people around there have defined most of what I consider is important to me at the moment. What has also had a great influence on me was my stay in other countries, for example, to the United States or the UK, and what has happened is that I have adopted some of the values and the experiences that I had interacting with other people in these countries.

OLGA I would say my family defines me a lot, because I'm looking after two small children now and erm, life is centred a lot on them rather than on myself, which is something quite different from when you're young and when you're just thinking about your own prospects in life. I think that says a lot about my identity at the moment.

LIAM I think of my identity partly in terms of my friends and people around me. I like to be around people who I find fun and entertaining and interesting, people who like books and music, and ideas, debate, that kind of thing. And so I suppose I like to think that I'm reflected in the people that I like and the people that I get on with. Erm, I see myself, I like to see myself as, erm, as a traveller I suppose, as someone who can adapt to different cultures. I've lived in France and I've lived in Vietnam, I spend a lot of time around Italian people. So I think I'm probably largely a product of where I come from, but I like to think that I can adapt to other cultural situations as well.

JANE When I was, erm, younger I really didn't know who I was or what really defined me, but I think, I think now what defines me is probably my, my job and my friends. Erm, I need to feel part of a close circuit of friends and a close set of friends. I see myself as a happy person, a fun-loving person, somebody who loves their job and also loves the social aspect of life as well.

1.12

1 says 2 saw 3 knew 4 was 5 'd seen 6 'd decided 7 was sitting 8 came 9 chatted 10 called 11 've been 12 have 13 work 14 're having 15 came 16 would have met

1.13

A **AMANDA** So, Uri, would you like to say a little a bit about yourself first, just to get the ball rolling, you know?
URI Well, yes, I've been interested in this field for, for many years now. So, when I saw this job advertised, you can imagine I was very interested in, very interested by it. The thing is, I've been out of work for a while now and I saw this as an opportunity, and so, here I am!
A Right. So, why is it that you're interested in working with us?

B **MICHAEL** So, Ms Faber, it's nice to meet you at last!
SANDY Yeah, yeah, well, after all these months of emailing each other, it's kind of nice to see someone face to face, see what they look like. I couldn't imagine what you …
M Yes, that's right, it's always good put a face to a name.
S Yes, yeah, you're … younger than I imagined you would be.
M Really? Well, it's time for you to meet the others now. Come this way, please. The seminar begins in a few minutes.

C **AMANDA** Mrs Santos, it's really nice to have you back here with us.
CARMELO Thanks a lot. It's great to be back. And you are?
A Amanda Woods.
C Oh yes, I remember. So I suppose the other … candidates are here. Should I go through?
A Erm yes, we're keen to get started as you can imagine. Erm, is there anything else you need?
B You know, I forgot my pen. The nerves …
A Of course, no problem. Follow me.

1.15

A I thought they had real talent – especially the guy on the keyboard, he was amazing.
B I think she has tremendous leadership skills – she's exactly the leader that Europe needs.
C You've got plenty of natural ability, but you also need to practice, or you won't get anywhere.
D They lack basic skills in reading and writing. That's the main problem we're trying to address here.
E It's very competitive, there's so much new, young talent, and designs go out

of fashion so quickly, it's very difficult to stay ahead of the game.

F We need someone with proven computer and technical skills. Academic ability isn't so important.

1.16

A They spend the summer in the Côte d'Azur, in the south of France. They've got a massive villa.

B A villa? How wonderful.

A Yes. Well, not really a villa, more of an apartment, really, but with its own private beach.

B Amazing.

A Well, when I say private, it's kind of private, I mean, not literally private, but it is pretty empty most of the time. That's to say, not all the time, it is busy at weekends, and in the summer of course.

B But still, an apartment right by the sea. That's wonderful.

A Well, to be honest, it's not strictly speaking by the sea, but it's not far from the sea – about 10 minutes' walk, or well, 15 minutes, I should say, or perhaps more like 20 ...

Unit 3

1.17

PRESENTER In this programme, we ask explorer and writer Ian McDonald to tell us about a book that changed his life.

IAN It's a very obscure book but it really meant a lot to me. It's a book by Fridtjof Nansen, the Norwegian explorer and scientist. It's called *Farthest North*. I must have read it when I was a nerdish lad of about 12.

P And what is the book about?

I Well, it's an account of an attempt in the late 19th century to drift through the Arctic ice in a wooden ship called the *Fram*, which means 'forward'. It's a kind of meteorological, biological and geographic expedition. The ship got stuck in ice, so Nansen set out by dog-sled and kayak to reach the North Pole. He was accompanied by one other crew member. They were eventually forced to head back, but they got closer to the pole than anyone had done previously.

P And what was it in particular about this that made an impression on you?

I It was one of those very daring, very, very daring books. The stuff they did was unbelievably brave; it was a bit like Scott of the Antarctic, but much less well-known. I vividly remember reading it and being absolutely fascinated. It must have been a thousand pages of tiny type, enormously long, enormously detailed and enormously discursive, so it was quite a struggle to read, but it was worth reading it. It gave me the idea that I'd like to go on expeditions and discover things.

P It must have been quite a formative book for you because in fact for many years that's exactly what you did.

I Yes. Also, I think it was the first book I'd ever read about the way science was done, rather than about science itself. And I really liked the idea of getting out there with nature and looking at things. It also gave me a real interest in maps. I remember being absolutely fascinated by them.

P Did you ever manage to read the book again later on in life?

I Yeah. I re-read *Farthest North* as an adult, a condensed version that was about a third as long.

P And how was it again?

I Well, I was amazed first of all that I'd read the whole thing when I was a young teenager. But secondly and sadly, I was depressed by how boring it was. Maybe that's just the way it is, and the books that changed you as a youth are always going to be a disappointment, if not an outright embarrassment, as an adult.

1.18

LIAM Norman, your English is excellent. When did you learn? When did your English get to this level?

NORMAN Thank you. I think most of my basic-level English I have picked up at school. Actually the school education there in terms of English is sort of basic but quite good and it helped me to get to grips with the most important vocabulary in order to get by. But other, sort of, conversational English I mostly learned in the context of having had exposure to native English speakers.

L When was that? What were you doing then? Was that work or study or ...?

N That was mostly during my studies, when I had many friends from the US and the UK and that helped me a lot to express myself a little bit more.

L So, school in Germany gets you a kind of working knowledge but still quite basic level of English. So, I mean, most German people that I've met speak pretty good English. Erm, why do you think that is?

N I think it's probably because of, erm, in Germany you're expected to speak at least basic English once you leave school. And also in Germany people consider themselves often quite in a more international context.

L So why do you think, I mean, why are people expected to speak English?

N It's very important to speak English in order to find work for example, but also there are many many people from other countries living in Germany. And for example, in places like Frankfurt where there is a big international community there, conversations can happen quite often in English and in everyday life situation as well.

1.19

JANE So tell me about coming to the UK for the first time and being immersed in, sort of, this culture and the language. What was it like having to speak English?

PILAR Erm, well, at the beginning, at the beginning it was very difficult because I had to translate what I thought in Spanish into English, so it was very difficult to even have a basic conversation. Erm but as, as time went by, I felt that people helped me get to grips with the language quite a bit, they were, if I got stuck with a word they would help me, so, erm yeah, and I also, I was very lucky that I got a lot of exposure to different accents quite early on, so that helped me with the language.

J And have you ever learned any other foreign languages apart from English?

P Erm, I tried to learn French for a while, but I didn't have enough time to, erm, to commit to it, so and – I don't speak a word of Italian or Portuguese either.

J So obviously now you're fluent in English, have you ever thought about learning any other languages, or have you?

P Well, I took up French some time ago, but no, I didn't quite get to grips with the language, because I don't think it was like when I came here that there were lots of English people around me, erm, I didn't get a lot of exposure to the language. So, I don't think, I don't think I learned French, for example, as well as I learned English, mainly because I didn't put as much effort into it, maybe also.

1.20

1 get to grips with; get by 2 exposure to
3 express myself 4 being immersed in
5 have a basic conversation
6 took up; get to grips with

1.21

SYBILLE I feel quite confident with talking, sharing my thoughts, listening to people and so ... This is for me no problem, probably because I'm talkative. So it helps a lot, I think, when you have a lot of things to say, you learn fairly quickly how to, to say them. I think I personally need to concentrate on my writing, on checking my writing, because I write quite fast and I think quite fluently but I never take too much care to re-check if I used the proper word. Sometimes it sounds a bit stupid to read it afterwards. My main problem in English, actually is, I still have a hard time catching the regional accents. For instance, Scottish accent, or Welsh accent, or very deep American accent, Texan accent, I have a hard time. I think I probably need a bit more exposure to these regional languages from all around the world. I think the best way to do this is first watch movies coming from all these different countries. And second, when you have a bit more money, to travel to these countries and spend more time learning the special expressions that are used in these countries. For instance, I went to Australia twice already, and I learned a lot of their expressions that are typical Australian. And it's nice as well to be able to recognise: oh, this guy is Australian because I recognise these expressions! I think it's part of the richness of the

English language that it's spoken everywhere in the world, but you have everywhere different cultures using it.

1.22

1 It takes a long time to get there, but it's just amazing, it was really worthwhile going there. It's such a fantastic, wild place. I've never seen anything like it.
2 It was a really disappointing speech, I thought. He had absolutely nothing worthwhile to say at all, just empty phrases. I don't know why he bothered.
3 Oh yes, I definitely support them, they're a very worthwhile organisation. It's not just animals, they do a lot for the environment and for communities as well.
4 The stock market's certainly worth your while if you're investing over a long period – 10 years or more.

1.23

INTERVIEWER You read *Chinese-English Dictionary for Lovers* as a Chinese person living in Britain. How did the novel strike you?

SZE Yes, in fact it mirrored my own experience quite closely. Because when I came here, when I left China, everything was very new, very exciting for me for the first half a year. And this is same feeling I got from this novel. Guo Xiaolu comes to a new country and she has to go back to the beginning, like learning everything for the first time, and she captures this feeling very well.

I One fascinating thing about the novel is the way the language changes, so it reflects the character's own progress in learning English. As a Chinese speaker, do you think this is convincing?

S Yes, I do, I like the way she sets up the broken English in the first part of the novel, say the first 20 pages. So, she uses the present tense in a certain way, for example, by using *-ing*, because in Chinese we don't have tenses like in English, so everything is spoken in the present tense. Then later in the book, the sentence become longer, more complicated, the character start to use past tense and then the future tense. So I think that's a difficult job to do ... and I guess, er, I mean, that you do need to pay great attention to what is happening with language, not only making a good story. So, for me, it's wonderful to have these two sides to the novel, it's a wonderful achievement, and it works very well.

I Another thing that interests me is the difference between the Chinese and the English languages. In the Chinese alphabet, the characters are sometimes equivalent to whole words in English. In English we have an alphabet comprised of letters that mean nothing in themselves, but we assemble them together in words. So, the way you get your message across must be very, very different?

S So, yes, the writer said when she writes a Chinese character, she ... actually, she makes an image of that word. For example, if I write about the mountain, if I write the word *mountain* in Chinese – it's *shan* – I can see the mountain. I make the shape when I write. And then I think that shapes Chinese way of thinking. And sometimes it's difficult ... if I try to say something in English, I need to be very clear to find the words to give the emotion I want to ... to convey. So, I think that's the difficulty with a new language, especially English. I do find it's a complete different way of thinking, and in a way I need to kind of take out the Chinese way of thinking and ... replace it with English way.

1.25

1 I couldn't follow the presentation very well, the speaker kept beating about the bush. We were told to always stick to the point when you do these things.
2 My advice is to get on and make your point as quickly as you can, speak clearly and slowly and, above all, confidently. The electorate don't like politicians who don't seem to have a clue what they're talking about.
3 It was my turn to say something but the salesman just wouldn't shut up. That's their technique – they don't you let you get a word in edgeways.
4 In the oral part, I got really tongue-tied. At one point, it was just nerves. I just couldn't string a sentence together and I know I can do so much better. My partner wasn't much help either – she dried up as well!

Unit 4

1.26

A Well, one thing that is apparent from these maps is how little has actually changed. I mean the balance between rich and poor countries has pretty much stayed the same. You can see even in 1500, Europe, that is Europe and the Mediterranean, were right up there among the richest countries. And then Europe stayed wealthy, in fact it got wealthier technically at the expense of other countries. Maybe that's just beginning to change now. And you can see if you look at Africa, those countries weren't wealthy in 1500, and that's stayed the same. In fact as the maps show, the difference between rich and poor has got bigger, not smaller.

B I'm actually not really sure what the significance of the maps is. What do they really indicate about wealth? I suppose they're based on the GDP of countries, so it tells us how much countries produced, but it doesn't reveal much about say, lifestyle, or quality of life. So if you, if you look at the map of 1500, North America is shown very small. So I suppose this means that it wasn't producing much wealth. Obviously that's because it didn't have developed technology. But that doesn't necessarily mean that they were poor. They probably had a good, sustainable way of life. In a sense, they were probably very well off, though not affluent in a material sense.

1.27

Well, I think one very significant thing that happened to Britain was joining Europe, joining the European Union in the 1970s, and erm, I think this had all kinds of consequences for the way people live, some of them very far-reaching, for example food, people's attitude to food. I remember before Britain joined Europe, things like olive oil or French cheese or Italian pasta were luxury goods – they were quite difficult to get hold of. And then after we joined Europe you could buy anything from France or Germany or Italy. And I think this had an impact on people's attitude to food and to cooking. And this gave rise to a whole new style of British cooking which was based more on Mediterranean food. So British food became really cosmopolitan, and this led to a new wave of TV chefs and cookery writers, people like Jamie Oliver, whose books are now best-sellers even in other countries. So it was like a renaissance really of British food, very different from the stereotype of bad British food that foreigners used to have. So I'd see this as a really positive development – people eating well, eating much better, and this was a direct consequence of joining the EU, I think.

1.28

1 This had all kinds of consequences for the way people live.
2 This had an impact on people's attitude to food.
3 This gave rise to a whole new style of British cooking.
4 This led to a new wave of TV chefs.
5 This was a direct consequence of joining the EU.

1.29

1 Low pressure will build up on the coast and it will get more humid as the day goes on. Tomorrow, fresh easterly winds will cool things right down.
2 That's looking nasty ... now make sure you change the dressing or it will get infected, at least twice or even three times a day for a week.
3 Don't worry about this, you'll learn it on the job. Please ask if you have any serious doubts. But take it easy ... it's easy to get overwhelmed on your first day.
4 The thing is, he just timed it wrong, didn't he? He made a break too early and he got left behind on the last lap there ... so our chances of a medal have gone, or so it looks ...
5 **A** How do you justify your actions, Mr Rossi?
B Erm, I got carried away in the excitement of it all. Erm, I didn't mean to do anyone any harm, you know ...

1.30

1 A How was Athens?
B Oh, it was great. I must say though, I was a bit disappointed by the Acropolis. It wasn't nearly as impressive as I thought it would be. Looks much bigger when you see it in photos ...
2 A Still enjoying university?
B Oh yes. Mind you, I have to work quite hard for exams this year. So I don't go out as much as I'd like to. But the courses are really good.
3 New York has really changed. It's much safer than it was when I first went there. It used to be really dangerous to go out at night.

Unit 5

2.1

The social character of public spaces is influenced by architects, building owners, the police, and many others. But although urban activities are becoming more and more homogenous, there still exist spaces in the city that are unpredictable, and go against what architects designed. Looking at the city as organic and alive, the *Post-it City* project examines how public spaces are used, and challenges us to think about more flexible, more informal models of urban planning. The very term *Post-it* comes from the idea that city dwellers make improvised, alternative use of their city, depending on their needs. These 'no-man's lands', or leftover spaces can often have a new and surprising purpose. Pavements may be transformed into makeshift street markets; underpasses may become refuges for the homeless. And like *Post-its*, these informal, do-it-yourself spaces are spontaneous, short-term, and likely to disappear without trace.

2.2

JANE It was really late at night, it was about two in the morning. And the light was changing to red, and so I drove straight through, and there was a flash, so obviously, like, I'd had my photograph taken. And so they made me pay a £200 fine and they made me go to a special education, sort of session at the police station over a weekend. And I suppose, they were really strict because it is a crossing by a primary school, and I understand that road safety's really important, but I did think it was a bit over the top, as you know, I wasn't really doing anything that dangerous. And it's not as if any schoolchildren were actually crossing the road at two in the morning. So yeah, I do think it's a bit unfair.

URI I think they serve no purpose whatsoever. Drivers know exactly where they are, so they just slow down when they come to them. There's one on the bypass I go on every morning to work, everyone goes batting along at 80, 100, then they all slow down to 60, and then they speed up again, it's quite ludicrous. What they're really there for is so the police can earn some money.

PATRICK Yeah, I think they're probably necessary, but sometimes I think it's just a bit out of proportion. I mean last time I went through, I had to take off my belt and my shoes and they looked through everything. There was even a small tube of shaving cream I had. You either go back and buy a special bag to put it in or you couldn't take it through. But at no point did they actually ask to see my passport, it was ridiculous. Talk about getting priorities wrong.

TINA I do think they're a very sensible idea, I mean if you think about it it does make it safer to buy things, as long as you remember your PIN that is. I remember when they first came out. I'd be at the supermarket buying loads of things and then you'd get to the till ready to pay and all you have is your card. And I couldn't remember the number, there was a huge queue of people standing behind me. It was really embarrassing.

2.3

Harras as the central square of Sendling has a lot of problems at the moment. The main problems are really caused by traffic, which is completely cutting off the functions of the square from each other. Like, people cannot get from shop to shop, or people can't go to the post office, or there is a problem getting on the bus and the underground, so there is a lack of communication between the bits of the square. And this is mainly caused by traffic which flows all around the square, leaving the actual square in the middle completely cut off from the sides. So the access to the middle is, ridiculously at the moment, only through underground tunnels. And there are these wonderful old plane trees in the middle, which would provide shade and a nice place to stay, but they are in the middle of a, an island which is surrounded by traffic, so nobody really wants to stay here. The square itself is a very unusual shape. It is a triangular shape, and it is surrounded by some very, very fine buildings. Some of them, in the north part and also in the east, come from the turn of the century, and they are, they are *art nouveau*, and Bavarian renaissance, whereas the post office in the south is a fantastic building, a fantastic Bauhaus building, and they create a very nice ensemble together. In order to turn this square into an urban space with high quality it needs reorganising and it needs a new concept for the whole layout of the square. First of all, the road, the spaces taken up by the road need to be reduced, but enabling the flow of traffic for the same amount of vehicles and without causing traffic jams. Also, short-term parking needs to be enabled for quick shoppers, because people obviously want to stop, get their things quickly and go on, on their way home. Then the bus routes need also be reorganised, and the access to the bus stations must also become easier, and also accessible from all parts of the square. And priority to pedestrians and cyclists is important, because they need to occupy the space now.

The main aim is really to create an urban space for the inhabitants which would have high quality, which would be done in very nice materials, where people would want to come, spend time, meet with each other, use it as the centre of their communication and also have enough space to probably create some Christmas market or have some festivities here, which would actually be the heart of this part of Munich, the heart of Sendling.

2.4

Well in our design for the square, first of all we looked at this island concept, and we thought 'Well, this island needs to be linked to the shore'. We imagined it as a tongue of land rather than an island, so we connected the island to the shore and made it into a peninsula, which gives a 'platform' for all the activities. This platform includes the main underground access, and we closed some side accesses to the underground. That gave us a lot of space in front of the houses, for cafés and pedestrian areas and meeting points. We also placed a fountain in the middle of the square under the trees, where there are seats, where people can meet, and the fountain is also a place, a focus, where people can say 'Meet you at the fountain at 7.00'. We re-arranged the traffic, we had some special planners for the traffic who calculated the amount of traffic and the flow of traffic, which now flows around this peninsula. We also put in some additional pedestrian crossings that would put pedestrians into a position where they can easily go from shop to shop, from side to side. And we left these wonderful old plane trees, and added some other kinds of trees which would have a different aspect, like a different colour of the leaves in the autumn, so that they would make the square look very nice in every season. We used white paving stones for the square to stand out in comparison with the surrounding pavings and roads, and also to attract people because we thought white is a very friendly colour and it's also full of light, so we thought that would attract people and make it into a very special space. We also created some circular seats around the trees where people could sit and look in all directions in the square, so it's very communicative. The space is basically open, so installations can be made, like you can put in some market stands, or just leave it open and use it to walk in all directions.

2.5

DAVID I think to me it's about having time to myself, or time with my girlfriend. I mean we have quite a lot of friends and we have quite a busy social life I suppose, and so there's quite a lot going on, we go out and see people quite a lot. And after a weekend I really enjoy and also need two or three days where I don't see other people. And that's OK if I'm on my own, watching TV or something or if Emma, my girlfriend's in the room it's not – so privacy isn't necessarily being on my own, there's no real difference for me between the two really. And I think, I suppose people are either extroverted or introverted, I suppose I am quite introverted – I definitely need time and space to kind of process what's happened to me. And I've known extroverts in the past who just don't need that, they can spend time with people, lots of things happen, and then they can see people all the time and process all that whilst they're still socialising, and I mean I'm quite sociable I think, but I sort of need that time to sort of process what's going on in my life I think.

INTERVIEWER And what do you do in this time where you have privacy , how would you typically spend your time?

D Reading, writing, I write fiction, and go online, listen to music, play my guitar, talk to my girlfriend, cook. It's very nice to do, you know, something practical with your hands I think, it's very therapeutic. It's quite funny because it's completely different when I lived in Egypt for a while and, I mean, people move around in groups all the time, you rarely see an individual walking on their own down a street. All I know is, when I came back was, you know, stayed with my parents they lived on an estate in Britain, and you know, you walk home in the evening and there's literally no-one around. And you look in all these little separate houses and everybody's got their curtains drawn. You can see light behind the curtains, but you can't see anybody. And yet, you know, the place is obviously full of people, and it's such a, sort of, culture shock in reverse, really.

2.6

1 reorganising 2 a new concept
3 to be reduced

2.7

1 Over 60% of trains were delayed over the last year, and far too little money is being invested in new stations and equipment. The whole system is in need of a complete overhaul.
2 The school was built in 1965, and although considered a landmark building at the time, is now urgently in need of repair.
3 Military helicopters have spent days rescuing survivors from the floods, but thousands of people are now in desperate need of food and shelter.
4 The council has set up a new community project to help the poor, the elderly and others in need of assistance. Help is offered in completing forms, providing transport and giving legal advice.

2.8

Well, good afternoon. My name's Len Griffiths, I'm the manager of Petit Bacaye and first of all I'd just like to thank you very much for coming this afternoon. So, I'd just like to give you an idea of what the hotel is like and what it's like to stay there. I'll talk about the hotel in a minute. But first I'd just like to give a general idea about where we are. ... The hotel is on the island of Grenada, which is just here, in the Eastern Caribbean, where I'm just pointing to now – that's Grenada there ... Not a very big island – and one thing about it is that it's covered in forest, so it's really green and tropical, as I'm sure you noticed from the first picture just now ... There's only one main town, St George's ... which you can see here, this is the harbour, this is a general view of the town ... and here's a quick glimpse of the market, quite bustling as you can see ... and this is also where the bus station is, if you want to travel round the island. ... And this is where we are on the island, not too far from the main town, as you can tell from the pink splashes here, but it's in quite a peaceful little bay. ... OK, so let's go on now to Petit Bacaye itself, the hotel, and here it is ... This shows you roughly what it looks like. So if you look at this picture you can see that it's not so much a single hotel but rather a collection of chalets or cottages. And as you can see, these are built in traditional style, quite simple, single storey, thatched roof, and quite spread out so you get a lot of privacy. ... OK, let's just home in on one of the cottages, this is a closer view of it here, it's got a bedroom and a small kitchen, all the cottages are self-catering ... And here's a shot of the inside, very simple style as you can see. It's not really visible in this photo, but all the bedrooms have got netting on the windows, to keep the insects out. ... And this is the view from the cottage looking out. As you can see, just palm trees and the sea, really peaceful – and of course what you can see here all belongs to the hotel, it's the hotel grounds ... OK ... so if we just zoom in on this ... this in fact goes down to the beach. It's not a private beach, there are no private beaches on Grenada, so fishermen bring their boats in here ... here it is from a different angle, you can see the beach and a fishing boat here ... and this is a close up view of them bringing the catch in – and this is in fact what you get in the hotel, we've got a small restaurant – and they go out every day and catch fish for supper – so the food's certainly fresh, and also very good ... So, that's it, really. I hope I've given you some idea of what the hotel is like. If anyone would like to ask any questions, I'd be very happy to answer them.

2.9

1 first of all I'd just like to 2 I'd just like to give you 3 I'll talk about the hotel
4 first I'd just like to give 5 let's go on now to 6 hope I've given you some idea of
7 If anyone would like to ask
8 I'd be very happy to

2.10

1 We think we've come up with a practical solution to the problem of how to develop the central space. Our proposed solution is to relocate the bus stations, to create space for people to sit and meet friends ...
2 The cease-fire provides an interim solution to the crisis, but discussions will continue with both sides in the hope of finding a diplomatic solution to the conflict. Meanwhile, we are calling on the United Nations to provide observers to monitor the situation.
3 We are willing to work together to search for a mutually agreeable solution. However, we feel that the only long-term solution is to invest more money into equipment and to provide better facilities for workers.
4 It's a global problem, so it clearly requires a global solution which needs to be agreed on by all the countries involved. So far, individual member states have suggested partial solutions to the problem, such as strengthening border controls. But ...

Unit 6

2.11

OK, so if you compare the two photos we can see what's been done to the original image of Stacey. You can see the skin here has been enhanced, so it's much smoother, so now she has flawless skin. And look at the teeth, they've been whitened, and the eyes also they've been whitened. Erm, the face has been thinned down a bit, and the spots around the mouth they've been removed, and also the lines below the eyes. Er, the lips have been reddened, so they are now a brighter red. And if you look at the eyes – longer eyelashes have been added, and the eyebrows have been thinned slightly, so they're a tiny bit less bushy. Erm, the background, you see the background has been changed slightly, so it's now whiter. Erm, the whole thing took about five hours altogether.

2.12

INTERVIEWER 1 From art forger to genuine fake, we have the pleasure of talking to artist John Myatt today. Welcome John.

JOHN MYATT Thank you.

INTERVIEWER 2 So, I really think that this is a really fascinating story, and it's been described as the biggest art fraud of the 20th century, so I think the best place to begin is have you tell us something about how this all happened, how you got involved in art forgery, what you're doing now, so just begin somewhat at the beginning.

JM It started about 1983, 1984, when I was, I was a single parent, I had two very small children, I was a school teacher at the time. But my wife had left home and she wasn't coming back, and they, there were two very young ones to take care of. So I was trying to find a way of working from home, and you know keeping the family together really. And one of the things that, that cropped up was this idea of putting an advert in the back of *Private Eye* magazine, which is a sort of satirical magazine we have in England. And it just said 'Genuine fakes. Paintings from 150 to 250 pounds.' And I got quite a lot of replies from, from that advert, I ran it for about two years. And one of the people who replied was different from all the other customers really, and he kept coming back for more paintings, over a two-year period he probably had about 14 or 15 paintings off me. And I, I got to know him very well, became friends with him. He introduced himself as Professor John Drew from, from the Institute of Physics, you know, he was a very well-to-do and important person, I thought. I liked him a lot, I liked him very much. And anyway one day he, he took a painting, a small Cubist painting off me, and he must have taken it down to Christie's, and he had re-framed the painting, presented it differently to the way I'd left it to him. And Christie's had said that they would sell the painting I think for 25,000 pounds, which is probably about 40,000 dollars.

I1 Was that, was that Cubist, was that Cubist painting a, a painting that actually existed at one point, or was this the ...?

JM No, it was a made-up one, it was totally kind of invented out of my head, with the help of some drawings I'd seen in a book. There's no point in, in doing copies because any art expert worth their salt knows that, you know, if ... Well, to put it bluntly, if you had a Mona Lisa hanging on, you know, they'd know perfectly well that the real one is in France, and so that's not the Mona Lisa – so it becomes a bit silly. But if you had a study by Leonardo da Vinci on, on the wall of your house, you know, and it was a tiny bit of ripped paper and it was all beaten up and all that, well it's much more credible if not necessarily believable. Anyway ... to cut a long story short he said to me would I be interested in having half of the 25,000 and I said yes. And I took the money, and proceeded really to go into ... a career of art fakery with this man over the next six or seven years.

2.13

1 We need to be there by six, so we're aiming to leave at 5.15 at the latest.
2 *Women's Pages* is a broadly focused, popular magazine aimed at women aged 25 and over.
3 The average theatre-goer is aged between 55 and 85, but our new play is aiming for an audience aged between 15 and 30.
4 The tour started with a visit to Beijing this weekend, aimed at improving relations between the two countries.
5 She made the mistake of marrying a man whose sole aim in life was to have a good time and spend lots of money.

2.14

1 "Wouldn't it be wonderful to just fly away somewhere?" said Edward. "Oh yes, how wonderful that would be!" cried Marianne, her eyes sparkling with excitement.
2 They reached the house at 2.30 in the morning. All the lights were on, glowing dimly through the fog.
3 Her pulse quickened when he saw him standing at the business-class check-in, leaning on the counter, chatting to the clerk.
4 There were around 20 desks in this open-plan office, and he threaded his way between them. At each sat a man or a woman, gazing at a computer screen.
5 She shaded her eyes with her hand, searching for him, and spotted some people in the distance, strolling along the beach towards the house.

2.15

1 They tried to blacken my name but at the trial, the jury found me innocent.
2 We don't eat tuna anymore. They're an endangered species in this part of the world, because of over-fishing.
3 I enclose my CV along with the cover letter. Please let me know if there are any vacancies at the present time.
4 We were 5–2 down at half time, but this just strengthened our determination to win.
5 Can you enlarge the picture a bit? It's important that people can see the presentation clearly.
6 He tried to soften the blow with the pay-off, but now I'm out of work. What happens when the money runs out?

Unit 7

2.16

arthritis diabetes asthma hay fever chest infection high blood pressure heart attack stroke prescribed drugs pills injection immunisation antibiotics painkillers

2.17

The contemporary art installation 'Cradle to Grave' dates from 2003, and was made by Susie Freeman, a textile artist, David Critchley, a video artist, and Dr Liz Lee who is a GP. Together, they call themselves Pharmacopeia. The installation explores our approach to health in Britain today. The piece comprises a lifetime's supply of prescribed drugs, sewn into two lengths of textile, drawn from the composite medical histories of four women and four men. The image shows a small segment of the installation. The textiles are fine, pale grey net, 13 metres long and just over half a metre wide, one telling the man's story and the other the woman's. They are laid side by side in a long glass case. Each length contains over 14,000 pills, tablets, lozenges and capsules, the estimated average number prescribed to every person in Britain during their lifetime. This does not include over-the-counter remedies, vitamins or other self-prescription pills. There are large and small tablets wrapped in foil or unwrapped in different shapes: round, oval, triangular, diamond-shaped. There are many different colours: blues, greens, pinks, browns and scarlet. Some capsules are a combination of two colours: blue and yellow, red and black, pink and blue, each tablet individually sewn into a pocket in the fabric. Laid out in groups, the tablets form solid blocks of one colour, interspersed with vivid geometric patterns where different coloured tablets lie together. The result is a visual chronology of the drugs we take through the different periods of our lives, from a child's aspirin to medication for common conditions such as asthma and indigestion, through to drugs for arthritis, high blood pressure and diabetes in later life. On either side of the case, accompanying the length of fabric, are photographs and objects that trace typical events in a person's life. Both the man's and the woman's side begin with birth: a photograph of a baby boy with an oxygen tube in his nose; a tiny lilac-coloured footprint on a baby girl's identification form. Photographs in black and white and colour taken from family albums from the 1930s to the present day are arranged in order of the subjects' ages. The photographs come from many different sources, forming a composite image of life. Each has a hand-written note underneath, explaining its context. A rosy-cheeked toddler crams himself in the shelf of a kitchen cupboard; the caption reads 'Anthony exploring'. Two little girls in snow-white hats and muffs stand in front of a Christmas tree. A young man stands proudly by his motorbike. A young woman in childbirth breathes deeply from an entenox gas and air mask. An emaciated man cradles a sleeping baby. A group of four middle-aged women blow cigarette smoke defiantly at the camera. A group of young men lift an old man's coffin onto their shoulders. Intermingled with the photographs are personal objects that also relate to the course of the man's and woman's lives. Childhood vaccinations are indicated by a set of syringes, and childhood asthma by an inhaler. An x-ray of a boy's fractured ankle shows the pins used to rebuild it. On the man's side, an ashtray full of cigarette butts are placed alongside the tablets used to treat his high blood pressure; and a glittering silver blade on the woman's side turns out to be an artificial hip joint. At the age of 75, the man's story ends abruptly, as a stark white death certificate informs us he has died of a stroke, and that his daughter was by his side at the end. By contrast, the woman is still going strong at 82, despite being prescribed medication for diabetes. The end of the fabric is rolled up empty, waiting for more pills to be added.

2.18

ANNOUNCER Professor Irving Kirsch devised his own experiment to see whether merely believing you have had something can have the same effect as actually having it. He showed that this could significantly affect people's co-ordination skills. We talked to Doctor Thomas Hässler about his experience of working with Professor Kirsch on the project.

INTERVIEWER So how did Professor Kirsch devise this test, one that could prove that what people believed could really affect their bodies?

HÄSSLER Well, the first thing he wanted was to take an example from daily life. And one of the things that people do is they drink coffee or tea, that has caffeine in it. People report all kinds of effects: they get jittery, they're able to concentrate better, they become more alert, and some of these effects are clearly effects of caffeine, but perhaps some of them are also effects of thinking that you've taken caffeine, thinking that you've had a caffeinated beverage. So, the experiment involved testing people's responses before and after drinking. What would happen to people's ability to respond quickly, to concentrate, if they were given decaffeinated coffee without them being aware of it?

A So, the idea was to test whether having decaffeinated coffee would have the same effect on people's co-ordination as real caffeine. Their performance would be assessed before and after they'd been given a caffeine-free drink.

I So, when a volunteer turned up to do the trial, what would they experience?

H The first thing we did was we gave people some tests of cognitive abilities and motor skills.

I And then what?

H We asked people what they thought would happen to their ability to do these tests.

I So, it's kind of looking at their expectations of what the coffee's going to do?

H That's exactly what it is. We went through the whole ritual of brewing the coffee, and we used a very professional looking machine to make espresso strength coffee, though what was really in it, they didn't know, was decaffeinated coffee – placebo coffee, if you will. We had just emptied out the bag of coffee and put in decaffeinated coffee.

I And presumably you used coffee with a great aroma, so it was really convincing, that that was really what they were getting.

H Yes, we used a well-known brand. It was very important to be completely convincing. We brewed the coffee, poured them a cup, had them drink it, and then we waited for a period of time, about 15 minutes, to let the coffee go through their system, let the caffeine (which didn't exist) take effect, and then re-measured their performance on these various tasks. These activities tested the volunteers' co-ordination. That included the ability to concentrate, remember strings of numbers, to follow with their hand a moving target, the ability to react very quickly when a particular stimulus would be shown, you know, that kind of thing.

I So a kind of concentration test, an accuracy test and a speed test.

H That's right.

A But did it really work? Did drinking something with absolutely no caffeine have the same effect as drinking the real thing? Well, incredibly, the answer was yes.

H In more technical terms there was a correlation, a significant correlation, between what people believed the effects of coffee would be and what the effect of (unknowingly) decaffeinated coffee was on their behaviour.

I So, just believing that something's going to make you better can make you better, regardless of whether you actually have any of the thing?

H That's exactly what Professor Kirsch's data suggested, yes.

2.19

INTERVIEWER So, how dangerous is malaria?

DANIEL Well, the first thing to say is that malaria is a very dangerous disease, although it doesn't kill as many as it once did. It's also not as dangerous as Europeans think it is. When people in Africa get it they treat it like a cold or flu – so it's not as if you get malaria and you'll die.

I Bit it is one of the world's killer diseases, isn't it?

D Yes, very much so, it is a killer disease. It's also very dangerous to vulnerable groups of people – such as babies, small children, poor people. Also people with no access to healthcare, people who live in villages, or a long way from the nearest hospital. These people generally use traditional treatments, comprised of herbal remedies which don't generally help. Another factor in this is the lack of available medicines, they're too expensive so they're beyond the reach of poor people. So, because of this, malaria is partly a health issue but it's also partly an economic one.

I So, what's the solution? Erm, how can malaria be prevented?

D Well, malaria is in fact preventable but not by taking expensive anti-malarial drugs – these can't be taken for the rest of your life anyway. But by providing good mosquito nets. This has tried in certain countries and has proved to significantly reduce malaria cases there.

I So, why hasn't this been done on a larger scale?

D Well, it's partly a question of providing education, getting people to change their habits. People in villages don't necessarily know how malaria is caused. It's also got a lot to do with providing infrastructure. How do you manufacture mosquito nets? How do you distribute them? How do you make sure they're used properly? Corruption is a big issue, so this is also an issue when it comes to funding; where does the funding actually go? It's really not as simple as you might think.

I So, what about anti-malarial drugs?

D Yes, this is another solution. Firstly, you need to drastically reduce costs to make them available for developing nations. This is really important but this isn't really a long-term solution. The main problem is the problem of resistance. New strains of malaria keep evolving that are resistant to the new drugs, so it's just a vicious circle. The only long-term solution involves developing a vaccine. Work is being done on it, but far more money needs to be put into research. If the same funding was put into research on malaria that, say is put into heart disease, which is only a problem for rich nations, progress would probably be made much more quickly, in my view. So it's a partly a political issue as well, but there are signs that attitudes are changing.

2.20

1 factor in this
2 a health issue
3 a question of
4 don't necessarily
5 a lot to do with
6 a big issue
7 The main problem
8 The only long-term solution
9 attitudes are changing

2.21

PERCY A very common way of fighting malaria is to sleep in mosquito nets. The average homes, which have a higher chance of mosquitoes being present, would have poor ventilation. Mosquito nets are quite hot to sleep in, and so they will compromise on enough air and therefore, not sleep in their nets. So that's where attitude comes in. Because there are a lot of programmes which World Health sponsors and, you know, mosquito nets are distributed in the villages, in the rural set-ups, but people don't sleep in these, or people don't set them up properly. People just leave them hanging loosely, and then the mosquitoes can just fly under, so now you have smaller enclosure with more mosquitoes to feed on you, which defeats the whole purpose. The, the new technique people are using is a total house netting. We are looking at a whole room with a net, a permanent net. So this net is a permanent net covering all the walls, all the holes, all the nooks, crannies, every point of entry, so that you don't have to set it up every night.

And then with this there's more air space and so you get better ventilation and air circulation.

INTERVIEWER So you can open the windows? So it's like a tent inside the room in fact.

P Yes, that's the best way. So there's a permanent tent, which is a mosquito net in the room.

2.22

1 The majority of people who attend motor racing events are male. This is starting to irk the car companies that organise them, as women comprise nearly half the driving population and therefore half of their potential customers.
2 For decades, travel between America and Europe involved weeks or months of sailing. Nowadays, breakfast in London, lunch in New York is entirely possible.
3 Near the centre of Old Havana lies the Casa de los Arabes, a Moorish-style 17th-century building that now comprises a bazaar piled high with carpets, robes and pottery, Havana's only place of worship for Muslims, and a lovely restaurant tucked away in the courtyard.
4 Minneapolis-St.Paul International Airport was in the midst of a construction program that includes a new runway, new terminal and other improvements. But airport officials have sent 2,000 construction workers home in an attempt to keep its debt in line with falling revenue.
5 For Britons trying to enter the US, the situation is about to get worse. From the end of October, all British subjects will need a visa or a passport containing biometric data: fingerprints and a digitally-enhanced picture.

2.23

2 The United Kingdom comprises England, Scotland, Wales, and Northern Ireland.
3 A return flight from New York to Paris costs $695. This includes in-flight meals, insurance and airport taxes.
4 There are many threats to wildlife in the Danube Delta. They include drainage, new building projects, and air and water pollution.
5 My job with the PR company involves sending out press releases, organising events and contacting journalists.
6 The 'Placebo effect' experiment consisted of giving coffee to volunteers which contained no caffeine, and then conducting co-ordination tests.
7 The game of chess involves two players, and comprises a 64-square board and 16 pieces. These consist of a king, a queen, two bishops, two rooks, two knights, and eight pawns.

2.24

1 But hang on a minute, hang on.
2 Yeah, yeah quite. You're absolutely right.
3 I think you're exaggerating.
4 I think Tina has got a point
5 Yeah, but that's not really what it's all about.
6 I don't see that at all.
7 Yeah, but it's not as simple as that.
8 Yes exactly. I think that's the problem.

2.25

1 The atmosphere at the MTV offices is extremely casual. Everyone looks about 23 years old, music posters are plastered everywhere and CDs are stacked against the walls.
2 It was a girl's room, a schoolgirl's. Rather small, with conventional flowered curtains, a white spread for the bed, a desk with schoolbooks laid tidily, a school timetable pinned on a white cupboard.
3 When I came back to the car, I found a parking ticket stuck on the windscreen. The warden was still there, a few cars further down.
4 Today, Bagni di Lucca retains its elegance and pretty surroundings and the atmosphere is fairly subdued. If you want to spend a day or two soaking in the salty or sulphurous waters, there are a dozen hotels spread out along the valley – most of them reasonably priced.

2.26

1 A Painkillers and even prescription drugs don't normally work. In fact, it's very difficult for doctors to treat. When I feel it coming on, I just have to lie down in a closed room, in total darkness.
B For how long?
A Well, it depends how severe the attack is, the pain can last for a long time.
B Is it often related to stress?
A I don't know, but I find if I lie down and stay really still, it calms my nerves and that helps.

2 A He has a really high temperature, I suppose the best thing is aspirin or paracetamol. What do you think?
B What other symptoms did he have?
A The usual, a sore throat, a cough. But that's gone, his body aches, he says. I think he's on the road to recovery.
B How long has it been going on?
A About ten days.
B Oh, that's a long time. And you didn't think of antibiotics?
A You can't get them over the counter and I didn't think it was worth going to the doctor.
B Mm, I always take a double dose of vitamins to prevent this stuff happening. It seems to work – I haven't been ill in a while.

3 A I'd had this sort of thing before, but this time I couldn't move. I was literally prostrate on the floor, when it went.
B So what happened?
A I managed to drag myself over to the phone and call a doctor, it was agony.
B And then?
A It was a case of staying in bed, you know, convalescence. Really boring, but what can you do?
B And now, how are you going to prevent that from happening again?
A Well, there is no treatment as such, you just have to look after yourself, you know. Posture's really important, of course, being aware of that all the time, doing stretching, that kind of thing – keeping yourself straight, you know.

Unit 8

2.27

LYDIA Brands are really important because I think, brands are for me – they carry information, they say something about the person who's wearing them, and also they are a symbol of style. If I say, for example 'Nike', I know that that is something really sporty, that people are fast who wear them, and they will give me a feeling 'Yes, I'm fit' if I wear Nike. Or if I wear something like a top designer label, then I belong to a small club of people who can say yes I can afford it, you know, so it is really really important. And people also recognise what you wear, so they will put you into a kind of category as well. It defines you as belonging to a group.

INTERVIEWER But it's not real, is it? I mean, if I wear a Boss suit, it doesn't make any difference to my personality. It doesn't change me.

L Yes, but it will make people see you in a different way. First of all, the cut is important, they enhance your appearance, because brands of course are also very carefully made, and they are made to a certain style. So if you wear a Boss suit, first of all it will be very well cut, but they will also make people see you in a different way, so your appearance will be enhanced by the cut of the garment, and also people will recognise you as a person who can afford it as well, because these things are not very cheap as well. So you definitely have more attention, or that people will definitely see you in a very positive way if you do that. But brands define also your attitude towards life, and your attitudes towards certain things.

I But you see it as a positive influence on people, do you? You think it's absolutely fine?

L I think, I think it is fine, because I like wearing brands, yeah. I think clothes and identifying with the label gives you this, kind of, wonderful feeling of being part of a group. You are individual because they have so very different things, like, you know, they have different colours and different cuts and so on and so forth, so you can have your individual style within the brand, and by wearing the brand you belong to a large family, a large group of people who all wear the same brand. So you are part of it but you are also allowed to be individual. And I think that is a good feeling just to be ... And you feel accepted as well, I think. And you see yourself, like, it is very important – you put something on, and you feel 'Aha, I feel good with this.' And so, you have much more self-assurance if you wear something that you feel positive in as well. You know, if you have something that has a positive effect on you, then your whole personality is, is more positive, so you have a much more positive effect on people, and it gives you something that you, you gain from.

I So what would you say to somebody who says 'Well I'm not influenced by brands at all, I don't care about them.'?

L Ah, I would admire him, I would look at him and I would definitely see how individual his style is or her style is, this person as well. Because not wearing brands is also a brand. I mean, it is also defined by something, isn't it? I mean, the things they put on, they are also a brand, which are probably not a well-known brand, but there isn't anything in the world that's not a brand.

I So you mean they also have their own image?

L I think that people who negate brands, they also form their own category of brands.

2.28

1 make any difference
2 make people
3 be enhanced
4 define
5 has a positive effect
6 not influenced

2.29

A JANE Erm, they make me think of erm definitely sport, erm, of keeping fit and also erm, of being fashionable, because they're quite trendy, erm, makes me think of ambition, getting to the top of your game, erm, being excellent in your game, erm, definitely comfort because they're comfortable to wear. I think they make you look good because they're quite attractive, erm, I think they make me think of ambition and striving for something, erm, yeah.

B KLARA I think the first thing they make me think of is top quality definitely, reliability, it's a technology that's reliable and innovative springs to mind as well. They sort of suggest perfection, that they have perfect sound quality, perfect technology, sort of great to listen to. I think they also suggest a kind of executive lifestyle, something that's not quite average, a little bit premier. Success, I think that's what they suggest.

C KEITH I think the first words that would come to my mind are things like fast, erm, dynamic, small, erm, they're easy to park, erm they come in these primary colours, these very bright colours, so, and I think that gives an image to them which is all about fun and enjoying yourself. They're for people who, you know, appreciate good design, erm, they're a little bit retro because they used be fashionable in the sixties, and then there was a new version of them, came in a few years ago. And they're pretty speedy and powerful cars as well, so good on motorways.

2.30

This is a really strange viral ad campaign. It was never actually planned, either by the Coca-Cola Company nor by Mentos, you know those peppermint sweets. It started out as an experiment on a website called Eepybird. It's a video showing two men adding Mentos to a bottle of Diet Coke. It all fizzes up and shoots out like a geyser. And then they made more videos, with more bottles of Coke, so it was like a firework display, with Coke shooting out of bottles. It's hard to know how many people viewed it, but it was probably more than 50 million globally in total, including both the original and all those user-generated videos. So this was a very unofficial campaign but it generated loads of PR. Thousands of people contributed their own eruption videos, with groups of bottles together, or people running about, or on bikes or whatever ... A lot of the hype around it was caused by discussions of whether it would be dangerous, or even lethal, to actually drink a Diet Coke and eat Mentos at the same time. So both Coca-Cola and Mentos got plenty of publicity from it, it was very very successful.

2.31

1 Police say they have stepped up efforts to tackle street violence. Tough new laws will come into effect next year.
2 Much of this advertising takes time to take effect – it's subliminal.
3 Any change in lifestyle, however slight, can produce a negative effect on your sense of well-being.
4 Drinking alcohol and taking certain other prescription drugs can reduce the effects of the medication.

2.32

1 Maintaining a balance sheet is essential, whatever business you're in.
2 I had a talk with him which left no doubt whatever in my mind.
3 Whatever do you want to do that job for? It's so badly paid.
4 A What would you like to drink?
B Oh, whatever.
5 A Come on! You know I'm right...!
B Oh, all right then. Whatever you say
6 Web 2.0, whatever that is, was mentioned a lot.

2.33

1 I was in a no-win situation where I could not afford to stay here or buy something else.
2 The hotel forgot to give me my wake-up call so my siesta lasted three hours.
3 Meanwhile, traffic on the peer-to-peer network continues to rise, despite the fact that more than 5,000 copyright infringement suits have been brought against individual file sharers.
4 After further questions, she added: "Few of us in the White House have had hands-on experience with a crisis like this."

Unit 9

3.1

PAT The painting's called 'Two young men' and it's by a Dutch painter Crispin Van den Broeck who lived in the 16th century. So as you look at the painting, what's anybody's impressions of it?

URI The obvious element is the apple. A very symbolic fruit.

JANE Yeah, that's true, and of course it's commonly known that the apple represents the forbidden fruit.

PAT Of course yeah, that's the, that's the, the first connotation that comes to mind, *Book of Genesis*.

JANE And also the apple was supposed to have a symbolic value in Greek mythology well before Christian tradition. And yeah, it was associated with Aphrodite, the goddess of love ...

PAT So if we go back to the Bible though, of course, the story of Eve seduced Adam with the apple in the Garden of Eden, so the apple became associated with various things, with knowledge, love, temptation, death and of course, sin.

URI It's no coincidence that in Latin, apple and death are almost the same word – *malus* and *malum*.

PAT But if we go back to the painting, what's any deeper impressions of it?

PILAR It's difficult to know what, what the painter intended. What stands out for me are the expressions on their faces. The young men are smiling, they're cheerful, they're unself-conscious. It appears that they know each other very well.

URI They could be brothers, they have the same red hair.

PAT And quite similar-looking faces, too.

JANE I don't know, is he offering the other man the apple? It's hard to tell whether he's offering it or the other one's pushing it away from him. Also, that's not the top of the apple is it? That's the bottom of, of the apple. I wonder if that would, I don't know if that's got any meaning?

PAT It strikes me that there's a whole lot more going on here.

URI Yeah, I think we're supposed to look a bit at the background behind them and see the other parts of the painting, maybe that will help us to interpret it.

PAT What else have we got? I mean look, we've got two birds. What do they mean?

PILAR There's three birds actually, if you have a good look. Yeah, there's a crow's head jutting out from behind the head of the boy in red, and there are two dark owl's faces peering over the boy in black's shoulders. I think it's a bit creepy.

PAT So what's it supposed to mean then?

URI I think it has something to do with a reminder of death. Owls and crows, they had morbid connotations at that time.

PILAR Yeah, like in Shakespeare's *Macbeth* the owl and crow are considered as symbols of death.

URI So, you think the painting seems to be saying that behind the happiness of youth, of life, lies the frightening reminder of death.

3.2

1 was supposed 2 difficult to know
3 stands out for 4 appears that
5 hard to tell 6 strikes me that
7 are considered 8 seems to be saying

3.3

Well, this is an image from the 2009 US presidential campaign. It was actually created by the artist Shepherd Fairey who had been well-known for his political satire and parodies and it was quite strange when he first came up with this image because it shows a very positive image of Obama, and it's true that he obviously felt that Obama was then a very special candidate and one that was worth putting some effort into. So, he felt that he should make something that portrayed Obama as having vision and the ability to lead and that's something that's very abstract. And so what you've got here is an image that immediately captured people's imagination. He started selling these images, 300 at a time, from a stall in the street and then it just snowballed and by the end of the campaign he was selling 300,000 stickers and half a million posters. Why it became such an iconic image is an interesting question, but I think one of the reasons is that Fairey wanted to create something that was mainstream, that was accessible. He felt that he wanted something that he felt was going to transcend the counterculture, that was going to make an impact with lots of different people, and I think that is why the image has lasted and is still very resonant today. It seems to me that his objective in creating this image was just to make people curious about Obama, and that hope, the message of the poster, was one that really captured voters' imaginations at the time. He claimed that he didn't make any money from the posters and that he put all the money back into the campaign itself and he also stated that he didn't mind that the image had been parodied and copied. In fact, it's true to say that all the knockoffs and parodies say how much really the image has resonated and become a reference point, a symbolic reference point. And I think he must have been very happy that this icon was copied, because it shows that Barack Obama's campaign had worked and that the image had helped it work.

3.4

TINA I like this one, I think it's a very, very powerful image. When it appeared during his campaign it really captured people's imagination, didn't it. It was really, it meant a lot at the time. I think we should go for it.

JANE Yeah I see your point, but I'm just not really convinced that it's, its going to last, like as an icon. I mean it's, isn't it pretty out-of-date already? I just don't see that it's an enduring image. Erm, I'd much rather include, erm, an image of someone who's going to be remembered for something else, erm, maybe something more worthy than just politics. Erm, what about a more creative figure like, erm, I don't know, John Lennon, or ...

URI Erm, yes, I agree with Jane, yeah I'd be in favour of that, yeah John Lennon I think, yeah.

PAT I don't know. Obama was a great leader. He's much more important than, than, than an artist. This portrayed what American people wanted at the time. I think it's valid. As you say Tina, it captured people's imagination.

T That's right, I mean he was the first African-American president, that's quite an achievement, who knows when that might happen again, so he certainly won't be forgotten, will he?

U Yeah, I agree with, I agree with Tina and Patrick. I'm quite happy to go along with that. Can you live with that, Jane?

J Yeah, yeah I can. I agree.

3.5

NORMAN The way Germans use English words has increased a lot in recent years I think, especially in the language of marketing for example, 'cool' or 'event' or 'image'. And then also in other fields like, for example, computer language there are many words that have partly no German equivalent, but erm, it's most common to use the English expression, anyway. For example, 'email', 'URL', 'keyboard', 'headset', 'hard drive', and so on. But then, there are also other expressions that have an English meaning but are used in a different context in German. For example the word 'handy' is used for a mobile phone in Germany, whereas it is used to say 'useful' in English.

OLGA For quite a long time, the Soviet Union was cut off from the rest of the world, and it was just Russian, predominantly. But then as a reaction, the last 20 years, it became very popular to use English words. A lot of new words which don't have equivalent in Russian, er, English words are used for it. Another thing which I noticed, erm, for shop names ... would be called 'supermarket' because the owner would think it's very trendy to do so. But the last few years, there is a reaction against it. There was a law passed that any shop name should be done in Cyrillic as well as in English, so people can actually read it. And I think it's quite good because there should be some balance. It's nice when cultures mix, and I think it's inevitable that words from different cultures come to Russian, but Russian should be still predominant, I would say. Some people might say there is a danger of too many English words coming into Russian unnecessarily when there is a perfectly good Russian word for it – 'training', 'marketing', 'manager' of course. In my opinion, there should be a balance – the language itself should develop, instead of just blindly borrowing words from different languages.

3.7

1 **A** Look, I got this octopus, but I don't really know what to do with it. Do you know anything about them?
B Not really, I think you're supposed to bash them to make them tender.
A Bash them?
B Yeah, with a bottle or something.

2 **A** Ah, great ... Yes ... Lovely ...
B Careful, Chloe, you're a bit close. Come back in the car.
A No, it's fine, don't worry. Just one more ...
B Come on, supposing it suddenly charges at you? Come on, you're provoking it.
A OK, got it ... Let's go.

3 **A** We're going to be here for hours. Such a waste of time.
B Well, it is supposed to be a really good exhibition.
A Yeah, if we get in. It's just not worth it, just for a few paintings.
B No, you're right – OK, let's go and get a drink. We can always try tomorrow morning.

4 **A** Bye, mum.
B Just a minute.
A What?
B I suppose you couldn't take the rubbish out, could you?
A I can't, I'm late. I'll do it later.
B No, do it now please. It won't take you a minute.

5 **A** Hi. Good flight?
B Yes, it was fine.
A What's that?
B That, oh I got in Brazil. It's a wish bracelet.
A What, does it bring you good luck?
B Yes, you make a wish when you put it on, and if you leave it on the wish comes true, supposedly.
A So what did you wish?
B Well, I can't tell you that, obviously ...

Unit 10

3.8

INTERVIEWER What was your experience of being in the army and belonging to this organisation?

GROVER I was in the army for four years and I would say I enjoyed my four years in the military. There was definitely a sense of family, erm, I felt a part of, as if I was part of a larger group, and yeah that's, it's so true, and, one of the things, one of the first things that they drill into you in basic – it's called basic training that we have – is something called *esprit de corps*, it's pride in and loyalty to a unit displayed by its members and that's something that we, everyone had to memorise and learn and practise and so

– how can I say this? – at the beginning you don't see the purpose of it, you really truly don't but you do see the purpose of it when you are in a situation and it's relevant because you must depend upon the person that's standing to your left and to your right, and so you develop a sense of family, you develop a sense of loyalty to these people.

I How did that affect you personally?

G Erm, I've always thought of myself as an open, honest, and loyal person, I just thought of it as, I'm just extending myself to other people. Erm, however, there are other people out there who were not like that naturally and these are things that they had to learn, whereas you have somebody who is an only kid and now all of a sudden he has to share his toys with other people, with 80 other guys for example, when I was in basic we had to share, I had to share a bathroom with 80 men. And so that can be, you can't get territorial about things. And if you do they will cause problems, so you have to learn, so, I think that is not more or less for me but more or less for those persons who wasn't quite used to sharing, or belonging to a larger group.

I What do you think are the good things you got out of being in the army?

G I think I became a stronger person. I learned that I was a lot stronger than I thought I was, so that was definitely cool, I've made a few lifelong friends. Erm, I learned yeah, I liked me. I like myself and I'm worth being here.

I Did you miss the army after you left?

G I will be honest. I missed my friends. Because I lived with the same people for four years, day in and day out, I ate breakfast with these people, I went shopping, I went drinking you know, went partying, these are friends from the last fours of years of my life, so of course I missed it and there was a strong temptation to rejoin the army, and that's how they get you, you know, they make you, because you are so bonded with your group, and it's kind of sort, of hard to leave.

I Is there a temptation to stay in the army because in some ways life must be much simpler?

G It is because you don't think, you don't think ...

I Because everything is arranged for you?

G You don't think, thinking is not required in the army, only *doing* – someone gives you a piece of paper, you do it, that's it yeah there is a huge temptation for people to stay in the army, because, because it's just easier.

3.9

1 part of a larger group 2 a sense of loyalty 3 belonging to 4 get territorial 5 bonded with

3.10

1 Believe it or not, I got very involved in politics at university, I even joined the Scottish National Party for a time. I was really keen on independence for Scotland. Seems funny to think of it now.
2 Well I teamed up with a few colleagues from work, and we set up this software company together, we called it relax. com. It all went fine until the tech bubble burst in the 90s.
3 Well, I signed up for one of their training courses, and it was really good. After six months I was working in a bank.
4 I wanted to do something in the evenings, so I enrolled in this drawing class. I wasn't any good at it, actually I was hopeless, but I got to know a lot of new people.

3.11

Well, I only became a member, er, of this, erm, specific group recently. Erm, I got involved with the organisation because a friend of mine said that I might enjoy it, that it's quite a supportive environment. And, erm, I had some free, erm, afternoons, so erm, so I thought yeah great, I can, I can devote some time for, erm, to this. Erm, I suppose as a carer you do lots of different things, erm we help each other, especially when somebody new joins, to show them the ropes and, you know, just help them get started. And for example this week I'm looking after an elderly couple, they, they're still in their house and they want to be independent, for example, the lady's in a wheelchair and they need assistance just a few times a week. So I go over and I do housework; maybe I cook a little bit for them and, erm, then I take them out for a walk. Erm, so sometimes I team up with other carers, erm this means that as well as me being able to talk to the carers, the old people can meet up and they can get to know new people that way. Erm, they can create their own little groups of friends, and they call them their gangs. So, erm yeah, socialising and just getting out of the house, it really makes a difference to their lives and I suppose it makes a difference to my life as well. It's great to be of help to these people, yeah. I suppose, erm, one day I'll be in their place ...

3.12

1 For not only had you escaped from the clanking machinery of this lesser life, but you had escaped with most of your mates and neighbours.
2 No single world religion can match its geographical scope.
3 Football has not merely been consumed by the world's societies, it has been embraced by them.
4 Exactly when chaos comes into our life, is when we must never lose hope.
5 As for their interest in football, yes, they are genuinely interested and passionate about football. They wanted to go to the matches.

3.13

PRESENTER It's the highlight of the footballing calendar, the day when the city wakes up to the big match of the year. David Kleberson is here to tell us what to look out for this season. Could you tell us David, why these rivalries are still so important today?

DAVID One reason these rivalries provide such high-profile matches is because of all the money that surrounds them. Media coverage is massive and almost overshadows the matches themselves, which can, at times, be disappointing because of all the tension involved.

P You've chosen three rivalries for us today?

D Yes, that's right. I'm going to start in Argentina, with the the biggest rivalry being the Buenos Aires one. Boca Juniors – famous for their yellow and blue strip – and River Plate fight it out four times a year in what's known as the *Superclásico*. Both clubs have origins in La Boca, the working class dockland area of Buenos Aires. However, River moved to a wealthier district in 1925. Since then, Boca Juniors has been known as the club of Argentina's working class, or the people's club, with many Boca fans coming from the local Italian immigrant community. In contrast, River Plate are nicknamed *Los Millonarios* (*The Millionaires*), with a supposedly upper-class support base. *Superclásico* matches are noted for the gigantic flags and banners which each club's supporters hang from all over the stadium.

P I've heard that many people plan a trip to the Argentine capital just to catch the *Superclásico*. What about in Europe, David?

D In Italy, a key derby is between Inter Milan and AC Milan. It is called *Derby della Madonnina* in honour of the statue of the Virgin Mary on the top of Milan's cathedral. In the past, Inter was seen as the club of the Milan middle-classes, whereas AC Milan was the working-class team.

P And the greatest of them all for you?

D Well, surprisingly, we need to turn to Turkey for that. Recently, Istanbul was voted the most exciting derby of them all, and it's between Galatasaray and Fenerbahçe. It's a unique rivalry because although both teams call the same city home, they're based on different continents. Fenerbahçe, traditionally associated with a more working-class fan base, has their home stadium on the Asian side of Istanbul. Galatasaray, whose supporters are historically thought of as being from the upper classes, are based on the European side. Interestingly, Galatasaray has something of a fan base in Australia because some of the country's best-loved players went to play there. That shows how globalised a sport football has become ...

3.14

1 I should add that not once have I, or anyone on my behalf, received a complaint.
2 In no way does the crisis threaten their business.
3 Seven years I've known him, and at no time has he let me down.
4 Usually you audition for things so many times. Very rarely do you get the dream call.
5 Only recently have we discovered what the real problem was.

3.15

1 No way will United win the league. They haven't got a chance.
2 No way did he write that himself. He copied it from the Internet.
3 It's great for a holiday, but no way would I want to live there.

Unit 11

3.16

NEWSREADER The billionaire entrepreneur Richard Branson is offering $25 million to anyone who can identify a way to reduce greenhouse gases. John Holm reports.

REPORTER With former vice president Al Gore lending his support, Richard Branson says he will award $25 million to anyone who can develop the technology to remove CO_2 and other greenhouse gases from the atmosphere at a rate of a billion tonnes per year. His statement comes just a week after the United Nations panel on climate change said 'Global warming is more than 90% likely to have been caused by humans, and predicted temperatures are likely to rise one to six degrees by the end of the century'.

3.19

Yes, well this is a poem about society in the future and it's called *2084*, which is obviously a reference to George Orwell's novel *1984*, which was about a totalitarian society in the future. So, this is a poem about society in the future, and what's happened is that normal civilisation has come to an end because of climate change. So, these are the survivors, and this is a very strictly controlled society they live in, and probably very religious – it says it's 'scripture safe'. And it's also like a small farming community – the poem talks about fields and keeping bees in beehives. So in a way, they've gone back to pre-industrial society. And anything that contributes to global warming is forbidden or it's controlled – so they're allowed just one computer, the airports aren't used any more, they use windmills, there's an interesting contrast between tradition and technology running through it in fact. It's a traditional lifestyle, but they also have technology like solar panels and computers.

So in a way, the poem is quite optimistic – everything is probably going to be OK. But it's also very critical of our generation. In the second half, it describes how the children want to use up energy, they want to light fires, they want to be children, but they aren't allowed to. And they blame the parents for creating this situation – they say we stole the magic brand, we stole fire, in other words, we misused the sun's energy. And the last part refers to the story of Phaethon – how he borrowed the sun god's chariot and he drove it to destruction. And this is what our generation did, or is doing right now, in fact. So really, this poem is partly about how we will be accountable to our children for what we're doing now – what they will say to us.

3.21

INTERVIEWER Scientist and writer James Lovelock has just brought out a new book *The Vanishing Face of Gaia* in which he makes very gloomy predictions about the future of our planet. He predicts that by the end of the century climate change will make the Earth almost uninhabitable for humans, and that it's already too late to do anything about it. We talk to Moira McCann, who read the book. Moira, is this book a very depressing read?

MOIRA Well, it some ways yes, it's certainly a very disturbing book. If he's right, then global warming is already out of control, and not only that, but it's us that caused it.

I So it's humans that are causing climate change, according to this book?

M That's right. The way the book describes it, it's like somebody walking in a forest somewhere and they pick up a gun, and they accidentally pull the trigger and it goes off. They didn't intend to do that, they kind of pulled the trigger by accident. And that's what we've done: we've pulled a trigger on climate change, and now we can't stop the process.

I So this could have happened anyway, but we've just kick-started the process?

M Exactly.

I So is it reversible?

M No, it isn't, not according to James Lovelock. That's the main point of the book. That a lot of people round the world, particularly politicians, the people who organise the climate conferences, they think that if we're good and we stop burning fuels and everything, it'll all go back to where it was. It won't. Once it's started moving, you can't stop it.

I Can we slow it down?

M Well he doesn't say we can't, but he doesn't think we can, no.

I So does that mean we should just enjoy ourselves?

M Well you could take it like that, yes. Fly off on lots of holidays while you've still got a chance.

3.22

1 Synthetic trees resemble real trees in many ways. For example, they have the equivalent of a trunk and branches which hold up the leaves.
2 The DNA analysis found that the bloodstains were identical to those on the victim's body.
3 One euro is now equivalent to 1 dollar 25 cents.
4 Traditions run deep. On special occasions, people still sing traditional folk songs, just as their parents and grandparents used to do.
5 We believe that banks should be regulated in the same way as other institutions which have a responsibility to society, such as government departments or the police.
6 Her refusal to answer the question in court was tantamount to admitting she was guilty.
7 I'd prefer to cycle to work as opposed to walking or taking the bus.
8 Many antibiotics are not available over the counter in pharmacies in the US, in contrast to pharmacies in Europe where many can be bought without prescription.

3.23

1 don't really agree 2 think he's exaggerating 3 I partly agree 4 don't really see that, though 5 think he's got a point 6 think that's a valid point 7 think what he says is spot on 8 he's absolutely right.

3.24

1 What he's really saying is that global warming is already happening and we can't stop it ...
2 His point really is that politicians are never going to say how bad things really are ...

3.25 3.26

JANE Well really, the only thing that's ever going to stop people *(travelling by plane)* is if it becomes just much too expensive and people can't afford it. Erm, because actually it's so important to be able to get places and visit people and it's an amazing thing to be able to do *(so I just think people are always going to carry on flying)*.

TINA I just can't bear thinking about it *(I mean, the way they treat farm animals. You see those battery chickens all cooped up and they look so distressed)*. It absolutely breaks my heart when I see stories about it or see it on TV. I mean, you would never treat human beings that way, so I don't see why we should treat animals that way ... I really don't think people should buy them, they really shouldn't, I'd never buy one.

PILAR *(Of course I download music, everyone does it.)* It doesn't hurt anyone, does it, it's not like I'm going into a shop and you know stealing something, putting it in my pocket ... Artists are not going to starve, they get plenty of money from their record labels, don't they? And the people at the record labels get a lot of money. So, just listening to it, just listening to it in my house, it seems OK to me.

URI No, I don't agree with it *(I don't think war is ever a solution)* because you don't know what's going to happen, do you? You can't control it. I mean look at Vietnam, all those innocent people killed, you know – what for? It went totally out of control, it always does. And what did it achieve? Nothing. They just need to find some other way, I think.

3.27

1 I think one colour that works really well for a bedroom is light green.
2 I think what she's really trying to do more than anything else is get attention.
3 The people I hate more than anyone else in the whole world are rude shop assistants.
4 The thing I remember most clearly of all is our first holiday together.
5 What I like most of all about living here is that it's close to the sea.

3.28

1 Well, it's famous this one, almost reassuringly familiar. But, after all these years, it's still amazing how it can affect you, when you think that we were able to do that. However familiar, it's still an astonishingly powerful image.
2 I didn't know where this was but apparently it's the House of Soviets in Kaliningrad in today's Russia, hideously ugly, don't you think? In fact, it's well known for it. It sums up for some people the worst kind of post-war Soviet architecture.
3 What a great image of the 60s. This is one that I would choose to sum up that time. It's not just the music of the Beatles that it represents, but the crazy time it must have been. It's impossibly colourful and exciting. There was so much going on then.

Unit 12

3.29

LIAM So do you think that modern technology has a downside to it?

OLGA Erm, well it's hard to say, I would say there is no yes and no. For example, you go abroad and you need to eat somewhere. Before, you would just wander round the town and find a place yourself, but now – click click click, you've found a restaurant, you've found the review, so here you go. What do you think?

JANE Yeah, I agree with you. It's helpful, but it also takes away, as you say, it takes away the romanticism of just wandering around the city and thinking 'Ooh shall we go here?'.

L And you're thinking about saving time, this is going to save time, this is going to mean that I can get what I want more quickly, I'll have more time to kind of spend enjoying myself, that kind of thing. I think there's an instinct where, because it's written down, you trust it as well, so with restaurants, you know, you look at them and think 'Right, that's what it's going to be like'. Like kind of five-day weather forecasting – it's a myth, you can't do that. But you still look at it and think 'oh great, it's going to be sunny on Tuesday'.

J That's so true.

O So you think technology sometimes replaces your own knowledge or your own initiative to investigate and find out things?

J It brings out the lazy side, I think probably.

O At the same time, it's a new thing that people have less time and want things quicker, they want to live their lives quicker, and they get more and more value, in a way, in a certain time, in the very limited time they have now.

J That's true. One good thing is things like transport. If you, erm, commute to work or, erm, whatever, then you can always look up on, say your phone or your computer before you leave for work, and find out if there's any, like rail closures or any traffic problems, and that's actually invaluable because then you won't be late or you can tell someone in advance if you are going to be late.

L There are clear practical benefits to that kind of thing, definitely yeah. The article suggests that people these days don't value general knowledge as much as people used to, erm, because of, you know because it's so easy to access, to acquire ...

J I think that certainly that it's so easy to find the answer that they're looking for, that they don't actually have to, in inverted commas sort of, go on this sort of learning journey to get to their answer. They don't have to go through a process, thereby also getting more information about something to find their answer. They just find it and that's that.

O I quite agree with that but I think it's new time, new technology. People don't need all this, kind of, dead knowledge. Erm, they have this easily available information, and they can extend their knowledge when they need it and where they need it, erm, opposed to what was before, that somebody would be an expert in one field but not in the others.

L Right. I don't know if this is a problem necessarily, but I think that the information that people get when they just look up, say for example, an event in history in a search engine, you'll get a very concise view of the key points of that event in history, but you won't necessarily find out about the context of it or any kind of broader detail, so what you're getting is quite shallow in terms of knowledge and information.

O That's a very fair point.

3.30

The children are falling over themselves to look at something new. It's a computer. There are some children in India who have never used one before, let alone seen one. This nine-year-old girl comes every day to use it, playing with the educational games. This, the Hole in the Wall project – which would go on to inspire the hit movie, *Slumdog Millionaire* – began when a Delhi scientist decided to install a computer in a wall in a poor part of the city and see what happened. Children would be able to use it unsupervised. Before long, the children started to learn things they wouldn't normally learn in a classroom. In short, the children were teaching themselves.

This 12-year-old has no computer at home. He's been coming here from the start, learning by watching others. Before long, he had learned how to operate a computer.

The Hole in the Wall project has spread like wildfire. There are now 48 computers installed throughout the Indian capital. The idea has caught on and is spreading internationally. And just like *Slumdog Millionaire*, some of these disadvantaged kids are learning more than the adults – their parents or their parents' friends – giving a tremendous boost to their confidence.

Each computer has educational software, word-processing software and so on, installed. The project aims to connect the computers to the Internet at some point, giving the children access to a whole new world and valuable life skills. For these slum kids, it's not just fate that is shaping their lives – it's also the hard work of a handful of good people who know what children are capable of.

3.31

INTERVIEWER You set out to turn traditional media on its head back in 2006 when you started Demand Studios. Three and half years later, how have you redefined media?

RICHARD Thank you for that. We actually didn't set out to turn it on its head. We set out to create a whole new form of content, it may or may not turn traditional media on its head, we definitely think that it's causing people in traditional media to rethink their business models. What we did was we added a science to the art of creating content. So the idea forever was let's make a piece of content and we'll see if it works. What we're doing instead is we're using, you know, search, social media and direct navigation – people typing directly in what they want – to figure out what type of people ... what type of content people want, match it with advertisements and then only make the content that people want that's profitable. So, imagine going from big, huge budgets of content which no one knows if it's going to work to small, micro pieces of content which we with surety, can tell through all the science and algorithms, is going to be successful.

3.32

1 We set out to create a whole new form of content.
2 We definitely think that it's causing people to rethink their business models.
3 ... we can tell with surety through all the science and algorithms, is going to be successful.

3.33
Thousands of nerds collectively staring into the screens, monitors which eventually go on to form mountains of rubbish in the streets of the developing world. The two images are poignant and shocking but may well give a distorted impression of computer technology in the world today. Of course, the inequality continues and every technological innovation that appears in the developed world may well end up a decade later on a rubbish dump thousands of miles away. But that's only half the story. Is the digital divide as apparent as these two images suggest? Is the developing world really losing the information revolution? Sarah Vernes reports on the subject of mobile phones ...

3.34
From Spain to Brazil, Poland to Australia, people are working via text message, viewing their bank accounts on their mobiles, using their phones as video or music players. In India, handsets sell for under $25, with one-cent-a-minute phone calls across India and one-cent text messages and no monthly charge. In the US, on the other hand, consumers pay a relative fortune just to own the latest gadget. The USA and other parts of the world seem to be moving in different directions. American companies are concentrating on fancier, more expensive devices which give their customers status. In developing countries, the focus is on creating more and more uses for cheap, basic mobiles.

Americans don't seem to have fallen completely in love with the mobile. Text messaging, so vital to Indians, for example, has yet to become mainstream, where most chatting seems to be done via the Internet. Compare this with India or Kenya. Here, mobiles are truly universal technology. It is always with you, cheap and easily repaired, opening a new frontier of innovation. One Indian company offers a text message service for job hunters. Even without the Internet, job seekers can register by texting information about themselves. They will get a list of potential jobs, along with employers' phone numbers. In Africa, the mobile phone is opening up new ways of managing money. In the West, where most people have bank accounts, plastic cards have become the norm. But projects like PesaPal in Kenya have made the mobile a tool of personal finance, allowing you to convert cash into 'cell-phone money' at your local grocer, which can instantly be wired to anyone with a phone. In many places, the phone has moved to the centre of community life. In Africa, churches record sermons with mobile phones, sending them out to remote villages. In places like Moldova, phones helped to organise protests against the government. In India, the mobile allows voters, via text message, to check on election candidates' incomes and criminal backgrounds. All this suggests an *innovation gap* between the richest societies and the poorest – not in how fancy or expensive your phone is, but in how you use it. And will the United States, which gained so much from the Internet revolution, be able to profit from the billions of mobile users in developing countries – a massive worldwide middle class with a simple mobile and a less-is-more sensibility? Will domestic demand for sleeker, faster, more elegant devices make it harder for the US to innovate for the huge developing world outside, still dominated by everyday needs?

3.35
1 It was a sure sign that we'd hit the 'terrible twos' when my daughter started crying a lot.
2 It is a sure bet that no classical music release this season offers better value for money.
3 What was once a sure thing suddenly became much more competitive. Hong Kong now faces competition from mainland China.
4 Being English, she thought that a sure way of greeting her new friends would be to shake hands.
5 Ahead 7–6, 2–1, Mauresmo looked like a sure winner, but she lost her concentration in the third set.